Searching for Freedom after the Civil War

Searching for Freedom after the Civil War

KLANSMAN, CARPETBAGGER, SCALAWAG, AND FREEDMAN

G. WARD HUBBS

THE UNIVERSITY OF ALABAMA PRESS

Tuscaloosa

The University of Alabama Press
Tuscaloosa, Alabama 35487–0380
uapress.ua.edu

Typeface: Minion Pro

Manufactured in the United States of America
Cover image: The most notorious political cartoon of its time,
A Prospective Scene in the City of Oaks first appeared in the Tuskaloosa
Independent Monitor on September 1, 1868, and was then reprinted in
newspapers from coast to coast; courtesy of the Alabama Department
of Archives and History, Montgomery, Alabama

∞

The paper on which this book is printed meets the minimum
requirements of American National Standard for Information
Sciences—Permanence of Paper for Printed Library Materials,
ANSI Z39.48-1984.

Library of Congress Cataloging-in-Publication Data

Hubbs, G. Ward, 1952–
    Searching for freedom after the Civil War : klansman, carpetbagger,
scalawag, and freedman / G. Ward Hubbs.
    pages   cm
    Includes bibliographical references and index.
    ISBN 978-0-8173-1860-4 (cloth : alk. paper) — ISBN 978-0-
8173-8808-9 (e book) 1. Reconstruction (U.S. history, 1865–1877)
2. Randolph, Ryland, 1835–1903. 3. Lakin, Arad S., 1810–1890.
4. Cloud, N. B. (Noah Bartlett), 1809–1875. 5. Jones, Shandy Wesley,
approximately 1816–1886. 6. Reconstruction (U.S. history, 1865–
1877)—Biography. I. Title.
    E668.H94 2015
    973.8—dc23   2014038707

For Lawrence Frederick Kohl

Contents

Illustrations

Preface

On the first day of September 1868, a small woodcut appeared in a backwater Southern town's newspaper. *A Prospective Scene in the "City of Oaks," 4th of March, 1869* depicted a donkey, the letters *KKK* emblazoned on its side, ambling away from two men hanging from an oak branch. The stark black and white image, only three inches by four and a half, predicted what lay in store for at least two Republicans on the day that the Democratic presidential candidate Horatio Seymour would enter the White House.

Why a book about this particular political cartoon? It was—and is—repulsive. In any case, Horatio Seymour lost the election, and the threatened lynchings never occurred. The woodcut should have been ignored and forgotten. But its awful power has, if anything, increased.

For one thing, this nasty cartoon had an effect on the 1868 election. Republican newspapers from Maine to California reprinted *A Prospective Scene*, warning voters of what lay in store should the Democrats win. Such was the reaction that some claimed it helped Ulysses S. Grant to carry Ohio and to win the Electoral College. Nor did the ripples end with the election. Today the woodcut routinely finds its way into textbooks as a vivid visual expression of Ku Klux Klan (KKK) violence in the post–Civil War South.

Yet even that is hardly the whole story. Historians seldom note that the stick figures in *A Prospective Scene* did not represent just any Republicans, but rather well-known individuals actively engaged in the controversies of the day. The fellow holding the carpetbag labeled *OHIO* represents the carpetbagger Arad S. Lakin, a Methodist minister. The Reverend Lakin came south to Alabama after the Civil War to reestablish the national Methodist Episcopal Church, which had been excluded from the state after the Methodists split over slavery in the 1840s. Lakin succeeded in reestablishing the national church in Alabama—but at a price. Because he allowed black and white Alabamians to worship side by side and strongly supported the Republican Party, Lakin became a target of the Ku Klux Klan.

Neither was the other fellow hanging from a noose just any Republican. He was Noah B. Cloud, a native South Carolinian and physician who used his scientific training to find more efficient methods of growing cotton and other plants that would flourish in the South. Dr. Cloud published the most successful journal devoted to what was then known as scientific agriculture. But after the Civil War, he joined the Republican Party, i.e., he became a scalawag in the parlance of the day. From that base he won election as Alabama's superintendent of education and worked to establish free public education for all—black as well as white.

The *KKK* on the side of the donkey obviously stands for the Ku Klux Klan. The Klan's leader in Tuscaloosa, Alabama—and the editor of the newspaper who published *A Prospective Scene*—was Ryland Randolph. His childhood was spent bounding from luxurious plantation homes to exciting times on the high seas, but his war record was mediocre at best. In 1868 Randolph purchased the Tuskaloosa *Independent Monitor* and turned it into the South's most virulent pro-Klan and anti-Republican mouthpiece. Not content with hot words, Randolph sometimes used hot lead to advance his cause. One of his frequent gunfights resulted in the loss of a leg, and another violent confrontation left him unable to work.

Randolph was very much agitated during the days leading up to the 1868 election. Not only had slavery ended, but freedmen would be voting. So it is odd that the black man—the central figure in the controversies of the 1860s—seems to be missing from *A Prospective Scene*. He is there nonetheless. Randolph's extensive caption (fully reproduced in Appendix C) notes that the oak branch is long enough to hang any freedman who dares to vote for Grant. The editor had in mind Shandy Jones, Tuscaloosa's most prominent freedman.

Freed as a young child, Jones earned his living by cutting the hair of wealthy white men and by investing in real estate. He became relatively wealthy but remained unsatisfied. He soon began campaigning for emigration to Liberia, the colony for freed American slaves established in the 1820s. Jones never made it to Africa, but he did become a leader of Tuscaloosa's black community and in 1869 took his seat in the Alabama General Assembly as a member of the state's first class of black legislators.

Ryland Randolph's *Prospective Scene* certainly threatened what would be done to Lakin, Cloud, and Jones six months hence. But the woodcut also looked back on an incident just four days before its publication.

In early August of 1868 the Republican-dominated board of regents elected the Reverend Lakin as the University of Alabama's new president. When Lakin and his ally Dr. Cloud arrived in Tuscaloosa on the twenty-eighth to take formal control of the school, they were met with warnings and catcalls from behind locked doors. After failing in their endeavor and realizing that staying in Tuscaloosa might not be conducive to their health, they left town.

That night Lakin was pursued by Klansmen on horseback. Four days later Randolph published *A Prospective Scene*.

Here were the makings of an extraordinary tale: the lives of four individuals whose paths crossed during one of America's most critical moments, four individuals immortalized into the most notorious image from post–Civil War America. The first aim of this book is simply to tell the story of these four fascinating, interwoven lives—from the great woods of New York State to the court of the Haitian emperor, from Civil War battlefields to the Klan-infected streets of an Alabama river town—with all its noisy, smelly, and gritty details.

Recounting their tales, however, did not begin to exhaust the opportunities latent in *A Prospective Scene*. After all, Randolph, Lakin, Cloud, and Jones found their way into the woodcut because of their roles as Klansman, carpetbagger, scalawag, and freedman—the four archetypal figures at the center of struggles to reconstruct the South. A careful study of their lives before, during, and after 1868 thus presents an opportunity to see the rebuilding process in new ways. In these four men we can discern the traits they held in common with others: the violence of the Klansman, for example, or the nationalist perspective of the scalawag. Even allowing for each individual's uniqueness, Randolph, Lakin, Cloud, and Jones are symbols of post–Civil War conflicts.

At the same time we can draw back the curtain on how ordinary people dealt with the great issues of the mid-nineteenth century. Too often the post-war years are presented as radiating outward from Washington, DC. There, in the halls of Congress and the back rooms of the White House, critical constitutional amendments were hammered out and important legislation enacted. But the hinterland was where the heavy lifting had to be done. Everyone knew each other in the towns, villages, and neighborhoods of the South. Political colleagues and foes were also personal colleagues and foes. The names of Randolph, Lakin, Cloud, and Jones were known throughout Alabama, from Mobile to Huntsville. Simply passing a law in Washington would not do. Laws and directives were implemented, resisted, or ignored by individuals. Accommodation to local conditions was necessary. Violence was a constant concern.

The violence of those years warrants special comment. Although massed armies were no longer surging forward at the bugle's call in 1868, former allies were accosting each other on city streets. Instead of rifled muskets, their weapons of choice were pen, ink, and the occasional noose. And instead of donning infantry uniforms, some donned Klansmen's robes. So pervasive were the lynchings, gunfights, and raids that some scholars have started referring to the Era of Reconstruction as the second phase of the Civil War.[1] The violence in west Alabama matched or exceeded the violence elsewhere in the South, as the publication of the outrageous woodcut suggests. Placing *A Prospective Scene* in its larger context thus gives new insights into those troubled times and forms the second major aim of this book.

But violence and political activity are still tools—key tools, to be sure—for accomplishing larger goals. That moment in 1868 during Tuscaloosa's hot summer, timelessly preserved by Randolph's woodcut, brought together four individuals with four very different worldviews. Re-creating those four worldviews, which took four lifetimes to create, is a great challenge. Meeting that challenge is this book's third aim.

Worldviews are hard enough to discover at the best of times, but the problem is compounded here by the fact that none of the four individuals in *A Prospective Scene* numbered among the intellectual elite who usually write about such matters. Nor would simply lining up dates and places into short biographies get very far. I needed a different approach.[2]

So after years of looking at them, I decided to look within them. I *became* Ryland Randolph. I *became* Arad S. Lakin, Noah B. Cloud, and Shandy Jones. I realized that the beliefs, values, and ideas they had in 1868 were the result of experiences and decisions made decades earlier. Patterns began to emerge. I started to see that Randolph wore his Klansman's robes and defended his former Confederates because he wanted to reestablish a society—his own society—whose freedom he believed to be threatened. The Reverend Lakin's unflagging efforts began when he accepted Christian beliefs that radically turned his life in a different direction. Dr. Cloud, the former Whig, believed that individualistic Americans must be committed to ongoing self-improvement, largely through education. And Jones always seemed to act from a deeply held hope that things could be better for his people.

From their four very different lives emerged four very different worldviews. They would express those worldviews in countless ways every day, but none more profoundly than in their lifelong quests to be free, as each understood it.[3] The different meanings that Randolph, Lakin, Cloud, and Jones gave to freedom thus expressed the essence of each one's character. Many others shared those same varied understandings of freedom in 1868.[4] And many share those same understandings today.

Here then, in a small woodcut, lies an exciting tale of intersecting lives. Here lies a new way of looking at the second phase of the Civil War. And here lie four different understandings of freedom. Some will find it implausible that we search for freedom in a black American's obsession with moving to Africa or in a physician's experiments with growing better cotton. Others may be offended at the mere suggestion that we can glean insights from a violent racist. Alternative visions are often difficult to grasp and easy to dismiss. Randolph, Lakin, Cloud, and Jones stand apart from us in obvious ways; yet they stand near to us in essential ways. We are the poorer for turning a deaf ear to unfamiliar ideas that come from the mouths of those long dead or from those who seem strange or vulgar. But if we persist, we will find that these four still have something to say.

XXX

A few years back some boxes arrived unexpectedly at the Methodist archive, part of my bailiwick at Birmingham-Southern College. When at last I got around to opening those boxes, I pulled out two notebooks with the simple word *Lakin* on the covers. These raised my interest. A fellow professor, Larry Brasher, had asked me to be on the lookout for any information related to one Arad Lakin, a nineteenth-century Methodist minister who figured in Brasher's excellent study *The Sanctified South*. Beyond a professional interest, Brasher had a personal interest in the Reverend Lakin, for his grandfather had not only been named for the minister but as a child had even been bounced on Lakin's knee. I knew about Lakin from another direction entirely, as the president of the University of Alabama who had been driven from Tuscaloosa by the Ku Klux Klan and then threatened in the famous (or infamous) political cartoon. So I opened the notebooks. To my delight the first contained a typescript of Lakin's previously unknown personal reminiscences; in the second was correspondence with Lakin's descendants.

This discovery led me to other surprises of a more personal nature. From notes in the second of the Lakin notebooks, I was able to track down the exceptionally generous Bill Mapel, Lakin's descendant, and his wife Gail. They flew to Alabama to present the outstanding oil portraits of Arad and his wife, Achsah, to the North Alabama Conference Archive. I regret that Bill did not live to see this book in print.

Although he would never know it, of course, Shandy Jones had descendants who are keen to preserve his memory. Among these is Ophelia Taylor Pinkard, a lovely person who wanted me to be sure to reproduce his photograph.

Other acknowledgments would fill pages, but I will try to keep them short. Archivists at Samford University, the University of Alabama's W. S. Hoole Special Collections Library, and at the Alabama Department of Archives and History once again did their excellent job of helping me knowing all the while that I could be a well-meaning but trying patron. The Wednesday morning breakfast bunch—Ian Brown, John Hall, and George Rable—insisted that I eat crow along with my biscuits, and Ian kindly found me an office to which I was able to escape in order to write this manuscript. Mills and Brenda Thornton took me to Dr. Cloud's home, renamed Cloud Nine, where we enjoyed a lovely lunch with the present owners, Joe and Wendy Slaton. In the course of their own research, Tuscaloosans Chris McIlwain and Jim Ezell provided me with so much primary material from nineteenth-century newspapers that I am almost embarrassed to call the research in this book my own (but that won't stop me). Brenton Rose, my former student, took time from his law studies to locate material for me at the Amistad Research Center, Tulane University. My college, Birmingham-Southern, generously extended to me a semester's sabbatical.

Several individuals—including John Lawrence Brasher; Joshua Burgess; Michael W. Fitzgerald; Philip Herrington; Matthew R. Keogh; V. Markham Lester; Christopher Lyle McIlwain, Sr.; Paul M. Pruitt, Jr.; Pamela P. Sawallis; Thomas R. Sawallis; and Margaret M. Storey—read my manuscript and offered welcome suggestions. Frances Osborn Robb found some of the photographs and improved the text in many places. As we have for approaching twenty-five years now, Larry Kohl and I spent hours drinking black caffeine, thinking, and talking—this time mostly about freedom; I am both a wiser and better person for his words.

All of these friends' contributions came not from any sense of professional obligation, but as personal favors. I am more grateful to them than these few words can convey.

Most Saturdays my wife has us retrace Lakin and Cloud's 1868 walk between downtown Tuscaloosa and the University of Alabama. Pat calls it cardiovascular exercise; I call it drudgery. Still, I am blessed to walk with her.

Prologue

The center of Tuscaloosa—a public well at the intersection of Market and Broad streets—marked a good spot for two out-of-towners to reconnect on the twenty-eighth day of August, a Friday, in the year 1868. Neither the Reverend Arad Lakin nor Dr. Noah B. Cloud came from Tuscaloosa, but rather from other locales, most recently Huntsville and Montgomery. Nor was Tuscaloosa their ultimate destination. That would be the University of Alabama, which lay a mile to the east.[1]

Tuscaloosa, as Lakin and Cloud could easily see, was laid out in a grid. During the 1840s water oaks had been planted down the middle and the sides of virtually every street in the square mile that comprised its corporate limits.[2] The resulting green parasol, especially welcome on that hot August day, gave the town both a certain charm and a welcoming nickname: the City of Oaks.

Looking south down Market Street, Dr. Cloud and the Reverend Lakin could see the usual sorts of buildings one finds in a typical Southern town. A bar and pool hall were on the near left corner, a rooming house beyond; in the next block the clockface on the courthouse tower poked out above the trees. Speaking from the courthouse steps, the fire-eater William Lowndes Yancey had once called for Southern secession—but that was a decade and 750,000 lives ago. Across the street from the courthouse was the city hall, its cupola surmounted by an imposing weather vane depicting a running Indian with bow drawn. Further down Market Street, obscured by the oaks, were the Baptist, Methodist, and Presbyterian churches; and beyond them, a series of grand homes.

Turning right, clockwise, the dome of the former state capitol towered at the end of Broad Street, four blocks to the west. The capitol dated from

1. Market Street, Tuscaloosa (*The City of Tuskaloosa Its Many Advantages . . .* , 1887)

Tuscaloosa's two decades as the seat of state government, chosen because it was accessible from the north by the Huntsville Road (Broad Street within the town's limits) and by steamboat from the south. A leading architect had designed the capitol and other important public structures, including the University of Alabama. Tuscaloosa's time as the seat of government were years of spectacular success as the once-rough frontier town became a place of beauty where professors and local literati created an island of culture in the Old Southwest. But the government was removed to Montgomery in late 1847, and Tuscaloosa's population and fortunes plummeted. The capitol that Lakin and Cloud saw above the trees became a female academy; the once-elegant state bank (on the north side of Broad), a private residence.

One visitor claimed that no other Southern town its size (some 1,800 souls) had been more blessed by nature and embellished by "genius, learning, and the enterprise of trade." But if the City of Oaks had been blessed, it had also been cursed; for the same correspondent noted that "perhaps no place in Alabama to-day presents more 'mouldering ruins, the mournful vestiges of her former grandeur,'—the devastation of relentless war."[3] What the removal of the government started, the Civil War finished.

By turning again to the right, Lakin and Cloud could see the first cotton bolls in the fields that stretched out in the distance to the north, for Tuscaloosa lay atop a hill. Immediately below them, at the bottom of the hill perhaps a hundred yards away, flowed the Black Warrior River. Along each side of the river lay the stone foundations of what had once been a covered bridge, which Union cavalrymen had burned when they invaded Tuscaloosa during the first week of April 1865. Nor had they stopped with the bridge: Along the river to the east, the bluecoats burned the cotton factory. They burned the Leach and Avery Foundry, which normally made plows but during the Civil War had cast a small cannon or two.[4] And they burned a nearby tanyard and the public arsenal.

The "mouldering ruins" of the town's major hotel, Washington Hall, lay immediately in front of Lakin and Cloud at the northeast corner of Market and Broad. Washington Hall had long served Tuscaloosa under the proprietorship of a series of Irish hotelkeepers. In this unofficial state capitol, politicians made deals, lawyers kept offices, traveling troupes staged theatrical presentations, and practical jokers played out pranks on the unsuspecting.[5] During the war, Washington Hall had served as a prison for captured Yankees and then as a hospital for injured Confederate soldiers.[6] Nathan Bedford Forrest had stopped there on his way to Selma, just a few days before the enemy entered Tuscaloosa. With the war's end, occupying Yankee troops took over. Then, early one evening in November 1865, fire broke out. Flames illuminated the sky, the engines pumping water from the well at the intersection were unable to put out the fire, and within an hour the great hotel was no more.

All that remained of Washington Hall was on the corner: a brick pillar surmounted by a life-sized picture of General Washington holding a grey horse by the bridle. A small shelf—probably designed to assist in mounting a horse, carriage, or wagon—afforded an ideal location for loafers to sit while discussing the issues of the day. Now, on that twenty-eighth day of August 1868, the occupying Yankee troops were gone, having only left a few weeks earlier.[7] The loafers were left undisturbed by the impending November 3 presidential election that pitted Republican Ulysses S. Grant against Democrat Horatio Seymour.

They also discussed the reopening of the University of Alabama. Dr. Noah B. Cloud, the newly elected superintendent of education for the state, was the *ex officio* head of the university's board of regents. A native Southerner, Cloud had risen during the 1850s to become among the most respected advocates of scientific agriculture in the South. He served as a Confederate surgeon during the war but afterwards joined the Republican Party, thus earning the Democrats' contempt and the disdainful title of scalawag. He and the other seven board members had recently selected the Reverend Arad Lakin to be the university's new president. Lakin was a native of New York State who, for more than three decades, had served as a Methodist minister. While chaplain of an Indiana regiment, he had participated in Sherman's March to the Sea. After the war, the Bishop of Cincinnati had sent him to Alabama to reestablish the Methodist Episcopal Church, which had been gone from the state since an 1840s split over slavery. Lakin was thus a carpetbagger, a recently coined term to refer to Northerners who had come into the former Confederacy after the war. Parson—now President—Lakin was meeting Dr. Cloud in Tuscaloosa to assume control over the University of Alabama.

Dr. Cloud and President Lakin began walking down Broad Street toward the university. To their left, next to the vacant lot that had once been Washington Hall, Shandy Jones may have been out in front of his barbershop.[8] Jones, born a slave, had been freed when still a young child. Since the Confederacy's defeat he had become increasingly involved in Republican politics and church work. Jones's barbershop was the first establishment of the two blocks along Broad Street that comprised much of Tuscaloosa's retail district.

On the near left corner of the next intersection, where Broad and Monroe streets crossed, the two men passed in front of Glascock's general store. An aged oak there neared the end of its life.[9] Over Glascock's store was the office of a newspaper, the Tuskaloosa *Independent Monitor*.[10] The proprietor and editor of the *Monitor* was one Ryland Randolph, leader of the local Klavern of the Ku Klux Klan.

In the next block was a bakery. The smell of yeasty baked bread floated out of its doors to mingle oddly with the town's other smells: dust, horse manure, and rain. Showers were a usual part of August afternoons in west Alabama. By dropping the temperature while raising the humidity, the rain both relieved and discomforted Tuscaloosans. Newspapers carried hints for coping with hot weather: "Empty your coffee grounds into your spittoons; it will keep them sweet." Drink well water often in small amounts and avoid ice water. Eat sparingly, mostly vegetables. "Above all things, keep your patience—if you can."[11]

Tuscaloosa was located at the fall line, the point where the Black Warrior River dropped from the rocky Appalachian foothills to the sandy coastal plain on its way to the sea. The fall line was as far as boats could ascend upriver, for there began a series of cascades that stopped navigation. Thus Tuscaloosa's original settlement had come from the need for an entrepôt where goods and people switched from wagon to boat, or vice versa, in order to continue their way northward or southward. The river dropped some thirty feet over two miles, thus creating the extensive Warrior Falls and a ceaseless monotone that could be heard in every quarter of the town. One citizen compared the sound of the falls to the "moan of pines shaken by the winds," mingling "with the busy hum of life on our streets," or floating by night "like an echo from the past, and a voice of the ever on going present, blended in one stream of sound."[12]

That busy hum of street life included the usual clop of horse hooves on the red clay streets. A "perfect jargon of voices" sounded out above the clopping as boys called the names of competing hacks, or the latest theatrical production, or the best hotel in which to stay. Some carried poles with attached placards, like commercial gonfalons.[13] But on that particular Friday other sounds drowned the busy hum of street life and the moaning monotone of the falls. As Cloud and Lakin walked toward the university, they heard unearthly sounds—"men screaming, and groaning, and grunting"—coming from behind the doors and windows along Broad Street. The sounds were meant to intimidate the two into returning to Huntsville and Montgomery, for Cloud and Lakin had ignored the prominently displayed printed warnings to leave that they had already passed.[14] The two continued their walk to the university, the lanky (six foot two) and bearded Dr. Cloud[15] conversing with the stocky (five foot ten) and ruddy-faced President Lakin. In contrast to the husky-voiced Cloud, Lakin had a "round, full, baritone singing voice" and may have been attired in his usual domestic jeans with a soft slouch wide-brimmed hat.[16]

After the two blocks of commercial stores, the pair passed along four blocks of houses set well back from the street. Huge gullies occasionally split the street, and the duo would have to get off the straight path. At Tuscaloosa's legal limits of East Margin Street, Broad Street bent to the right and became the road to Huntsville.[17] The magnificent Dearing home sat on the left, its six-columned portico looked straight down Broad Street at the former capitol. Dr. Cloud and President Lakin were away from the town now. The houses were set farther apart, and the chirping of birds and the muffled roar of the shoals were the only sounds they heard. In the hot summer the walk from the Dearing home to the university took about fifteen minutes. The men reached the campus, turned left, opened the fence gate, and entered the grounds.

On either side of the path in front of them lay mounds of rubble—rubble that contained the remains of what had once been a renowned architectural gem. The same Yankee cavalrymen who had burned Tuscaloosa's bridge

2. The University of Alabama, c. 1868, with the newly completed Centre Building
(now Woods Hall) visible through the rubble of the antebellum university
(Courtesy Hoole Special Collections Library, University of Alabama)

and factories three years before had also destroyed the university because, as
the state's military academy, it had been used to train officers for the war. As
Cloud and Lakin walked through the rubble, they passed the octagonal guard
house, or sentry box, on their left. Straight ahead lay the newly built and still
vacant Centre Building. Its towers, crenellation (matching the guard house),
and barracks-like rooms stood as a modern version of a medieval fortress,
defying the Yankees to invade again.

They approached William Stokes Wyman, professor of ancient languages
and president of the university under the former regime, and asked him to
hand over the keys to the university. He refused.

With nothing to show for their efforts and sensing that their lives could
even be endangered, the two returned to town. Dr. Cloud departed for Montgomery, probably by stage during this dry season.[18] The Reverend (he could
hardly be called President now) Lakin gathered his things, ordered his horse
and buggy, and proceeded rapidly towards Huntsville. Eight miles out he
stopped for the night at the same house where he had stayed on his way to
Tuscaloosa. Sitting on the porch about nine o'clock, he heard the sounds of
approaching horses. "Sit still," his host warned. Some two dozen armed horse-
men in disguise swept past, a rope clearly visible. Lakin went to sleep later
that night with three armed black men standing guard. The next morning he
continued his way back to Huntsville and arrived without further incident.

The following Tuesday, September 1, a small woodcut appeared on page

3. Tuskaloosa *Independent Monitor* 1868 September 1

two of Ryland Randolph's *Independent Monitor*. Titled *A Prospective Scene in the "City of Oaks," 4th of March, 1869*, the cartoon boldly depicted Lakin (with the carpetbag) and Cloud both hanging from the branch of an oak tree, a donkey with the letters *KKK* walking out from under them. Printed two months before the presidential election, the caption to *A Prospective Scene* laid out "the fate in store for those great pests of Southern society—the carpet-bagger and scalawag—if found in Dixie's Land" after the Republicans were swept from office and the Democrats once again had assumed their rightful place in the White House.

Editor Randolph's extensive caption hammered home the point: The carpetbagger, Lakin, was in the habit of sneaking in unknown places and "habiting with negroes in dark dens and back streets." He looked like a hound and smelled like a polecat. The scalawag, Cloud, was more contemptible, for this local leper had betrayed his community: "Once he was respected in his circle; his head was level, and he would look his neighbor in the face. Now, possessed of the itch of office and the salt rheum of Radicalism, he is a mangy dog. . . ." The invective directed at the scalawag continued for three paragraphs. The freedman was not depicted in the cartoon itself, but the last lines of the caption made up for that oversight: "P.S. It will be seen that there is room left on the limb for the suspension of any bad Grant negro who may be found at the propitious moment." And Shandy Jones, the barber, was Tuscaloosa's most prominent black supporter of U. S. Grant. (Although not specifically named in the caption, subsequent editorials and cartoons made the identification clear.) As for Professor Wyman's refusal to give up the keys: "We think Professor Wyman did exactly right," Randolph pleaded elsewhere in the same issue. Allowing Lakin and Cloud to take over would have created "the everlasting stigma of having once been polluted by the obnoxious presence of a nigger-worshiping faculty, and of black and white spotted alumni."

The twenty-eighth day of August in the City of Oaks: an unlikely time, an unlikely place to search for freedom.

ONE

Klansman

. . . we will be free. We will govern ourselves.
—Jefferson Davis

When in 1894 Ryland Randolph sat down to write his rambling and informal reminiscences—he titled them *Ryland Randolph's Scribbles*—he did not begin by describing his nomadic childhood. He did not begin by recounting his adventures during the Civil War, nor his gunfights on the streets of Tuscaloosa. He did not begin by summarizing his long career as a newspaperman or his short career as a Klansman. No, when Ryland Randolph began to write his reminiscences, he began with his decision as a young man to renounce God.[1] During the nineteenth century, many others also abandoned their belief in a separate realm—whether it be Truth, Beauty, Goodness, or God. They all had their reasons: Scientists found materialism adequate. Romantic artists did not want to be confined. Randolph renounced God because he deemed absurd the Bible's claim that God favored the Jews.

Ryland Randolph was born in a log house between Eutaw and Clinton, some forty miles southwest of Tuscaloosa. This was on the northern edge of the Black Belt, a great stretch of fertile land curving southeasterly from northeast Mississippi through west Alabama to Montgomery and Tuskegee. Here was the site of the most intensive cotton production in the country. For nearly two decades before his birth in 1835, the Black Belt had witnessed a mad rush to make fortunes. Men on the make bought land, brought in slaves, planted cotton, and then sold out, moved west, and started all over again.[2]

It was wasteful and destructive—of enslaved black Americans, obviously, and of the land, obviously as well. The cycle of buy, plant, sell, and move was also wasteful and destructive in another way. Friendships were fleeting and as thin as a dollar bill, for your friend might be gone next week, never to be seen again. Individuals who left town for six months would recognize no one when they came back. With neither an enduring population nor enduring institutions, reputations were not earned but announced. A newly arrived clergyman might be a fleeing criminal, and an itinerant schoolteacher might be utterly uneducated. If anyone raised an eyebrow, a quick show of the knife would put a stop to that. People had no communities in the traditional sense of the word, only short-lived voluntary associations that they could join or leave behind on a whim. It would take decades and a Civil War before the region emerged from its frontier days. This was the world into which Ryland Randolph was born.[3]

In an era and region marked by transience, young Ryland's rootless upbringing was more accentuated than most. While still an infant, his family moved across the state line to Columbus after the rich lands in northeast Mississippi had been taken from the Indians. Columbus was very much like Eutaw: just another parvenu Black Belt town where cotton and fatal diseases proliferated. Before Ryland reached the age of four, his mother died. She was originally from Norfolk, Virginia, where her father had been a merchant captain and where she had met and married naval officer Victor M. Randolph. Young Ryland was bundled off to live with his grandmother Granbery and aunt in Norfolk, while his father went back to sea. Ryland never mentioned what was done with his older siblings or even how many he had.[4]

Ryland's father and grandmother were devout Episcopalians, while his aunt was a committed Methodist. The trio raised the child accordingly: "[U]nder the strictest religious rules. . . . [f]rom the sixth to the twelve year of my age," Ryland recounted, "I was forced to attend one church in the forenoons of Sundays, and the other in the afternoons or nights. I never escaped Sunday School." Along with a healthy dread of eternal damnation, he learned from his father the grievous sin of reading any book "impugning the sacredness of the Scripture."

The family never allowed young Ryland to stay put. He was sent back to Alabama to stay for awhile with his father's brother, Dr. Robert Carter Randolph. Judging from the words he later devoted to recounting this episode, the time that Ryland spent with his uncle was one of the two most influential events of his youth.

Like his brother, Dr. Randolph had served in the navy. Unlike his brother, however, this Randolph was an assistant surgeon who did not make the navy his career. In quick succession he resigned, opened a large practice in New Orleans, married a wealthy widow (who happened to be his first cousin), and relocated to Alabama. There, near Greensboro (twenty miles southeast of Eutaw and forty miles south of Tuscaloosa), he gave up medicine and took up the life of a planter. Ryland described his uncle as "the embodiment of hospitality, the prince of gracious hosts," a handsome man who "commanded the respect of everybody." His vault into wealth and prestige may seem extraordinary and even opportunistic, but it was just the sort of step that young men in the Black Belt coveted. Nor did his uncle's position seem particularly unnatural in a zero-sum world where success was built on the backs of bound black men.

Dr. Randolph lived sumptuously at Oakleigh, probably the region's finest Greek Revival mansion in a region known for its architecture. Evenings were particularly memorable. An immense Chinese gong summoned guests for dinner; and before the meal Dr. Randolph would ask someone, perhaps one of the many ministers in attendance, to offer grace. Some evenings the Randolphs held parties; other evenings the doctor would treat the family, guests, and servants to a lantern show in the parlor. "Everywhere were indications of luxurious wealth," recalled Ryland. Dr. Randolph's wife efficiently managed about a dozen servants. Life generally "was conducted in a style bordering on the extravagant."

Oakleigh was often filled with relatives—some close and others quite distant—who would stay for weeks and even months. Ryland well remembered the visit of his father's first cousin Robert Beverley Randolph. Like Ryland's father and uncle, this Randolph had also been a naval officer with a commanding appearance. While a lieutenant, he had been charged with financial mismanagement and demanded an inquiry. The examining board acquitted him of any intention to defraud, but President Andrew Jackson dismissed Lieutenant Randolph anyway. Some years later, while Jackson was stopping briefly in Alexandria, Virginia, the cashiered officer received an audience with the president and proceeded to pull the president's nose. Although authorities attempted to arrest the brazen former lieutenant, the matter was dropped. When the aggrieved Randolph recalled the incident before the family at Oakleigh, Ryland recalled that his own "young blood boiled with indignation" at his relative's ill treatment. It mattered neither a jot nor a tittle whether the insult had come from a lowly servant or the most powerful man in America, the lieutenant "did just what any impulsive, high-toned gentle-man would have done who saw himself robbed of his fair name and the rob-ber in his presence."[5]

Certainly Ryland was impressed by stories of how an honorable man dealt with an unwarranted insult. Certainly he was impressed by an elegant life at Oakleigh built and maintained by slaves. But just as certainly Ryland was impressed and influenced at least as much by, of all things, his uncle's reading tastes. The library was Dr. Randolph's place of seclusion. There he would stay day and night, missing meals and indulging in his large and valuable collec-tion of books. His hermit-like passion for reading may have seemed merely exceptional; but it was more than that, for amidst all the books ranging from history and science to politics and philosophy were those written by Enlight-enment freethinkers. That Dr. Randolph was himself a nonbeliever left its mark. For the rest of his life Ryland would carry the image of a well-read, cultivated, and wealthy individual—a patron, ever sensitive to the demands of hospitality—who could ask that grace be said before meals even though he thought such observances nonsense. His uncle was living proof that doubt was not the hellish and frightful thing that his Episcopal and Methodist rela-tives had depicted.

His stay at Oakleigh at an end, Ryland continued to be bounced from place to place so often that the details are not always possible to reconstruct. Some-time about 1843 the boy, now eight or nine, was sent to live with other rela-tives in Tuscaloosa. As a student at Pratt's school there, he started to make acquaintances with others who would go on to play prominent roles in the state and significant roles in Ryland's life, especially James Holt Clanton. Seven years older than Ryland, the red-headed Clanton was then a student at the University of Alabama. The two would cross paths time and time again.[6]

In 1846 the United States went to war against Mexico. Ryland's father served aboard the *Vixen*, which took part in the attack on Vera Cruz.[7] Ryland joined his father the next year when Captain Randolph was made second in command at the Pensacola Navy Yard. That war ended in 1848; but by the summer of 1849 some three to five hundred men, many of them Mexican War veterans, set off to overthrow the Spanish government in Cuba. President Zachary Taylor declared the filibustering expedition a violation of American law and sent the captain, then senior officer in the Gulf of Mexico aboard the *Albany*, to end the Round Island Affair (named for the island off Pascagoula, Mississippi, where the force was encamped). Ryland again joined his father, having earlier gone aboard the sloop-of-war *Ontario* as a seven-year-old.

Captain Randolph ended the expedition by declaring martial law, laying siege to Round Island, and threatening force. The filibusters backed down, and Ryland learned a lesson on the advantages of staring down one's opponents.

From Round Island, Captain Randolph sailed the *Albany* to Havana and from there up the Amazon River to the city of Para, Brazil. In the tropical climate, Ryland came down with yellow fever. Two officers and several sailors died during the few weeks there before the ship returned to the open sea. Then the *Albany* called at various ports in the West Indies, including Haiti, on the way back home. Ryland was soon to learn another, even more valuable lesson.

Haiti had once been the French colony of Santo Domingo, but from 1791 to 1804 the island had endured the bloodiest slave uprising in the Western Hemisphere. Calling for a West Indian version of the French Revolution, former black slaves mercilessly butchered their former white masters. Of those who escaped, many made their way to America and many of those to the rich Black Belt lands near Greensboro, Alabama, where Napoleonic refugees were building a French colony. The Santo Domingo exiles brought back horrific tales of the consequences of freeing slaves, tales that were still being recounted nearly a century later—tales that Ryland would certainly have heard.[8]

Both Randolphs disembarked and called upon Haiti's ruler, Faustin-Élie Soulouque, who would later appropriate the title Emperor Faustin I. Many of his officers, Ryland recounted with amazement and ill-conceived delight, wore threadbare cast-off uniforms salvaged from pre-Revolutionary European regimes. The officers rode donkeys, not horses, and their feet nearly touched the ground. "The court-officials had some ludicrous titles, such as the Lord of Lemonade, Duke of Marmalade, &c. &c."[9] But what may have made Ryland, by then about fifteen years old, see more than the ridiculous in their display came when he attended a ball. There some of the *Albany*'s lieutenants danced with "the negresses, who flourished in the titles of countesses, dutchesses &c. &c. and a big buck negro officer waltzed with a daughter of the American consul."

Recalling the visit a decade later, Captain Randolph began, "I believe that bondage is the normal condition of the African race." Under French rule the beautiful island of Santo Domingo had been cultivated like a garden, and its exports exceeded all others in the West Indies. "*Now*, what is the condition of that island? The negroes on it are semi-savages," he continued. The beautiful sugar and coffee estates have been abandoned and consequently are of no value. "The Emperor, whom I know, has absolute power, and is a brute."

4. Faustin-Élie Soulouque, emperor of Haiti, sixteen years or so after
Ryland Randolph's visit (*Illustrated London News* 1856 February 16)

In sum, the captain concluded, his subjects would be infinitely happier under
French masters than "they can ever be under the rule of Negrodom."[10]

The Americans left Haiti and sailed on to Cuba, where Captain Randolph,
now commanding both the *Albany* and the *Germantown*, each with twenty-
two guns, faced a new problem. The Spanish navy was bringing into the
Havana harbor two captured American merchant ships, presumably for pi-
racy or filibustering. Captain Randolph tried to persuade the Spanish authorities to release the vessels because they had been captured on the open sea.

When that failed, he informed the Spanish that he was sailing out to reclaim the ships by force and would set free the American crew by sundown. The Spanish captain-general replied that Randolph was risking war. "Then let it be war," declared Ryland's father. The two American ships sailed out and within an hour or two sighted two Spanish naval vessels followed by the two American merchant ships. The *Albany* and the *Germantown* prepared for action while Havana's citizens lined up on shore to watch. As the American ships bore down, their big guns primed and ready, another American naval ship, the *Saranac*, steamed toward them at full speed. Captain Josiah Tattnall ordered his close friend Captain Randolph to break off any engagement with the Spanish, who sailed past them into the Havana harbor. "I never saw a madder set of men," recalled Ryland who witnessed the entire episode, "than those who reluctantly left their guns, and my father was terribly disappointed." And so the Americans returned to the navy yard at Pensacola. Captain Randolph spoke of the incident in later years as his greatest misfortune, having missed the opportunity to rescue the Americans and sink their lawless captors. "This would have made of him a hero in the eyes of his countrymen, who were tired of the outrages perpetrated by Spain, and would have welcomed war."[11]

All in all, the voyage had been instructive in ways that Mr. Pratt's classroom could never have been. Ryland had seen his father face down insurgent filibusters. He had been ushered into the court of black Haitians trying to emulate white Europeans. And he had witnessed an arrogant and remote government in Washington stand in the way of his father's glory. The world was a brutal place—out of joint with the order and gentility of Oakleigh—and when not brutal, then ridiculous. His behavior as an adult suggests that he learned his lessons well: Men of integrity stand alone and unafraid, whether in the face of Spanish ships of war, or the Haitian emperor, or even President Andrew Jackson. And men of integrity are not distracted by illusion, whether of social equality or of a supernatural being prescribing dos and don'ts. Another person, needless to say, would have drawn different lessons from these experiences: that the older Randolph was out for glory, that his proposed actions were more drastic and impulsive than those allowed by his superiors, and that his extremely prejudicial judgments were based on superficial observations. Could it be, for example, that beneath the aristocratic robes and diamond-encrusted crown lay a clever and effective ruler of Haiti?[12]

In keeping with the pattern of his youth, Ryland did not stay in Pensacola long but headed back to a succession of schools: In Alabama at a plantation school in Greene County and then at the renowned Professor Henry

Tutwiler's Greene Springs School north of Greensboro and on to Archibald's school in Eutaw; in Virginia at Pike Power's school near Staunton and then in Alexandria; and finally back in Florida at the Pensacola Navy Yard. "[T]oo many schools for my own good," Ryland later concluded. By this time the year was 1853, and he was seventeen or eighteen years old. Commodore Tattnall, under whom Ryland's father served directly, suggested that Ryland leave school and offered him the job of clerk at a substantial salary of $80 a month. Ryland took him up on the offer.

Ryland did not last long in Pensacola either, for he entered the University of Alabama as part of the class of 1855. The year before he graduated, he then took up the station of planter in Greene County. Ryland did not stick with that, but in 1858 sold out and moved into his father's home in south Montgomery, just six miles from another plantation belonging to his father. The Montgomery home, which the elder Randolph had purchased from the same red-haired James Holt Clanton whom Ryland had first met in Tuscaloosa, was located on Ferry Street only a few doors down from William Lowndes Yancey.

Ryland soon made acquaintance with the state's powerful secessionist and arguably the most influential Alabamian of the nineteenth century. He appreciated Yancey's "transcendent clarity" but did not admire his manner. "To me he seemed to be cold," no "*bon homme*." As the country moved toward the critical 1860 presidential election year, Montgomery became a vortex of excitement, and Yancey always seemed to be at the center of that vortex. Upon returning from a tour of New England in the fall of 1860, the state's—and the South's—leading fire-eater spoke in the Montgomery opera house. In "the grandest oration" Ryland ever heard, Yancey assured his tremendous and excited audience that "the South had nothing to hope for from the North, and must rely solely upon herself and the god of battles." The people "almost went wild with enthusiasm."[13]

When Stephen A. Douglas, the national Democratic candidate, appeared at a reception held in his honor at the Exchange Hotel, Ryland was close enough to find the Little Giant less than imposing, at least physically. He "seemed to be all head and body and no legs," wrote the astonished young man. (Others were even less impressed, for someone threw an egg that hit its target.) At noon Douglas moved to the steps of the capitol and addressed the largest crowd yet assembled in Montgomery. Randolph, who was about a hundred yards from the speaker, reported his great voice to be "distinctly audible above the din of the multitude."[14]

Young Randolph was marching with Yancey and those who wanted

Alabama out of the Union. In perhaps his first published piece, he scolded a local minister who was "endeavoring to instill into our minds ideas of submission to the domination of a party which numbers among its requisitions 'anti-slavery Bible, and anti-slavery God.'" If ministers were to discuss political issues from the pulpit, Randolph chided, then he expected them instead to emulate "the patriotic and Christian examples of the noble old clergymen of '76" by preaching Southern independence. He signed the piece "Hint."[15] Detestable meddling ministers preaching submission and social equality— these were the sorts of things that men of integrity could not countenance. But why did Randolph support secession? His connections with powerful Virginia families and successful Alabama planters explain a great deal, especially when coupled with his disgust with Haiti. But secession may also have appealed to a young man attempting to gain some direction. His entire life had been spent bouncing from relative to relative, from school to school, from port to port. He had no particular skills. But he did respond to the fire-eaters' message: that independence would end the possibility of another mass slave insurrection, that secession would end the possibility of a race war, that secession would end the possibility of a ridiculously dressed Haitian dictator emulating European royalty. And secession would end the rootless uncertainty in Randolph's own life.

Not long after coming to Montgomery, Randolph joined an elite military company, the Montgomery Mounted Rifles. He may have been able to join by renewing his acquaintance with the company's captain, James Holt Clanton. Since the two had first met in Tuscaloosa, Clanton had "increased his ugliness by turning out a fair crop of whiskers in full red uniform with his hair." Such volunteer companies as the Mounted Rifles combined fraternity with security. In return for a certain autonomy in selecting officers, uniforms, and the like, Alabama's 1837 military reorganization bill and new 1860 military law had placed the primary role of state defense on these elite local companies. They were expected to lead in the defense of the state and bide time while the general militia formed. They were also expected to impart their *esprit de corps* into the almost laughably inept general militia. These companies drilled in splendid uniforms, led the parades, and received flags from the prettiest girls. The state was now ready to cash in on its deal.[16]

Events followed one another at a bewildering pace following the election of Abraham Lincoln on November 6. Governor Andrew B. Moore called for a December 24 election for delegates to a convention that would determine Alabama's place in or out of the Union. Anticipating secession, the governor also ordered the state's forces to take over Forts Morgan and Gaines, guarding the mouth to Mobile Bay, and the federal arsenal at Mount Vernon, some sixty miles to the north. Alabama forces accomplished those tasks bloodlessly on the fourth and fifth of January. Two days later, the constitutional convention met in Montgomery and, after a few days of speech making, formally removed Alabama from the Union on January 11, 1861.

Upon hearing the vote, Captain Randolph immediately resigned his commission, "the very *first* officer of his rank to resign from the old Navy and to offer his services to the new," according to Ryland. The governor of Florida appointed the elder Randolph the commandant *pro tem* of the Pensacola Navy Yard. His Civil War career would be undistinguished, according to his son, because he was only given unimportant commands by his "remorseless enemy," Confederate secretary of the navy Stephen Mallory. Instead of adventure on the high seas, the old captain would instead be given charge of batteries along coastal Virginia and "the almost worthless 'mosquito fleet'" guarding Mobile.

Ryland's career would be equally undistinguished. Even more, it would be marked by the same inconsistency of his youth. He jumped from one company to another with a frequency that makes reconstructing his four years in uniform difficult at best, unreliable at worst. And given the disastrous record of one of his units and the obvious exaggerations of his responsibilities, the whole suggests deliberate attempts to distort the less-than-stellar record of a young man protected by his father.

The details of what Ryland Randolph was doing in the first months of the Confederacy are unclear. He was listed as a corporal with the Montgomery Mounted Rifles at the same time that his name appeared among the members of the Montgomery Independent Volunteers. He claimed to have gone to Pensacola to visit his father in January or February, but the records suggest that it was not until April. He boasted of having witnessed the formation of the provisional Confederate government in early February and to have made acquaintance with its leaders while in Montgomery. It is clear, however, that when the war began on April 12 with the Confederate bombardment of Fort Sumter in South Carolina, Ryland was then twenty-five years old; his papers listed him as five foot seven inches tall, with a florid complexion, dark eyes, and black hair.[17]

By July 10, the younger Randolph had left the Mounted Rifles to serve as secretary to his father, then at Mobile. But after the conscription law of April 1862 was enacted, Ryland was mustered into Captain Semple's Company of

Alabama Volunteers (a light artillery battery that went by various names) where he served as first sergeant. Henry C. Semple was a Montgomery lawyer and probably a family friend. The not-so-invisible hand of the elder Randolph was surely at work here. He wrote the secretary of war requesting a commission for his son and then wrote to General (and former Vice President) John C. Breckinridge requesting that Ryland be formally transferred from John Tyler Morgan's Partisan Rangers (Fifty-First Alabama Regiment, Mounted), in which he had supposedly been serving, to help in the naval defenses in south Alabama.[18]

Randolph was back in Montgomery by July 1863, this time as part of yet another unit: Company G in the newly organized Seventh Alabama Cavalry, commanded by Colonel Joseph Hodgson of Montgomery and one of the regiments that formed Clanton's brigade. Randolph joined as orderly sergeant, he joined again for the war, and this time it *was* for the war; for he would spend the next two years in the Seventh Cavalry. Once again, this was a unit with close family connections; indeed, it was Clanton who signed Randolph's enlistment papers. (Randolph, Hodgson, and Clanton would have occasion to work together again in Democratic politics after the war's end.)

The Seventh Cavalry, which was part of the Department of the Gulf, was a poor choice for anyone wanting to fight Yankees. Headquartered in Mobile, these cavalrymen were likely to see little or no action. At some point before the end of the year, Randolph was promoted to lieutenant in Company E and did encounter a little excitement. He was ordered to take two companies upriver by steamboat to impress slaves working in the Clarke County saltworks, whose labor was needed to help in reinforcing the Mobile fortifications. Randolph recounted with self-satisfaction that he and his men had to work at night, for "this work of impressing the negroes was dangerous, for their white owners & employers at the Saltworks were bitter against me; not mindful of the fact that I was only obeying orders." Randolph's detachment supposedly managed to capture and bring to Mobile some five or six hundred slaves; but to call the action "dangerous" suggests at the best naiveté and at the least exaggeration.

In fact, the troops in Clanton's brigade had little stomach for the war. In December 1863 the commander of the Department of the Gulf, Major-General Dabney H. Maury, reported disaffection among Clanton's troops. Rumors abounded that many had decided to desert on Christmas Day. The fear was real enough, even if the date was wrong. On the fifth of January, sixty men on picket duty laid down their arms. When Clanton sent the deserters to

Mobile for trial, Maury learned that they were members of a so-called Peace Society. They had taken "solemn oaths never to fight against the enemy; to desert the service of the Confederacy; to encourage and protect deserters, and to do all other things in their power to end the war" and thereby bring an end to the Confederacy. Maury proposed scattering Clanton's brigade into active field service far from their homes in Alabama.[19]

But the Seventh Alabama Cavalry, including Ryland Randolph, continued to serve between Mobile Bay and the Pensacola region. On April 2, the Seventh confronted Company M of the Fourteenth New York Cavalry at Nix's farm, near Gonzalez, Florida, some five miles north of Pensacola. "At the first volley from the enemy, the 7th about faced," or rather "turned tail." The correspondent to the *Mobile Tribune* who reported the incident observed that "if they can't do better in the future, they should be dismounted and set to work on fortifications. Their behavior is humiliating." A Union company had defeated a Confederate regiment many times its size. Confirmation of the Seventh's incompetence came three months later, in July, when the regiment was again overrun by Federal troops. After an initial attack near Pensacola, the Seventh had taken refuge in their newly constructed Fort Hodgson, which they considered safe and formidable. But after only a short contest, Colonel Hodgson and his men deserted the camp, leaving a large thirteen-star battle flag, a considerable amount of provisions and twenty-three head of cattle, seventeen horses, eighteen sabres, and twenty-three guns. They took with them more than thirty wounded. The Federals, by contrast, had only one wounded soldier, a member of the Eighty-Second US Colored Infantry. The Seventh's reputation was in tatters—and with it Colonel Hodgson's. He was forced into writing letters to the newspapers defending both the regiment's and his own reputation.[20]

The Fort Hodgson incident was the last straw. On September 25, Colonel Hodgson was ordered to bring his regiment to Verona, Mississippi,[21] just south of Tupelo and Corinth, where the men were assigned to a different brigade under the overall command of Major General Nathan Bedford Forrest, a demanding commander indeed. At the year's end, the Seventh was sent to help Lieutenant General John Bell Hood, who was preparing to order his Army of Tennessee to attack the Union forces in Nashville. This would afford Lieutenant Randolph his one moment of glory during the war—a moment that he would later recount in extraordinary length, detail, and typical embellishment.

In the middle of that last December of the war, General Forrest called for an officer and some men for "dangerous service." By the time it went through the line of command, Lieutenant Randolph was that officer, and the twenty members of the Seventh Cavalry he selected were those men. They were ordered to take three days' rations, cross over to the north shore of the Cumberland River, and proceed to the rear of Nashville, all the while destroying railroad and telegraph lines in an attempt to disorient the fresh Union troops who were arriving for the impending battle. It took them until dawn to find twenty horses about fifteen miles from their camp. They then crossed the river and waited in a secluded spot to avoid detection. About midnight the Confederates finally reached a railroad, which they began dismantling. Following the railroad tracks, they came upon a trestle that they resolved to burn. The wet brush and approaching dawn caused them to give up, however. This turned out to be the most damage that Randolph and his men inflicted during their "dangerous service."[22]

After making another camp, the detachment began to hear the sounds of cannon and gunfire from the direction of Nashville. The battle had at last commenced. The gradual fading of the sound convinced them that the Confederates were retreating south and that their mission was no longer needed. So the lieutenant led his men back across the Cumberland River to rejoin their unit. Randolph described the weather as freezing, the men barefoot and in rags, and their rations exhausted. They reached the north bank of the Tennessee River and camped in an old field. Even with a large fire, it was too cold to sleep. Fortunately, a sympathizer invited them for a hot meal on that Christmas Eve.

Ice was everywhere, and the wide river still had a strong current. The soldiers found a small skiff capable of holding only two or three men, so the day was spent ferrying men and horses back and forth. At one point the skiff capsized, and the men reached shore nearly frozen. Cold and hungry, the lieutenant sent three men to forage while the others set fire to a small hut to provide warmth. The foragers returned, loaded with biscuits, bacon, and even a bucket of coffee. "I thought it was the most toothsome meal that I had ever sat before," he recalled later. It had been a long and wearisome Christmas Day; and despite the cold the men slept until long after dawn. It would take several days before Lieutenant Randolph and his detachment rejoined their regiment, who by then were in retreat somewhere around Iuka, Mississippi.

Randolph discovered that he was infested with greybacks. Early in the war, the men in Clanton's Mounted Rifles would talk seriously of drumming out of the company anyone with lice. Now everyone had them. Randolph felt so humiliated that he went straight to General Forrest to procure a furlough home. When shown into the general's room, Randolph saluted. The salute was not returned; instead, General Forrest and his half-dozen aides and clerks merely stared at the young man. The insulted lieutenant proceeded to inform the general who he was, not forgetting to relate his experience across the Cumberland River. Forrest told his impertinent subordinate that no furloughs were being granted, that every man was now needed at the front. Randolph protested that he was "a disgrace to my commission and the army, and could be of no farther service unless he granted me a ten day's furlough so as to replenish my wardrobe." At last worn down, or perhaps realizing that Randolph in camp might be of even less use than Randolph at home, General Forrest granted the furlough. The brash young man had learned his lessons well having heard his father's cousin recount pulling President Jackson's nose and having witnessed his father's dealing with superior officers. But the Randolphs' bluster and arrogance had, in turn, deeper roots in their sense of entitlement as First Families of Virginia.

While Randolph was off to Montgomery procuring new clothes, Union cavalrymen under Brevet Brigadier General James Harrison Wilson invaded Alabama. He sent Brigadier General John T. Croxton with a force of 1,500 to Tuscaloosa with instructions "to destroy the bridge, factories, mills, university (military school) and whatever else may be of value to the rebel cause." On April 4, 1865, the cavalrymen put the torch to the University of Alabama.

Meanwhile the bulk of Wilson's invaders went straight toward the iron furnaces in Jefferson, Bibb, and Shelby counties. Forrest's men could only harass Wilson's 12,000 well-armed and well-equipped cavalrymen as they moved through the state with little opposition. Randolph finally rejoined his Seventh Alabama Cavalry in Montevallo, which fell March 29. After the Union overran the massive arsenal and military manufacturing complex in Selma on April 2, Wilson turned his men east towards Montgomery. At one point Wilson's vanguard was in pursuit when Randolph was thrown by his stumbling horse. While he lay concealed behind an osage orange hedge, the Yankee cavalrymen took the horse and left Randolph to walk to his father's farm only two miles away. Wilson's men captured Montgomery without notable resistance on April 12—a few days after Robert E. Lee surrendered to Ulysses S. Grant at Appomattox Court House, Virginia. Randolph claimed that he made his way to Gainesville, Alabama, where Nathan Bedford Forrest surrendered his troops on May 9.

If Randolph is to be believed, then his war had but one or two notable moments. Yet he, like so many of his generation, would be judged by the war. As the years passed, first Randolph and then his friends would turn the stories into epic tales: Lieutenant Randolph had not taken twenty men behind the lines on a futile attempt to disrupt communications; instead, *Major* Randolph (he would be a colonel by the time of his death) had saved Clanton's entire brigade by placing his *regiment* (not a detachment of a score of men) at a crossroads and directing the attack on the pursuing Federals. "They aimed with great precision and rapidly reloaded," recounted one veteran, with the result that "vast numbers of the enemy lay dead on this main road. It was one of the worst blows the Federals received at the battle of Nashville." Another would recount how in the retreat Major Randolph had drawn a gun and shot a Union soldier who was taking a Confederate prisoner. "Now you've killed me," the man gasped; "I reckon you're satisfied."[23]

But this sort of historical invention lay in the future. Now, in the spring and summer of 1865, the South had to deal with facts. First of all, slavery had ended, and many of the newly freed people were roaming about in search of lost relatives or merely satisfying their curiosity about the formerly forbidden world that lay beyond the confines of their plantations. Randolph's bitterest enemies—Union troops—occupied the major towns, including Montgomery, Huntsville, Tuscaloosa, and Greensboro.

Randolph and others believed that some problems might be fixed, and fixed rather easily. With a little tinkering under the lenient policies of President Andrew Johnson, the state could move beyond the turmoil of the previous four years to restore a semblance of the social and economic structure that white Southerners had developed over the centuries. During the summer and fall of 1865, Alabama complied with the president's directives for readmission to the Union. Another constitutional convention renounced slavery, Alabama's 1861 Ordinance of Secession, and the state's war debt. C. C. Langdon, convention delegate and the *Mobile Advertiser*'s editor, told a New York journalist that the convention was "to do just so much as is necessary to get back into the Union, and no more." Emancipation, in the end, would be rendered meaningless. The unrepentant Langdon explained that "most gladly would I vote for the substitute if the institution could thereby be saved." The New York journalist's conclusion: "Who believes that the State, left under the guidance of such men, will allow any real freedom for the blacks to exist within its limits?"[24]

Under the 1865 state constitution, a hastily organized general assembly sent former Unionist George S. Houston of north Alabama along with the military governor, Lewis E. Parsons, to the US Senate. Political reconstruction was now deemed complete. The editor of the Greensboro *Alabama Beacon* predicted that soon "the State will have been restored to all her former rights and privileges in the Union, the military withdrawn, the Freedmen's Bureau played out, and Alabama herself permitted to manage her own affairs in her own way, subject only to the Constitution of the United States."[25] It all seemed so easy.

Too easy, as it turned out. Southern states sent senators and representatives to Washington who had been prominent in the Rebel government, most notably former vice president of the Confederacy Alexander H. Stephens. The Thirty-Ninth Congress reconvened and refused to seat them. Reconstruction had not been completed. Reconstruction was just getting started.

And Randolph, too, was just getting started. He first headed to Texas, where his father owned land, and then back to Greensboro, where he still had family. There, in the quintessential Southern plantation town, he witnessed the troubles that former Confederates were having adjusting to the new reality—and he learned lessons.[26] "Our people are conquered, humiliated, ruined," declared a prominent Greensborian immediately after the fighting stopped. That summer, a minor altercation ended with a bullet through the brain of one of the occupying Union soldiers. The bullet was fired by Tood Cowin, a former member of the Greensboro Guards, who had spent the war as part of the Fifth Alabama, part of the famous Rodes' Brigade in Robert E. Lee's Army of Northern Virginia. Shooting insulting Yankees on the streets of Greensboro seemed not so different from shooting attacking Yankees on the streets of Fredericksburg.

Then in early 1867 Congress placed Alabama under military rule that was to last until another constitution was in place. Congress also stipulated that this time black Americans must be allowed to vote—for the first time ever in Alabama—to determine whether Alabama would hold a constitutional convention and, if so, who the delegates would be. Certain former Confederate leaders were denied both the vote and political office. Congress further required the state to ratify the Fourteenth Amendment, which extended federal citizenship to former slaves, forbade states from restricting individual rights, and mandated due process.

People were confused. At a public meeting in Greensboro, those who four years earlier had been reluctant secessionists suggested that the best course would be to accept the congressional mandates and work within the system to secure white interests. But only one agreed to speak at Republican rallies:

Dr. William T. Blackford, who had voluntarily served as a physician in the Fifth Alabama. Three thousand black men and women met in nearby Newbern, and twenty-five hundred assembled in Greensboro a week later. At those meetings the Republicans called for a convention to draft a new state constitution (as Congress had mandated), for a system of tax-supported common schools open to all, for governmental relief for the aged and infirm, and for harmony between the two races. They concluded by declaring the interests of the landowner and the laborer identical and inseparable and by avowing that the rights and privileges guaranteed in the Civil Rights Bill and the Constitution were unquestionably theirs.

If the Republicans' support for legislation was hateful to Ryland Randolph and the former Confederates, the claims of identical interests and possession of the same liberties as whites were simply incredible. These freed people were demanding to be included in a society that was simply not theirs. For one thing, they wanted to be regarded as equals, but experience made a mockery of their notions of equality. Moreover, with the exception of the scalawags and Yankee intruders, the white community was now an exclusive community based on duties and obligations to those with a common past, rooted in war and sacrifice, that these former slaves could never share. Had the freed people grieved over the whites' loss of property through emancipation? Had they wept to learn of the Confederacy's defeat?

As a first step toward fulfilling the terms of congressional Reconstruction, boards of one black and two white men began registering voters in June 1867. Alex Webb was the black registrar. On June 13, a Thursday, John C. Orrick, another former member of the Greensboro Guards, walked down Main Street smoking his pipe. Orrick saw Webb and called to him. The two began arguing. Orrick calmly drew out a pistol, aimed, shot the unarmed Webb three times, and rode out of town. Greensboro's black residents immediately demanded revenge, threatening to set fire to the town or to murder white residents. Crowds of armed black men paroled the streets until an officer from the Freedmen's Bureau arrived to calm the situation. A Yankee soldier and a freedman had been shot on Greensboro's streets. Ryland Randolph took it all in.

Former Confederates continued the fight. Soon they would all be Democrats; but in this particular election they styled themselves the Conservative Union Party of Alabama, described by one Greensborian as "old-line whigs and democrats acting together to put down the radicals." The Conservatives appealed to the freedmen; but when Alabamians, including for the first time freedmen, went to the polls in early October 1867, the Republicans won handily.

Just as the elections were taking place, Randolph took action. He stacked a cot, some bedding, trunk, and chairs into a two-horse wagon and headed northward. The next day he arrived in the City of Oaks, stopped into a hotel, and sent his black driver back to Greensboro. He had moved to Tuscaloosa to take control of the thirty-year-old newspaper the *Independent Monitor*, from John J. Harris, a former schoolmate at the Greene Springs School. The *Monitor*'s former editor had counseled Tuscaloosans to "obey the laws, remain quiet," and to accept the new federal terms "in good faith."[27] Randolph would turn the newspaper in a totally different direction.

Randolph had left a lively town for a worn-out one.[28] After the state government moved from Tuscaloosa to Montgomery in late 1847, a successful and prominent legislator pushed to establish the Alabama Insane Hospital on grounds adjoining the university, and that building program was the only significant development during the 1850s. The outbreak of war had done little or nothing to stem the decline. Tuscaloosa offered the graceful and vacant old capitol to the Confederacy for its seat of government, but the proposal was never given serious attention. A prisoner-of-war camp was established in warehouses and hotels near the river and put under the command of Henry Wirz, later in charge of the Andersonville prison camp. Refugees came seeking sanctuary. The Insane Hospital was used for war casualties. Along the river were small industries adapted to helping the war effort.

But none of that mattered. It was the University of Alabama that had made Tuscaloosa a military target. Trying to instill discipline in unruly boys and perhaps anticipating the coming conflict, the general assembly had turned the university into the state's military school, modeled on West Point. After Fort Sumter, the university was responsible for supplying the armies with skilled officers. Its cadets drilled the newly formed regiments. All of that ended on the morning of April 4, 1865, when Colonel Thomas W. Johnston of the Second Michigan Cavalry started up the Huntsville Road with his men. About a mile later they turned left at the gate of the University of Alabama—the same gate that President Lakin and Dr. Cloud would enter—and rode up the cedar-lined avenue. Professor André Deloffre pleaded unsuccessfully to spare the Rotunda, the center of the campus and the home of the university's library. After Colonel Johnston took a copy of the Koran as a souvenir, the cavalrymen launched torpedoes and destroyed one of the finest libraries in the Southwest. They then torched other university buildings, leaving in ashes Alabamians' hopes for their sons' futures.[29]

Federal troops soon returned to occupy the town, and the garrison's lieutenant reportedly stretched the Stars and Stripes above the sidewalk and arrested anyone, including women, who refused to walk under it. The venerable Washington Hall, Tuscaloosa's social center, burned while occupying troops were quartered there. Some white Tuscaloosans found it difficult to find food. "You can form no idea of the suffering among the Southern people," wrote one woman who had seen strong men weep like children because they could not feed their starving families. "We are all too poor to help each other."[30] In early 1867 workers did begin rebuilding the university, but no one had any idea who would run it.

This was the Tuscaloosa that Randolph found when he took over the *Independent Monitor*. He moved his few pieces of furniture to the *Monitor* office, above John Glascock's store on the northwest corner of Broad and Monroe streets,[31] where for the next two and a half years he would go to sleep with the smell of ink filling his nostrils. It was "a business entirely new to me," he confessed later, "in a place where I did not know a half dozen people, and whose political preferences were unknown to me.[32] I sat by an open window long after midnight, wondering how on earth I could fill ten or more columns of a newspaper with editorial matter," when he had never published more than one or two such things before. "The more I thought of the difficulties ahead of me, the more nervous and desperate I became, and . . . thought seriously of abandoning the project." A night's sleep and a good breakfast bolstered his confidence. Randolph could not see it then, but his life had at last assumed a direction.[33]

Randolph's account of the move was, like his account of his Civil War experiences, an exercise in self-promotion. Unanswered questions certainly remained. Why did he enter journalism without experience? Where did he find the $3,000 to buy the paper, when his family had lost most of its wealth by selling its plantations for Confederate bonds, now worthless?[34] One possibility is that Randolph had encouragement and financial backing from like-minded wealthy former associates throughout the state. In each of Alabama's larger towns, a phalanx of unrestrained Democratic editors were neatly ensconced: the Tuskaloosa *Independent Monitor*, edited by Randolph; the *Mobile Register*, edited by John Forsyth; the Selma *Southern Argus*, which Robert McKee would found in 1869; the *Montgomery Mail*, edited by Joseph Hodgson, Randolph's former colonel in the Seventh Alabama Cavalry; and the *Huntsville Democrat*, edited by J. Withers Clay, a close relation of Randolph's future wife. In their columns, these editors would defend each other, reprint each other's articles, and even adopt each other's rhetoric. Hodgson, for example, coined the term *carpetbagger*, while Forsyth used Randolph's term *the Menagerie* to describe the state senate.[35]

In many ways Randolph's newspaper would be typical of the age: a single sheet folded to make four pages, the format dictated by the limitations of the hand-operated press. The newspaper's front and back pages were filled with advertisements that ranged from announcements of the upcoming circus to new dry goods to the latest best sellers stocked by the bookstore. Readers had to turn to the second page for news and opinion, and this was where Randolph cut loose. The large pages were divided into long columns. Because photographs would not appear in Tuscaloosa newspapers for some years, the print was only relieved by decorous mastheads and advertisements. Thus Randolph's introduction of woodcuts into the *Independent Monitor* was visually striking. Working only with white and black (no half tones), the artist selectively positioned each character for greatest effect. The resulting images may seem primitive, but they, in fact, represented the peak of the woodblock art form, before engraving took over completely. When tied to outrageous depictions of black men as apes and Republicans hanging from nooses, the effect was electric, as attested by the resulting furor.[36]

Less a departure, but still unusual, was Randolph's announced intention to pursue "independent journalism"—a newspaper, in other words, unsupported by a political party. But in fact he openly aligned the *Monitor* with the Democratic Party and vigorously opposed the Republican Party (signaled in part by changing the masthead to read *Tuskaloosa*, the more phonetic spelling preferred by the Democrats). What Randolph meant was independence of a different sort. "The man who is sure that he is right," he wrote, "and then dares not go ahead because of unnecessary caution on the part of friends, or of impotent menaces from the direction of enemies, deserves the withdrawal of support of the one, and the thorough contempt of the other." The newspaper editor was responsible for exposing threats to the people. Because the only fit journalist was the one who had the interest of the community at heart, he must strike fearlessly, regardless of the consequences or status of the evildoers. Randolph's characterization of the editor as occupying an honorable and even heroic position in the community inflated his already ample self-confidence. "I was quickly transformed from a modest, timid, stonefaced novice devoid of self-reliance," he recounted later with typical hyperbole, "to a bold, self-sufficient, arrogant and full-fledged journalist. I held my head several degrees higher." Proudly donning his best clothes, Randolph "majestically sauntered" down Broad Street.[37]

His were not empty words. Self-assertion was not a posture that the editor could put on like a raincoat to fend off the elements; indeed, self-assertion was central to Ryland Randolph's personality, for he was a Romantic.[38] He faced the world without God, without a stable home, without successes on which to build, and most of all, without illusions—free of all, slave to none. Randolph had grown up in a society obsessed with preserving its own freedom from the threats posed by concentrated power: beginning with privileged finan- cial manipulators and a powerful government and extending to the threats posed by hordes of black slaves laboring on his father's plantations. Everyone had heard what Nat Turner and his band had done in Southampton County, Virginia. Turner's 1831 rebellion had ultimately failed, but the Haitian Rev- olution had created first a bloodbath and then a spectacle. Its distant echoes could be heard as defeated Confederates faced an occupying force also bent on social equality. Opposing this off-kilter world, a free people must act as one to assert its own will. Effort, unceasing self-directed effort: that was how the people recovered their freedom. Doubt and hesitation risked servitude.

Randolph's confidence contrasted vividly to the hesitation he found among white Tuscaloosans: demoralized, wavering on the fence, undecided whether their best interests lay in supporting or resisting Republican initiatives. The situation had deteriorated until "the leading negroes of the place had become quite insolent in their demeanor to white-folks, and, to their shame be it said, the latter had grown timid and actually afraid of the former." Some friends advised Randolph to go slower "but I went all the faster."[39] Randolph's edito- rial policy would henceforth link the Democratic Party to the protection of the superior white race.

In the first issue under Randolph's editorship—dated October 16, 1867— he penned "The Issues Before the Country." The North had not gone to war for the Negro, he insisted. In the two years since the close of the war, however, the national leaders had elevated what had been a side issue into the source of "national consolidation, national greatness, national development." The Radicals in Congress believed that by simple legislative fiat, they could "lift the negro from the barbarism to the summit of civilization." Now the peo- ple were beginning to think of these things, and "for the people to think in the United States is for them to act"—a statement that summed up much of Randolph's political philosophy. Another article in that same first issue pro- claimed that "being *white* in every sense of that word, we are ardently in favor of a white man's Government," which meant strenuous opposition to Radical misrule and electing Negroes to office. Randolph held special contempt for those "nervous dotards" who believed that safety for the Southern people lay in associating with the Republicans. "They believe that Radical thirst for cruelty and the desire to humiliate the pride of the South may be quenched and appeased by rushing forward *en masse*—negroes and all—to kiss the smiting rod." The new editor had set the tone for his newspaper.

Mere prose would never satisfy Randolph, who engaged in so many violent and sometimes deadly personal confrontations that he lost count.[40] The first of these apparently occurred within weeks of his arrival in Tuscaloosa. Hampton S. Whitfield, a local lawyer and editor of the rival Republican newspaper, the Tuscaloosa *Reconstructionist*, had reprinted an article that Randolph deemed "an abusive communication" and "personally offensive." Randolph found Whitfield responsible and challenged him to a duel across the state line in Mississippi. Whitfield declined but suggested instead a street fight, which Randolph in turn declined. As much of this was carried out through the columns of their newspapers, the authorities arrested both men and put each under a $2,500 bond. Whitfield would later be appointed professor of mathematics at the University of Alabama and his Republican newspaper taken over by Randolph's former printer, Dennis Dykous. When the new editor of the *Reconstructionist* described Randolph as "the petticoat hero" after so many Tuscaloosa women came to meet him upon release from prison in another affair, Randolph immediately became "piping hot" and started for his rival's office. As it happened, Randolph met Dykous on the way, "slapped soundly his jaws," and then pulled out a pistol. For once the confrontation ended without bloodshed, merely a $20 fine from the Republican mayor.[41] Not in reflection but in exertion—therein lay Randolph's future.

Randolph had entered Tuscaloosa just two weeks after the election for a convention charged with rewriting the state's constitution yet again. The Republican-dominated convention began its work the next month, in November 1867. The former Confederates, with Randolph in the lead, bitterly denounced the Republicans' efforts. As the convention finished drafting the new constitution, Randolph penned an editorial titled "Duty of White Men." Once again he aimed some of his sharpest barbs at the fence straddlers: "We would rather be a Radical; aye, we would rather be a *negro*, than one of these timid apologies for the white species, who does not maintain the supremacy of his race." The old boogeyman of buck Negroes marrying fair white daughters was once again trotted out. And then Randolph posed what was for him an ironic question: "Why did the Great God make such creatures in the shape of men?"[42]

5. The "Fence Straddler" (Tuskaloosa *Independent Monitor* July 14)

Throughout the state former Confederates organized to block the Republicans using a two-pronged approach: boycott and intimidation. Not voting in the February referendum to approve the new constitution could defeat it, even if all the votes cast were in its favor. This was because the Second Reconstruction Act passed by Congress contained a clause stating that the referendum had to be passed by a majority of registered voters and not merely a majority of votes cast. Randolph and other Democratic editors called for organized and violent resistance to prevent ratification. Their tactics succeeded, at least in the short run, as the minimum number of votes were not cast, although the majority of the votes cast were in favor of the new constitution. The boycott also called into question the status of a number of officials whose elections were held at the same time. "Alabama Redeemed!" read an *Independent Monitor* headline. Randolph could take pride in the fact that only 12 percent of registered white voters had gone to the polls in Tuscaloosa County. But that only left the source of political authority even less clear, especially as word was filtering back that the Republicans were about to impeach President Johnson and install a military dictator "in the person of the unprincipled ninny, Grant."[43]

The Democrats also began a more or less systematic program of intimidation. The January 22, 1868, issue of the *Independent Monitor* marked a departure. For the first time Randolph included the motto, emblazoned in all caps, for which his newspaper became notorious:

WHITE MAN—RIGHT OR WRONG—STILL THE WHITE MAN
AGAINST NEGRO EQUALITY—SOCIALLY OR POLITICALLY

That same issue called for "respectable white men" to rally the next Saturday to protect their wives and children. Each issue of the *Independent Monitor* ratcheted up the challenge for whites to prove their sentiments with action. Do not "trade with negroes, who registered their enmity against the welfare of the Caucasian race by voting for the wretched Constitution," Randolph proclaimed; nor should the "white skinned knaves" who supported the Constitution be given any patronage. He then went on to name those whose businesses should be boycotted. The first mention of the Ku Klux Klan in the *Monitor*'s columns seems to have been on March 25, and the next week Randolph devoted much of the paper to reporting on the organization in great detail, including descriptions of the Klan's initiation oath, secret ceremonies, and threatening posters that had been pasted on the walls of prominent Tuscaloosa buildings.[44]

According to Randolph, twenty or more Tuscaloosans banded together during the spring of 1868 to "strike terror into the hearts and minds of the worst elements of the tampered-with negro race, and to severely punish those whose insolence had become intolerable." The Klansmen also made a pact to assist any white man who had difficulty with a black man. They invariably worked in darkness wearing a sheet and mask in order to suggest that they were Confederate ghosts, which in a metaphorical sense they were. Each man kept one or more pistols in the holsters attached to his belt. They made it a point to single out the most vocal freedmen, take them to the old boneyard on the outskirts of Tuscaloosa, and "liberally applied the lash well laid on their bare backs. There they were left tied to trees till after our retirement. They invariably gave vent to yells which generally attracted the nearest neighbors and effected their release." The Klan would not stop with beatings. Randolph knew firsthand of these affairs, for he proudly claimed years later that he had been chosen the Tuscaloosa Klan's first leader.[45]

The intimidation, emerging violence, and Klan activity might suggest an attempt to continue the war. Many of their tactics were probably honed during the war, but these tactics were also familiar from the days of slavery. The purpose was a restoration of what former Confederates viewed as the natural order, the *status quo antebellum*, interrupted by four years of war and another three of uncertainty. For such failed, rootless, and frustrated individuals as Randolph, intimidation and violence gave them purpose. The three strands of the Republican Party in the South—carpetbaggers from the North, native white scalawags, and the black freed people—complemented each other and daily reminded the former Confederates that all had been turned on its head.[46]

During the time that Randolph was involved in organizing the Klan, an incident occurred that thrust him into statewide prominence. Even accounting for his dramatic exaggeration and self-satisfaction, the incident was clearly a turning point that secured his reputation as a man of courage, a champion ready to stand up to enraged, violent, and irrational mobs.

The Klansmen had already announced it their sworn duty to assist any white man who was having difficulties with a black man. Randolph had seen ample precedents in Greensboro. Then it was his turn. The opportunity came on Saturday, March 28 of that eventful year, 1868.[47] The day before, "an impudent yellow rascal" had struck a white man, who did not respond. Randolph interpreted the white man's passivity as emboldening the freedmen. Randolph was writing at his desk the next morning about eleven o'clock when the customary auction was going on in front of Rhea's store, diagonally across Broad Street from Randolph office above Glascock's store. He heard a commotion, pulled a derringer and long-bladed dirk from his desk, and rushed downstairs into the street. Two "burly negroes," according to Randolph, "had a small white man [John Hollingsworth] down on the side-walk, one of them [Balus Eddins] beating him unmercifully with a big bludgeon." Not only were the two black men assailing the single white defender, but other black men were egging on their black friends while "a score of white men looked on and did not offer to separate the combatants, much less take sides."

Randolph strongly suspected that the collision was partly in retaliation for previous beatings inflicted by the Klan, so he could not let the incident go. He hesitated but a moment out of concern that he could injure some innocent bystanders. Then he took his pistol, aimed it several feet above the black men's heads, and fired. The fighting stopped, but Eddins rushed at Randolph with his stick. With his left hand Randolph caught the stick as it was coming down, opening the spring-loaded blade of his knife with his right and stabbing Eddins until he fell unconscious. Meanwhile, the small white man, Hollingsworth, "crazed with pain and a desire for vengeance," took a large piece of flagstone in both hands and began pummeling the back of Eddins's head as he lay motionless on his stomach. Randolph stopped the unnecessary stoning, coolly and deliberately wiped the knife blade on the sole of his shoe, discovering that about an inch of the point had broken off in Eddins's back, and walked leisurely back to Glascock's Corner.

A crowd of some one or two hundred irate freedmen soon gathered on Broad Street. Randolph climbed the stairs into his office and took down his double barreled shotgun, already loaded with buckshot, and a repeater. Some half-dozen of his friends, fearing for Randolph's safety, rushed to his office and begged him to leave town by way of a horse waiting out back. The freedmen, they advised, were not only organizing to kill Randolph, but to burn the town (as they had threatened to burn Greensboro). He thanked his friends for their well-intentioned advice but informed them that if he were to leave, then "all the good I had just done would be cancelled, and the negroes would be worse than ever, and . . . that I was determined to settle the matter of race supremacy right there and then." Randolph walked down the stairs to face the mob. "I raised my gun as if to fire and, alone, started towards the crowd," which immediately retreated pell-mell "like a herd of stampeding buffaloes." The "skedaddle" was so great "that even I could not resist the temptation of laughing; and, to make the fun more complete, I sighted my gun at the fleeing mob." In less than a minute, not a freedman was to be seen on the streets of Tuscaloosa.

The incident made Randolph an instant hero, and those friends who had urged escape admitted the error of their ways. The next issue of the *Independent Monitor* contained all sorts of warnings. To the freedmen: "This will, doubtless, serve as a caution to those many insolent negroes, who essay to fight the ruling race of the land." To white Republicans: "Let those so-called white men, who have hitherto acted in concert with negroes, remember that whenever a true white man falls by black hands, not only all negroes, but themselves will pay the forfeit with their lives." To the fence-straddlers: "Let no white man, hereafter, tamely submit to abuse from negroes.—Let no white man stand passively by, and see a white man assaulted by a negro." To the former Confederates: "Let every true white man be thoroughly armed, by day and night, and be ready to begin the work of destruction upon both white and black niggers, in case a *drop* of pure Caucasian blood be spilt."

Neither the blood on the town's streets nor the ink on the *Monitor*'s pages would pass unchallenged.[48] A few days later the local justice of the peace ordered Randolph to appear in his court. Randolph was charged with assault and battery, his bond set at a significant $1,500 (soon paid by twenty of his friends), and he was ordered to report to the circuit judge. Randolph slipped out of town to present himself to authorities in Montgomery. Thinking he had escaped, federal troops were ordered to Tuscaloosa to search homes where they thought he might be hiding.

By this time, April 15, Randolph was in Selma meeting with his old class-mate and commanding officer James Holt Clanton, who offered to serve on Randolph's defense. Randolph left Selma a few days later for Montgomery to report to Brevet Brigadier General Oliver Lathrop Shepherd, the state's new director of the Freedman's Bureau and military commander (Alabama still being under military rule).[49] Shepherd received him cordially that evening; but the atmosphere changed when Randolph returned the next morning. As a guard stood in readiness, Randolph and Shepherd argued over which version of the events was to be believed. Randolph surely did himself no fa-vors when he vowed "to 'pitch into' scalawags, niggers, and carpetbaggers to the end of recorded time." (The irony that Randolph himself was carry-ing a carpetbag that he had just purchased in Selma was not lost on those in the room.) Shepherd then arrested Randolph, denied him bail, and had him marched through the streets to be confined in a carpenter shop that was serv-ing as the camp brig.

Randolph remained behind bars for a week. With the food, furniture, and flowers that his friends provided, things were not so bad. Then on April 25 he was unexpectedly placed in the filthy Selma jail, which he shared with eleven other inmates and his old pals, the greybacks. From there he wrote letters that were published in the Democratic press. "Time will bring us relief," began one, and urged Democrats not to back down before Shepherd or any other man who tries "to trample upon personal liberty and political rights." He also urged Alabama's white citizens to "keep the negro in his proper sphere of far inferiority. Make the vulgar race behave, or—but they know what."[50]

Randolph's friends met at the Tuscaloosa courthouse and adopted reso-lutions condemning the military for interfering with what should have been a civil matter. They also petitioned President Johnson to remove Shepherd (a rather silly move, for Johnson was then squarely in the middle of his im-peachment trial). Randolph's counsel, meanwhile, filed a writ of *habeas cor-pus* to move the case out from military jurisdiction into the court of Richard Busteed, US district judge for Alabama. All these the authorities disregarded.

Randolph's trial, before a commission of four army officers, finally began in Selma on May 4. After the charges were read ("unlawfully and with mal-ice aforethought did assault one Balus Eddins, a freedman of color, with in-tent feloniously and with malice aforethought to murder him the said Balus Eddins"), the defense protested that a military trial was unlawful—denied, of course. The prosecution called Eddins, who stated that Randolph had first shot at him (not as a warning over his head) and then had stabbed him *before*

Randolph had been hit with the stick. The prosecution's second witness, the son of a Tuscaloosa County scalawag, was unsure if Randolph had fired his pistol at Eddins and if Randolph had even stabbed Eddins. The four defense witnesses, all Tuscaloosans, essentially corroborated Randolph's account and condemned Eddins, one calling him "a notorious liar." A final defense witness, a one-legged black shoemaker, spoke to Eddins's truthful character. The last day of the four-day trial was devoted to closing arguments. The military commission then reached its verdict. But the verdict would not be made public until released by Major General George G. Meade, commander of the Third Military District in which Alabama was placed.

Four days later and to everyone's surprise, Randolph was released. The court had found him not guilty. Explanations abounded, focusing primarily on personal influence and an unwillingness to confront the federal courts. The most likely explanation was that the evidence—mostly conflicting—was simply not strong enough for a conviction.

Randolph's local supporters rejoiced, but the real celebration awaited Randolph's arrival back in the City of Oaks. When he neared, his lawyers rode out the Greensboro road to meet him, as did ladies who decorated his carriage and horses with flowers (thus earning him the despised title "petticoat hero" from the rival Tuscaloosa *Reconstructionist*). Church bells tolled, and that evening, May 14, a dinner was held in his honor at an oak grove outside of town. He had returned in triumph even surer, if that was possible, of his path.

While Randolph was engrossed in his trial, a federal judge sentenced some young men to lengthy terms at a prison in the Dry Tortugas for attacking one J. B. F. Hill, a white Northern Methodist minister and schoolteacher of black children in Greene County. The Democrats were outraged.[51] And less than two weeks after Randolph's triumphal entrance, President Johnson, too, was finally acquitted in his impeachment trials; but unlike Randolph, the innocent Johnson had been rendered powerless. Soon Congress would brush aside the Democrats' election boycott and declare the new state constitution ratified. By July the state's delegation would be seated in Washington while a new Republican-dominated general assembly convened and a Republican governor took the oath of office in Montgomery. And only a few months after that was November 3, the day of the next presidential election. Events were moving at a bewildering pace in unexpected directions.

Randolph and the Democrats faced these challenges in predictable fashion: through intimidation and confrontation. While Klan activity increased during the summer and fall leading up to the 1868 presidential election, the editor added a new tool to his arsenal. Back in December 1867, only two months after Randolph published his first issue, he had advertised for an artist to create political woodcuts for the *Independent Monitor*.[52] Nothing more was heard for six months. Then on June 16 the first crude cartoon appeared. *After the Presidential Election. Flight of the Carpet-Bagger!* depicted a man in swallow-tailed coat and stove-pipe hat striding off with his carpetbag emblazoned *US*; in the background can be seen a Klan poster such as those warning the freedmen. Nearly two dozen cartoons would follow. Some singled out scalawags, especially Tuscaloosa's appointed Republican mayor, aldermen, and marshal. Others turned on carpetbaggers and freedmen. None were subtle.

All this—the continuing harassment in print, Randolph's acquittal, the fracas over the "petticoat hero" comment—all this was too much for Brigadier General Shepherd. On June 23 the *Monitor*'s editor was charged with violating General Order No. 51, "publication of articles tending to produce intimidation, riot, or bloodshed." Randolph's particularly offensive lines read: "As for carpet-baggers, scalawags and political niggers—I will give them no quarter." Their choices are either to leave the county and quit politics, "or remain and risk the chances of suspension with hemp." When the June 23 issue came out, the newsboy was arrested, all copies seized, and a file of soldiers closed the *Monitor* office and put an armed guard at its entrance. Somehow Randolph learned of the plan in advance and, unwilling to revisit the lousy Selma calaboose, joined friends in Foster's settlement, southeast of Tuscaloosa on the other side of the Black Warrior River. Shepherd lifted his order on July 19. The effect was not what the federal authorities had wished. "The Spirit of Rebellion seems to have taken a renewed start," observed an agent for the Freedmen's Bureau in Tuscaloosa, and "all this disturb[a]nce is caused by that same Newspaper and its Editor," Ryland Randolph.[53]

Looming behind all this lay the bitterest fight of all: reopening the University of Alabama.

During the fall of 1865 the faculty had attempted to reopen the university in homes and what was left of the once grand campus—to no avail.[54] Their failure convinced everyone that a proper campus was necessary. Gradually the trustees cobbled together enough money to begin making bricks and to hire an architect. After setbacks and false starts, Centre Building, as it was first known, neared completion in spring 1868, and the trustees began looking to fill faculty positions. In June they tapped former Professor Henry Tutwiler

6. "Monitor office under Federal guard, 1868. Paper suppressed."
(Courtesy Alabama Department of Archives and History)

(whose Greene Springs School, Ryland Randolph had attended) to be president. If Tutwiler declined, the trustees specified that Professor William Stokes Wyman, the university's professor of ancient languages, would then serve.

But the decision on June 25 by Congress to affirm Alabama's 1867 constitution also affirmed the election of a host of state and local officials along with the new governor and Congressional delegation. This included a new state board of education and superintendent of education, the scalawag Dr. Noah B. Cloud.[55] These seven Republicans (one for each congressional district) and the superintendent not only had responsibility for creating a statewide system of public education, but served as the university's board of regents, its new name signaling a break with the former board of trustees it replaced. The regents' first task would be to select a new faculty and president free from any political affiliation with the party of secession—only Republicans, in other words. The board selected as president of the University of Alabama a carpetbagger, the Reverend Arad Lakin.

The reaction was predictable. "Cloud and his associate ignoramuses," sniffed the editor of the *Montgomery Advertiser*, have elected a president "who has been preaching politics to the negroes ever since he squatted in Alabama." A few days later under the heading "The State University—The Feast of the Vultures," the editor of the Tuskaloosa *Independent Monitor* warned that if the new president and his faculty "expect to live quietly here, and draw their salaries, extorted from the sweating brows of the toiling tax-payers of Alabama, *we tell them, they are mistaken.*" And to add to the point, "This community will be too disagreeable for them, and the sooner they resign the better." The following week Randolph reprinted an article from the *Montgomery Mail* titled "The University—What is to be Done?" penned by his friend and former commander Joseph Hodgson. The article reported that the four carpetbaggers and four scalawags who comprised the board of regents had elected four professors, three of whom hailed from Ohio, and as president "that political preacher who has been retailing his falsehoods throughout the poorer sections of our upper counties"—in other words, Arad Lakin.[56]

And little else was seen in the *Monitor* for two weeks.

✕✕✕

On Tuesday morning, September 1, four days after President Lakin and Superintendent Cloud had been rebuffed by Professor Wyman, Randolph published *A Prospective Scene* in the *Independent Monitor*. The beginning of the extensive caption read:

> "Hang, curs, hang! ＊ ＊ ＊ ＊ ＊ *Their* complexion is perfect gallows. Stand fast, good fate to *their* hanging! ＊ ＊ ＊ ＊ ＊ If they be not born to be hanged, our case is miserable."
>
> The above cut represents the fate in store for those great pests of Southern society—the carpet-bagger and the scallawag—if found in Dixie's Land after the break of day on the 4th of March next.

The allusion was to the inauguration of a new Democratic president, Horatio Seymour, and vice president, Francis P. Blair, who were running against the Republican candidates Ulysses S. Grant and Schuyler Colfax. The election was two months off. No mention was found in the *Independent Monitor* of the Klan's pursuit of Lakin as he left town, but Randolph did note that both Lakin and Cloud "would make first rate hemp-stretchers."

)()()(

Randolph did not anticipate the furor that his cartoon and caption would raise. Somehow a copy of the *Independent Monitor* made its way to Cincinnati, Ohio, where on the front page of the *Commercial*'s September 19 edition *A Prospective Scene* was reprinted along with the alarming headlines:

SPIRIT OF THE SOUTHERN DEMOCRATIC PRESS.
REBEL ILLUSTRATION OF SCENES WHEN SEYMOUR IS
    INAUGURATED.
EMIGRANTS FROM OHIO TO ALABAMA WARNED OF THEIR
    DOOM.

This was but the opening salvo. The *Cincinnati Commercial* reprinted the caption in its entirety below the cartoon and beside it detailed some of the more lurid lines from the same issue of the *Monitor*. The same *Monitor* material, including the woodcut, then appeared in the *Commercial*'s four-page political campaign edition that reportedly ran to five hundred thousand copies. The *Columbus State Journal* then reprinted the cartoon, and the *Cleveland Herald* printed an article titled "Spir[i]t of Southern Democracy. Gems from a Southern Democratic Paper—Ohioans to be Hung."[57] The message was clear: Here is what will happen if the Republicans lose in November.

The Democrats moved quickly to check the damage through a nineteenth-century version of spin control. Less than a week after the *Cincinnati Commercial* reprinted the woodcut, the editor of the Democratic *Montgomery Advertiser*, W. W. Screws, dismissed it all as "Much Ado About Nothing." The woodcut was a "joke." The artistic engraver could never have guessed that his accidental selection of Ohio on the side of the carpetbag was of any consequence. "Everybody knew" that the editor was using the cartoon as "a kind of local warfare of a jocose character" upon two or three local Tuscaloosa carpetbaggers. "Everybody knew" that Randolph was really "a brave and generous man, though somewhat erratic in his impulses" and "would not injure even his worst enemy if he had him at disadvantage." The *Advertiser*'s editor then tried to turn the tables. Because "everybody knew" how shamefully white Southerners were being misrepresented by the Radicals, who would use such matters to injure the South, the State Democratic Executive Committee generously condemned the woodcut as evidence that the Democratic Party in Alabama "is just as peaceable and loyal as that of the Radical party in Ohio."[58]

The *Mobile Register* took a different tack. The editor, John Forsyth, had been running hopeful articles predicting a majority of fifty thousand in Ohio for the Democratic nominee, Seymour. But then he began to have second thoughts, realizing that Randolph's cartoon might be used against them; so he shifted to advocating a "lynx-like vigilance" for every "unguarded, hyperbolical, extravagant, or ambiguous expression" spoken by a Southern orator or penned by a Southern editor that might "give the enemy any advantage." It was too late. After the *Commercial* reprinted the cartoon, Forsyth, too, tried to turn the argument on its head in an open letter to the editor of Cincinnati's Democratic paper, the *Enquirer*. All true Southerners were Union men, he proclaimed; it was only "the carpet-bag, Radical advocates of negro supremacy and white disfranchisement" who were the "partisans and artificers of disunion in practice and effect." The uproar in the *Commercial* was all political hyperbole and opportunism concocted over "a silly wood cut, and a series of injudicious articles copied from the Tuscalo[o]sa *Monitor*." Randolph was no villain, but a victim of Radical reconstruction, a man who "has been deprived of his liberty, assailed in his business and property, and threatened with imprisonment at the Dry Tortugas." In sum, the editor of the *Monitor* had "a right to hate carpet-baggers and military rule." Then Forsyth moved beyond the silly political cartoon to the real issue: the prospect of a people "of the master type, the fair complexion and Saxon lineaments, prostrate upon the earth, chained from wrists to ankles, while standing over it is a barbarian of terrible aspect, dark as Erebus in color." More than a mere prospect, the loss of freedom by Southern whites was a "sad reality, the disgrace of the age, a foul stain upon the records of American civilization and humanity."[59]

Randolph had already learned of his fellow Democratic editors' dismay. On September 22, five days before the *Montgomery Advertiser*'s attempt to dismiss *A Prospective Scene* as a joke and only three days after the *Cincinnati Commercial*'s front page reproduction of the cartoon, the *Monitor* published a follow-up cartoon lampooning its reception in the *Advertiser*'s office. And a few weeks later Randolph penned his own letter to the editor of the *Cincinnati Enquirer*, reprinted in the *Mobile Register*, which again tried to make light of the incident. This time he blamed the woodcut on one of his younger employees. "The sketch was understood by every one here to be a piece of pleasantry, gotten up, in a spirit of fun, by the devils of the Monitor office. . . . Had it been intended seriously, I would never have allowed it to go into the columns of the Monitor." Randolph, too, charged the *Commercial* with disingenuously perverting the woodcut for political purposes.[60]

The Democrats' efforts were ineffective, and they knew it. A few days after Forsyth's letter to the *Cincinnati Enquirer*, he was forced to admit that the *Commercial*'s reprinting of Randolph's woodcut had been disastrous, perhaps shifting 5,000 votes from the Democrats to the Republicans. (Other newspapers would up the estimate to 10,000.) Rather than merely silly, the woodcut was now obnoxious, damaging, and absurd, "another of the many indiscretions of hot-headed and impatient politicians among us." The Democratic Executive Committee, chaired by Randolph's old friend and attorney James Holt Clanton, expelled Randolph from the party.[61] But the Republican press saw the move as merely expedient. "The truth is," the Montgomery *Alabama State Journal* noted, "Randolph reflected the sentiments, views, hates and feelings of the Democracy." And telegraph lines spread the story of the woodcut across the nation—from San Francisco, California, to Bangor, Maine—just in time for the November 3 election.[62] The Democrats were soundly beaten in the 1868 election. The Republicans carried Ohio by over 40,000 votes, and in the Electoral College, Grant and Colfax would record 214 votes to Seymour and Blair's 80. *Citizens were disgusted*

Defeat at the polls only embittered the Democrats to look for revenge. Ten days after the election, Meredith T. Crossland, one of Tuscaloosa's two delegates to the state House of Representatives, was on his way to the regular session in Montgomery with one of the representatives from Pickens County. Crossland was a Republican who had won his seat in the February election that the Democrats boycotted. While he crossed the Sipsey swamp, the Klan's center in west Alabama between Tuscaloosa and Mississippi, he was ambushed and murdered. Republican governor William Hugh Smith sent investigators. Tuscaloosa's sheriff and the county solicitor both resigned. The governor's representatives noted that after a conference with Randolph in the *Monitor* office, one of the freedmen who was being held prisoner "was taken out of jail and murderously shot." Their conclusion: Ryland Randolph's paper "has contained numerous paragraphs directly advising assassination and house burning," and the recent murders and disorders were the fruits "of the lawless and

7. Reaction of the Democratic *Montgomery Advertiser* to *A Prospective Scene*
(Tuskaloosa *Independent Monitor* 1868 September 22)

8. "A Sample Grant Voter," according to Ryland Randolph
(Tuskaloosa *Independent Monitor* 1868 November 17)

revolutionary doctrines constantly inculcated by the *Tuskaloosa Monitor*." No indictments were filed and the murders and disorders would continue.[63]

Randolph was not slowed. He turned his attacks to the Republicans' attempts to reopen the University of Alabama. Not long after the regents met again in December, word leaked out that they had found a new faculty.

"Worse and Worse!" ran the headline. The regents had selected the Reverend R. D. Harper to succeed Lakin. Not only was Harper, like Lakin, a minister, but he had served as inspector and superintendent of schools for the Freedmen's Bureau and been in contention for the university's presidency at the regents' earlier meetings. Randolph described him as having organized Negro schools in north Alabama and as "inculcating ideas of miscegenation in brutish negro minds." The editor then implied that the Klan might show up again at the university and turn Harper's hair grey. Objectionable as Harper was, he was not as detested as Vernon Henry Vaughan, the newly appointed professor of history, logic, and metaphysics. Randolph knew Vaughan well, for the two had had served together in Clanton's brigade; but he was now a scalawag and thus a traitor. Of the others Randolph professed to know nothing, except for John H. Forney, former Confederate major general and now professor of mathematics, and W. K. McConnell, former Confederate colonel and now commandant of cadets, who both got Randolph's grudging approval.[64]

By mid-February 1869, the superintendent of education was steaming up the Black Warrior aboard the *Jennie Rogers*. This time he had with him several of the new faculty. Before the boat landed, some mischievous urchin wrote the letters *KKK* upon their baggage—not an auspicious beginning. The *Monitor*, of course, extended its usual greetings. Dr. Cloud, the visionary "scholarwag," had already announced in Selma that sixty or seventy students were awaiting admission—a claim that caused Randolph to howl with laughter. Two students was more like it.[65] Another cartoon, ridiculing the arrival of Professor Vaughan, appeared in the March 2 issue accompanied by another lengthy caption. This time Randolph came up with something new: a comedic farce. Performed at the courthouse two weeks before Vaughan's arrival, the skit featured the university's Republican faculty, a scalawag servant, and black students (including a son of Shandy Jones). The play ended with the students and professors running out pell-mell after seeing Klansmen.

The university would not keep this new president either. Harper left in March after receiving a copy of the *Monitor* with an editorial warning that the Tuscaloosa Klan had him targeted. Harper was succeeded by J. DeForest Richards, professor of natural philosophy and astronomy. He was originally from Vermont but had recently represented Wilcox County as a state senator. Under President Richards and Superintendent Cloud, who returned briefly to the City of Oaks, the university did manage to open with twenty students in early April. Randolph wasted no time. The next day he published another racist cartoon, this one portraying the black barber Shandy Jones as an ape hugging the latest president. Richards was soon gone and replaced on an interim basis by N. R. Chambliss who, according to the *Monitor*, had "commanded a Spartan band of three scallawag cadets at the close of last session." Randolph suggested that the regents select Raphael Semmes, former captain of the CSS *Alabama*, but they instead chose Cyrus Northrop, then a Yale professor, who promptly turned them down. In July the board of regents invited Commodore Matthew Fontaine Maury, famed oceanographer and Confederate chief of Sea Coast, River and Harbor Defenses; but Maury was unwilling to leave Virginia Military Institute. Later that year, Nathaniel Lupton, professor of chemistry at Southern University in Greensboro, was elected president; but he promptly resigned (he would accept in 1871). Finding a stable and enduring president for the University of Alabama was a frustrating experience for the Republican board of regents and would continue to be so.[66]

Through all this Randolph hardly confined himself to writing editorials in his office above Glascock's store. He ventured out for the occasional duel and street fight. He had already tried to fight a duel with the *Reconstructionist*'s first editor in October 1867, had struck Balus Eddins in late March the following year, and boxed the ears of his former printer after he left to edit the rival Republican paper. Sometime during those years he nearly fought a duel with a man who came all the way from Yazoo City, Mississippi, to challenge him for some unrecorded reason. Then in March 1869 John M. Martin—son of a former governor, a prominent Tuscaloosan, and Randolph's former schoolmate—decided to take up the cause of his father-in-law, Judge E. W. Peck, whom Randolph had been vilifying as an offensive Radical. Before Martin's friends settled the matter, Martin and Randolph traveled all the way to Memphis with the intention of dueling the next morning across the river in Arkansas.[67]

These confrontations ended without further incident; in fact, Martin would even serve later as Randolph's attorney. Not so Randolph's confrontations with the University of Alabama faculty. During that same spring of 1869, the University of Alabama's professor of belle lettres, J. C. Loomis (whose father was a founder and president of Shurtleff College in Illinois) refused to let the newsboy enter the university grounds to deliver a half-dozen copies of the *Monitor*. After frittering away many hours trying to meet the professor on the streets, Randolph sent him a "peremptory note of warning, informing him in language unmistakably plain even to one of his dull literary comprehension," that if he ever dared to interfere with the delivery of the newspaper, that Randolph would "on sight, proceed to give him a d— good whipping." The threat changed nothing, and Loomis continued to send the paperboy off the campus. "This was a little too much even for a man of peace like myself," wrote Randolph ironically. "I armed myself on Saturday . . . with a good stick, and put a repeater in my hip-pocket" and stood with a good view of Mayor David Woodruff's bookstore, the unofficial headquarters of the Republicans. When Randolph spied the professor there, he walked inside and "struck him over the head with my stick, and he keeled over in front of the counter." Randolph then jerked out his pistol and aimed. Loomis "begged so abjectly for me not to shoot that I could not avoid giving vent to a hearty laugh." Randolph gave the professor a lecture and walked off. The *Monitor* was henceforth always delivered to the campus.[68]

Curiously, for he regularly smeared the general assembly in his editorials, Randolph decided to run for a seat in the state House of Representatives—in fact, the seat formerly held by the murdered Republican Meredith Crossland. Clanton did his part by urging the local Tuscaloosa Democratic committee to secure Randolph's election by every means. The editor won by a six hundred vote majority. He at last took his seat "with some of those vile thieves and baboons," as he termed them.[69] True to form, his brief career as a legislator would be marked by uncompromising obloquy. Tuscaloosa's other representative in the state house was none other than Tuscaloosa's most prominent freedman, the Republican Shandy Jones.

Two days into the session, which began in November 1869, a Republican challenged Randolph's seating because of the duel he had nearly fought with John Martin a few months before. A committee of five charged with investigating the matter decided that there were insufficient grounds for dismissing him. Yet the committee's decision did not disappoint several Republican legislators who hoped that Randolph's outrageous antics would redound to his detriment and to their benefit.[70]

So Randolph was seated. With the seventeen Democrats vastly outnumbered by the sixty-five Republicans, he could exert little direct influence. Instead, he reported in his columns the activities of the "House of Misrepresentatives," where he served, and its counterpart on the other side of the statehouse, the "Menagerie." Randolph introduced only one significant piece of legislation during his tenure: a bill to declare illegal all marriages performed during the war. He claimed that his sole purpose in introducing the bill was to make the legislature look foolish. But more was at stake. The Republicans did not recognize secession and wanted to penalize those who had taken the state out. This could be accomplished by withholding legal recognition to the debts owed to slaveholding planters, whom the Republicans held most responsible. The Democrats, representing former Confederates, wanted to recognize all legal transactions incurred during the four-year war, especially those debts owed to wealthy planters. By lumping marriages with debts, Randolph's legislation implied that the state could not pick and choose which war-time contracts it would recognize and which it would not. Randolph's bill was strenuously and successfully opposed by the Republicans and especially by his Tuscaloosa counterpart, Jones.[71]

Only two months after he had entered, Randolph left the legislature—but not before making a scathing farewell speech. "I came here believing," he told them, "that you were a body of organized plunderers and thieves. I leave you fully impressed with the justice of my previous convictions." Then for good measure the House expelled him.[72]

He left the legislature, at least in part, to be married. On February 2 he wed Katharine Clay Withers, an orphan who had been brought up in some of Alabama's most elegant circles. Katharine's sister had married into Tuscaloosa's Battle family, whose home on Greensboro Avenue was justly prized for its elegant faux sandstone façade and the formal garden that framed it. Katharine herself had been informally adopted by her relative (described as a cousin but actually her uncle by marriage) Alabama's Senator Clement Claiborne Clay. Randolph had admired Clay, a strong proponent of slavery and states' rights who served in the Confederate Senate, and had even dined with him and his wife at the Montgomery home of Episcopal bishop Nicholas Hamner Cobbs. C. C. Clay and J. Withers Clay, editor of the *Huntsville Democrat*, were brothers. Katharine was the epitome of a proper Southern belle. It was probably she whom Virginia Tunstall (Mrs. C. C.) Clay described at a Washington, DC, ball in late 1857: "the tiny Miss Withers was, robed in innumerable spangled petticoats that floated as she danced, her gauze wings quivering like those of a butterfly, and her unusually small feet glistening no less brilliantly with spangles."[73]

The elegant Katharine Withers's attraction to the coarse Ryland Randolph seems at first puzzling. But both were well connected. Some of the most prominent members of the Withers clan lived in Greene County, not far from Randolph's uncle; and Randolph traveled in some of the same pro-secession circles as the Clays and the Withers while living in Montgomery. He was also exceptionally well read, despite his disrupted education. As he was preparing to enter the legislature, for example, he took Professor Loomis to task for citing Demosthenes's *Oratio pro corona* when it should have been *Oratio de corona.* The Greek original could be rendered in Latin either way, but that Randolph would quibble with a single preposition is telling. In his *Scribbles,* Randolph showed that he was conversant with Voltaire, David Hume, Constantin-Francois Volney, Auguste Compte, Thomas Paine, Thomas Huxley, and Robert Greene Ingersoll—all atheists. He would quote from Samuel Johnson and Oliver Goldsmith. Ryland Randolph may have been a brute, but he was neither an antisocial nor ignorant brute.[74]

Only two months after his marriage, Randolph engaged in his last fight on the streets of Tuscaloosa.[75] About noon on the first day of April 1870, a Friday, Randolph was standing on the edge of the sidewalk at Foster's Corner, conversing with an acquaintance, when a young man rudely brushed up against him. Randolph did not recognize the stout and "insolent rowdy," assuming him to be part of the circus, which was in town at that time. No matter, Randolph immediately struck him in the face with his right fist. The young man pulled a Colt Navy repeater from under his coat and fired straight at Randolph's heart. Fortunately, Randolph had only that morning put in his chest pocket twenty-five dollars in paper money paid him by the circus for advertising. The two- or three-inch wad of twenty-five and fifty cent notes stopped the bullet. Randolph was stunned but did not fall. His assailant started to back away and fired two more shots, missing Randolph. One of the bullets, however, went straight through the head of William H. Byrd, the elderly keeper of the town scales, who was standing behind Randolph.

Randolph recovered enough presence of mind to pull out his own pistol and shoot back at the retreating assailant. One of the bullets went through the young man's hat while another hit the large buckle on his pistol belt, which held a second Colt repeater. "Each stood within two yards of the other, almost hand to hand, firing repeaters at each other's heads, the powder from the pistols blinding each other's eyes, and burning each other's faces." Out of bullets, the assassin turned and started to run. Randolph fired his last shot, which struck home—the middle of the back—and the assailant hollered as dust came out of his coat. (Randolph had spilled some powder loading that cartridge, so the bullet did little damage.) Randolph threw his empty pistol at his retreating antagonist who, realizing that Randolph was out of shots, turned and renewed his assault, first with another repeater and then with a large knife. Randolph, too, had a large knife and drew it from its scabbard. The young man turned and ran through Foster's shoe store, firing backward. One of those shots struck Randolph in his left leg an inch above his knee, glancing upwards through the thigh and struck his femoral artery.

The unconscious editor was taken to the office of Dr. James Guild (who had earlier saved Balus Eddins's life). The blood expanded Randolph's thigh to immense proportions, which somehow prevented his bleeding to death. When he stabilized, he was put on a makeshift stretcher and taken home to be nursed by his bride. Several daily injections of morphine eased his suffering. A .44 calibre bullet was cut out from the underside of Randolph's thigh, nearly eighteen inches from where it had entered. But the mouth of the wound would not heal, and his thigh remained abnormally large. Gangrene set in after two weeks, and Randolph's mind began to wander. The doctors consulted with each other and decided that his only chance of survival lay in amputation. "All right," he replied feebly. A will was drawn up, the chloroform administered, and his leg removed about four inches from his torso.

For two months Randolph lay in his house, steadily improving. But he required morphine to ease the pain, so that by the end of six months he had become, in his own words, "a slave to opium." One day while looking in the mirror he saw an emaciated face and glassy eyes. He decided then and there to stop taking the morphine. "I suffered the tortures of hell upon earth," he wrote years later. Randolph bordered on suicidal and was closely watched. Even after he improved, he suffered from acute neuralgia thereafter. By the end of his life he had returned to a daily regimen of five to six grains of morphine.[76]

While friends and doctors attended to the fallen Randolph, the sheriff and everyone who could get a horse and weapon took off after the assailant, who was caught at the university and brought back to the jail. He turned out to be William Smith, an older student and former Yankee soldier whom the regents had hired at a fifty dollars per month salary to replace the steward.[77] More telling, Smith was the son of a regent, Union brigadier general Gustavus Adolphus Smith. The shootout on the streets of Tuscaloosa started to appear more like a hired assassination attempt than a jostling that got out of hand—as the *Independent Monitor* loudly proclaimed in its next issue.

Other evidence suggested that the *Monitor* may well have been right. There was the matter of timing, for example. The night before the attack on Randolph, some thirty armed and disguised nightriders rode into Eutaw, thirty-five miles southeast of Tuscaloosa. A dozen entered George Cleveland's hotel, went up to the second floor, and brutally shot and killed the Republican solicitor of Greene County, Alexander Boyd. The *Monitor* insisted that the disagreement with Boyd was entirely personal and that political considerations could not have prompted the murder. Never mentioned was the fact that Boyd had earlier announced that he would charge several local citizens with having murdered two blacks.[78]

More telling was Smith's apparent close relationship with Professor Vaughan. Randolph had long been harassing the professor, having a year earlier devoted one of his milder cartoons to lampooning him and typically describing him as being "on a bigger drunk than ever before."[79] Randolph was still ratcheting up the diatribes before the confrontation with Smith, and Vaughan was responding in kind through the Montgomery *Alabama State Journal*, a Republican newspaper. According to accounts, half an hour before the fight, Smith was seen at Vaughan's campus residence. The professor then left in a small Jersey wagon, which was later found to have concealed two large dueling pistols and a double-barreled shotgun under its white canvas cover. Vaughan was said to have dismounted from his wagon on Broad Street and distracted others while Smith approached Randolph. After the fight, the sheriff and his posse found Smith in the second story of Vaughan's house. They arrested Smith, charging him with murder, as well as Vaughan, charging him with aiding and abetting.

The preliminary investigation convened on Monday, April 18. Smith and Vaughan's counsel included John M. Martin, the same former schoolmate with whom Randolph had nearly fought a duel. An anguished Mrs. Vaughan wrote to the governor, "The 'Ku Klux' have been 'out' several nights swearing that they would hang 'Smith & *Vaughan*.' Last Friday night at 2 o'clock these bad men surrounded my house, and by shooting, hallooing and swearing, frightened me and my poor little children very very much. . . . Now it is thought my husband will be released this evening or tomorrow, but every body that speaks to me says that he must leave here at once or be murdered."[80] The court remanded the student to jail without bail and discharged the professor, who left the City of Oaks by way of the Huntsville Road on the following afternoon disguised with a slouched hat drawn over his eyes and an old shabby overcoat.

A week later, on the morning of April 27, Tuscaloosans awakened to learn that Smith had fled. Because he was under continuous guard by Union soldiers and the lock had been forced from the outside, he could only have been released by the guard or with the guard's compliance. The governor set a $400 reward—the highest allowed by law—for his arrest. The *Independent Monitor* had predicted it. While Randolph slowly recovered at his home, an editorial had correctly anticipated that neither Smith nor Vaughan would ever be convicted, or if they were, "the jail will be forced by a Radical band of disguised patriots, and the subjects of justice will be set free . . . to be appointed Governors of New Mexico or Idaho." Close enough. Within two months Vaughan was appointed by President Grant to be secretary and then governor of the Utah Territory; young Smith became secretary to his father, Brigadier General Smith, Collector of Internal Revenue for the New Mexico Territory.[81]

Randolph continued to edit the Tuskaloosa *Independent Monitor* through the rest of 1870 and all of 1871. Thereafter tensions eased. At the state Democratic convention in September 1870, Robert B. Lindsay was nominated for governor; his campaign was built around the freedom of white Alabamians to decide their own future. Concerning the new state constitution, he asked: "Is that the spirit of American freedom?" And then he continued, "I am here to carry the banner—to restore it to the men that ought to have the freedom of Alabama. . . . The white race of Alabama must govern their own race." He concluded with a rousing, "Will you rally around me, and say, 'We will be free?' And I say to you . . . You shall be free."[82]

At the same convention James Holt Clanton nominated *Montgomery Mail* editor and Randolph's old friend Joseph Hodgson for superintendent of education. He won in November and, with the help of local alumni, the new Democratic board of regents finally got the university successfully operating in October 1871. A month earlier, Randolph's red-haired friend Clanton—former Confederate general, head of Alabama's Democratic Party, and later identified as the head of the Alabama Ku Klux Klan—had been killed in a Knoxville gunfight.[83]

At the end of that year, Randolph negotiated the sale of the *Monitor* to Colonel Joseph W. Taylor of Eutaw, who renamed the paper the *Tuscaloosa Times*. Randolph claimed that his former patrons were dissatisfied with the way Taylor ran the paper, so that summer he started the Tuskaloosa *Blade*. The indignant Taylor charged Randolph with having violated a promise not to compete. Once again Randolph became offended—this time by an editorial in the *Times*—and made up his mind to assail Taylor on sight. The two finally met near the same spot where Smith and Randolph had fought. By this time Randolph walked with both a crutch and a stick. Denouncing him in "suitable terms," Randolph then hit Taylor on the head with his stick. Taylor's felt hat softened the blow, so he turned and rushed at Randolph, who latched on to Taylor and began pummeling him until blood poured out of his nose. The two were separated. When Taylor went to pick up his hat, Randolph thought he was getting ready to strike him again and drew a .22 calibre Smith & Wesson repeater from his pocket, cocked, and pointed it in his opponent's ᵗ

face. "For God's sake," yelled Taylor, "don't let him shoot!" This time, Randolph did not pull the trigger.[84]

Randolph published the last issue of the *Blade* in 1875 and, after some traveling about,[85] resumed his career in the new industrial city of Birmingham. He continued to write outlandish essays, this time in the *Birmingham True Issue*; and he continued to make enemies. In 1880, after one too many outlandish attacks on the rival *Iron Age*, its editor, A. O. Lane, shot Randolph in the neck as the two met on the sidewalk. The wound was not fatal, but it finally forced Randolph to retire from daily work. Lane was elected Birmingham's mayor two years later.[86]

Randolph henceforth wrote only the occasional essay, often under a pseudonym. These included bitter complaints about paying chaplains in the armed forces, a review of a book by the freethinker John E. Remsburg, and a critique of theistic arguments for a soul. Randolph also wrote privately to historians describing his role in the events of Reconstruction, and he penned several short sketches that substituted for an autobiography. The longest of his efforts was a series that he began writing about 1894. *Ryland Randolph's Scribbles* began with the words, "I very much regret ever having read the infidel and atheistic works of such men of gigantic intellect as Voltaire, Hume...." His faith in God and in a soul had gradually eroded before "the light of reason," an erosion that he had come to regret. Perhaps God was a First Cause, but it was the "height of impudence" to claim that man was made in the image of his maker. A hundred and thirty pages later Randolph began his twentieth essay with "I am beginning to feel weary of life." For someone not given to introspection, the *Scribbles* could be surprisingly confessional. He admitted that his misfortunes had been brought on by his own follies.

)(○)(○)(

As a Confederate soldier, Ryland Randolph battled Yankees in order to keep black Americans enslaved. As an editor, he campaigned to exclude carpetbaggers, scalawags, and freedmen from the political process. As a Klansman, he intimidated all who stood in his way. Merely dismissing such a violent racist would be easy. But the easy path misses the crucial element that propelled Randolph's decisions and actions: his need to restore his people's freedom.

Randolph's understanding of freedom arose out of his understanding of a person's place in a society. Society was primary. Individuals did not create societies; they were born into societies. It was an idea with ancient roots. Aristotle wrote that a man without a city was either a beast or a god. Those who

9. Ryland Randolph
(*Ku Klux Klan: Its Origin, Growth and Disbandment* by Lester and Wilson, 1905)

did not participate in the political and social commonwealth, in other words, were either brutish or divine; either way, they could not be fully human. Freedom was the natural consequence of being included in a community of self-governing people. The very word *freedom* itself is squarely in this tradition, for it comes from the same Germanic root word as does *friend*. Freedom is a consequence of membership.[87]

Randolph was building on this tradition when he called for a return to the natural order. Ordinarily, he believed, people lived freely together in self-governing communities. Certainly some might choose to live physically apart on remote farms or on the frontier. But that really mattered little because they were still members of a self-governing community and were all pretty much alike. They basically thought alike and valued the same things. They were comfortable with themselves and each other. The fact that their society was a natural society, confirmed by centuries of tradition, eliminated the need for self-doubt or reform. The whole inspired confidence. This was the way things were supposed to be. No one needed to prove the obvious. Life was good. Inclusion in such a society allowed the individual to act as he would wish: allowed the mechanic to live in town, the yeoman farmer to create his own little domain, or the adventurer to move westward in search of his main chance.

But the natural order was constantly getting out of joint. The cause could only lie with the enemies of the people. Once again, this was hardly a new insight. "Man was born free, and he is everywhere in chains," proclaimed Jean-Jacques Rousseau in 1762 when the people's foe was a powerful aristocracy. To the Americans in the 1830s, the great force threatening the natural order was the artificial concentration of wealth brought on by the Market Revolution. The people rose up in reaction, sending their champion Andrew Jackson to Washington, DC. He would slay the Bank of the United States and try to eliminate paper money with his Specie Circular.[88] Significantly, Ryland Randolph occasionally signed his editorials "Jacksonian." The next enemy came in the form of abolitionists. And by the late 1860s, Randolph and other defeated Confederates faced a conspiracy of carpetbaggers, scalawags, and freedmen who were denying the people their birthright. In such times of crisis, the people had to be loyal to each other, making betrayal the greatest of all sins and explaining the special contempt that Randolph heaped on the apostate Noah Cloud.

What made these enemies so threatening—and not something that could be ignored—was that the enemies' gain was at the people's expense. Wealth and power were limited commodities. When some benefited, others lost. Every inch given was an inch taken.

Freedom was a particularly limited commodity. Freedom needed its opposite in order to make any sense. It could never extend to everyone; for that some were free necessarily implied that others were *unfree*.[89] The freedom of one community implied the bondage of another. Those outside the community were not only presumed to lack freedom; they may not even deserve freedom. The result was a world in which the free and the *unfree* were engaged in a tense zero-sum contest—just as the South had been for generations.[90] Distinguishing whether someone was included in a free or *unfree* community had been based on a simple difference: race. Everyday life in the South was permeated by this contrast between the free white masters on the one hand and the black bound slaves on the other. But this was the way things had always been, the way things should be.

That started to change in the nineteenth century. When he was fourteen Randolph had witnessed what happened when the slaveholders' vision of the

2.

natural order was subverted and outsiders began to take away the people's freedom: Haiti's laughably pretentious Faustin-Élie Soulouque. What Randolph first knew as farce, came back as tragedy. The colluding efforts of those who would remake nature—the reforming abolitionists, Republican politicians, and evangelical Christians—used the power of the Union armies to take freedom away from white Southerners and to present it to black Southerners. Freedom had been extended "to four millions of negroes at the South," complained former Confederate officer and postwar Democratic politician Wade Hampton III in 1867, "but to secure their freedom, eight millions of whites are made slaves!"[91] Any method was justified in destroying the enemies of freedom and returning society to its natural order. Once "our people" had been a polite synonym for "my slaves"; after Appomattox "our people" became a synonym for "former Confederates."[92] The combination of a people forged in war with the reversal of the natural order only reinforced the former Confederates' understanding of the people's freedom as a precious and limited commodity. A nasty political cartoon and local Klan intimidation seemed a minor price for restoring the natural order.

More than anything else, what was needed was a courageous and unified citizenry—individually weak, together strong—to recover their lost freedom. With spectacular fervor, Randolph plunged into the task of rousing the people from their lethargy. He summoned them to be valiant, to rise up against the predators before it was too late. In this he surely sensed the powerful role that a visual image like *A Prospective Scene* could play in sharpening a group's identity. Randolph became the people's spokesman, a champion who would point the way against the tyrannous conspiracy intent on imposing a new and unnatural order. If he failed, he failed a hero.

Randolph did fail. His Manichaean world had turned topsy-turvy. The Southern states, once the wealthiest in the Union, were now its poorest. Thriving plantations lay abandoned. The price of cotton continued to drop. A once proud people were ruled by a gaggle of outsiders, traitors, and inferiors. Such were the makings of the Lost Cause. Randolph's failure also confirmed his personal disbelief. No God would have chosen the Jews, and no God would have let the Confederacy lose. With God he tossed out all forms of transcendence—from the Christian virtues of humility, mercy, and self-sacrifice to liberal ideals of universal liberation. His was a bitter end.

※※※

Randolph began writing his *Scribbles* In 1894. He sensed that his time was short. "I humbly ask forgetfulness and forgiveness. Remember that your . . . husband and father all his life has had to fight against an almost ungovernable temper, handed down as a legacy to him by his father. . . . My temper has ever been my greatest enemy; and the surpassing wonder is that I now live to tell it!" He considered suicide, but it was a cowardly. If only the bullets that severed his femoral artery or passed through his neck had taken slightly different paths, then neither he nor his family would have suffered.[93]

To his chagrin, Randolph had ten years left. His devoted Katherine died in 1901 and was buried by an Episcopal priest in the East Lake cemetery. Two years after that he was on a streetcar when it lurched forward. He lost his balance and hit the back of his head on an iron rail. A week later he was buried next to his wife.[94] Ryland Randolph died a bitter man painfully aware that the genteel life he once enjoyed at his uncle's plantation home was forever gone.

TWO

Carpetbagger

If the Son therefore shall make you free, ye shall be free indeed.
—Saint John

Like Ryland Randolph, Arad Lakin also wrote memoirs. But where the turning point in Randolph's life came with his decision to renounce God, the turning point in Lakin's life came with his decision to accept God.

Arad Lakin, who had been born in 1810, began his reminiscences with the bankruptcy of his father, Jonas, and the subsequent uprooting of the family when Arad was quite young.[1] They loaded up their possessions in an ox-drawn wagon and set out, probably from New Hampshire, through the thick forests for the Forks of the Delaware River (what is now Hancock) in New York State. After a week's travel, the family stopped at a finely timbered lot, and Jonas began felling trees. With enough to build a cabin, barn, and stable, he called on his far-flung neighbors who, fortified with strong drink, managed to put up the walls in a single day. With the roofs and chinking in place, the family moved in to their new abode a few days later.

Jonas did not use his new property primarily for farming, but rather for lumbering. All was toil. Each day began (at four in the morning) and ended (at nine in the evening) with foddering the horses. In summer and autumn the trees were cut and prepared for transport to the mill. In winter the logs were drawn across the snow to the ice-covered river. And in spring when the freshets raised the Delaware, the logs were joined into rafts and floated downstream to a mill. It was an enterprise that involved the whole family. The Lakin boys grew so strong, healthy, and vigorous that they became the envy of the Forks.

The long hours left no opportunity for the life of the mind, and their father rarely sent the children to school. (Some speculated that he rejected education because, "had he been unable to write, he could not have signed those bonds which brought his ruin.") Beyond the skills they learned on the lumber lot, the Lakin children were given practical advice and admonitions: "Never shun, nor deride, nor neglect the poor," for example, "because you may be poor yourself." "Avoid fighting. But if any man force you to fight, never turn your back upon him." Arad, the Lakin's fifth child, did attend a school of sorts for three months at age five, but the old woman who kept the school could scarcely read.

Of religion the Lakin children were left to their own devices. For one thing the Lakin homestead was near no churches. But that was merely an excuse. The fact was that Jonas was a disbeliever. He would welcome the itinerant preachers who occasionally dropped by, and he would talk with them on any subject—except God and religion. Such matters were not things that he could see or hold in his hand and thus not things to which he would commit. Perhaps he likened faith in an unseen God to the faith he had placed in worthless paper money; real money, after all, clanked in the pocket and shimmered in the sun. He might go so far as to admit, like Ryland Randolph, that God could have been the First Cause; but Jonas could not see God's hand at work in his everyday life and so had no use for such a notion.

Death was common on the frontier. Arad's first encounter came when a younger sister died from scalding—an event that, curiously, seemed to make "little or no impression upon any member of the family." Then, when in his twelfth year, Arad's maternal grandmother died. She had lived with the family, and he was her favorite grandchild. Being an amiable and kind-hearted member of the Baptist church, she had talked to him of their doctrines. These included, significantly it would turn out, "the necessity of leading a sinless life." She died without converting any of Jonas's family. This time Arad could not be consoled and refused all attempts at comfort.

Arad was fifteen in the winter of 1825-1826 and entered school a second time. He paid for his board with another family by working nights and mornings. The rest of the time he devoted to arithmetic, geography, and history. But after only three months, he returned to his father's house and worked in the forests, thus ending his formal education.

Arad grew tall and powerful as a lumberman. It was common for him to fell and top fifteen large trees in a day. He also gained a reputation for skill at piloting rafts of logs down the Delaware, for being able to outwrestle anyone, for an extraordinary jumping ability, and for his throwing accuracy. (He once killed a deer by hitting it behind the ear with a single stone.) Most of his time was still devoted to helping his father.

His life as a youngster seemed a series of adventures, but as an adult he would construe them in other terms. "There is no such thing as chance in the world," he declared in his reminiscences, "nor is there any event, however unimportant, that affects us, which has not been ordered and appointed." And yet, "we are free." This was not the sort of dilemma that philosophers and theologians could solve, much less a poorly educated woodsman. Still, it explained to his satisfaction the unlikely series of trivial events that led to the turning point in his life.

In August of 1828, the eighteen-year-old joined a party of young people assembled one afternoon at the comfortable home of Charles Leonard, about seven miles from the Lakin lumber lot. Arad was called upon to sing because he was passionately fond of music, had a good voice, and knew many songs. As he wheeled himself round in his chair to face the others, he found himself opposite a bedroom door. He had gotten through a couple of verses of a humorous song when the bedroom door opened and there emerged "a ghostly looking figure drooped in black, with a white cravat around its neck." All was silence. The hair on Arad's flesh stood up as the image intoned, "Shall mortal man be more just than God? Shall a man be more pure than his Maker?"

The sallow-faced figure was, in fact, the Reverend Sandford Benton, who was in the habit of visiting the Leonards. He stalked into the living room groaning "O, my Lord! O, my Lord!" When at last the singing ended, the Methodist preacher walked again past Arad and muttered, "O, my Lord, what a pity such a sweet voice should be spent in the service of the devil!" The passage of the dour minister ended the young people's fun "like the scorching blast of the desert upon the surrounding vegetation." The party broke up, and each went his own way.

The folks in the Forks were all astir the following February. They had arranged a great ball; and Arad, who was also known for his dancing, was one of those responsible for the event's success. The memory of the gloomy Reverend Benton had receded as the prospects for amusement grew. Then Arad learned that the Methodists were getting up a revival. At first he thought little of it, for their revival was to be at some distance away and not the sort of thing that should pose any competition for the greatest ball that the Forks had ever known. Yet with each day came news that the revival was spreading ever closer. "Like a great fire on the prairie it ran along with the rapidity of the wind, encircling, scorching, and burning everything with which it came in contact."

The Second Great Awakening had come to the Forks. The first half of the nineteenth century was a time of religious enthusiasm. The Methodists were at the forefront in large part because of their insistence that all could be saved, in contrast to the predestinarian Calvinists, who believed that only a select few would be saved. Ministers fanned out across the West spreading this message to ordinary folk, and western New York State became such a center of fervor that it would be known as the "Burned-Over District" because no one was left unconverted. The Forks of the Delaware was not quite in the Burned-Over District, but its sparks could still start a flame.

Arad did not care if the old folks went to the revival; that was to be expected. There was a real possibility, however, that the girls might skip the ball in order to attend the revival. So he saddled his horse and rode round to see if his fears were justified. The girls assured him that no revival was going to prevent their attending, even if the blessed apostles should be holding a camp meeting in front of the ballroom. Still, fresh reports kept filtering back. Drunkards, profligates, scoffers, and infidels were all getting religion. Arad saddled his horse again to check on the girls, and once more they all claimed that nothing could keep them away. Of the boys he had no fears.

Yet the Methodists would not quit. They announced a meeting the next Sunday to be held only six miles below the Lakin lumber lot. Arad decided to attend in order to find what the fuss was all about and perhaps have a laugh or two in the bargain. He entered to find a crowded room of solemn and reverential souls contemplating the business of life and death. They began to sing an old hymn:

> 'Tis down into the water
> Where we young converts go,
> To serve our Lord and Master
> In righteous acts below

Long before the singing had finished, Arad started to feel an odd combination of awe and reverence—similar but stronger than the feeling that had accompanied the Reverend Benton's intrusion. "Let us pray," said one revivalist. All were on their knees except Arad, whose Baptist grandmother had stood at prayers. Although embarrassed at his faux pas, standing allowed him to take stock of the congregation. He not only recognized the most respectable members of the neighborhood, but also some of the young ladies who had vowed to attend the ball. His attention shifted to the preacher. "How he describes the atrocity and wickedness of the human heart; in what hideous colors he portrays the exceeding sinfulness of sin; and man's black ingratitude to God, the beautiful giver of every good and perfect gift." Arad felt that the evangelist's words were directed at him, an utterly mean and worthless creature. An overwhelming sense of guilt came over him. "Oh! wretched man that I am, who shall deliver me from this body of sin and death?" Afraid of letting his feelings betray him, he left the meeting house while the congregation knelt in prayer. That week he started praying in the dense forest.

Arad set out the next Sunday for the meeting held at a house at Partridge Island, a mere three miles downstream from the Lakin lumber lot. When he got there he took a seat in the fiddlers' gallery, some two feet above the rest of the floor. Looking out he saw, to his chagrin, his own father and mother in the congregation. His overpowering sense of guilt and unworthiness returned when a hymn was sung. Arad asked Major Daniel Bradstreet, the blacksmith who conducted the meeting, to pray for him. "That's right, Arad," shouted the blacksmith. "Come forward here and kneel at this chair, and pray and shame the devil, and God will hear you and give you religion." As Arad stepped forward to the temporary altar, he saw his father's disapproving look but kept going. He knelt and prayed for forgiveness and deliverance, this time aloud. Before the prayer was finished, he felt peace and composure. Arad returned to his seat perfectly assured that he was a new man.

The convert hurried home, consumed with the zeal and joy wrought by his newfound freedom from sin, ingratitude, and meanness. Arad announced that God had changed his heart and that he now wished to have family prayer. Jonas swung his hat backward and forward between his legs and looked up with astonishment and pity. "You may pray if you have a mind to," he said, "but it won't be of a bit of use. It's all nonsense, mere nonsense." And then he left. Arad read and prayed fervently, having no apparent effect on his family, whom he had resolved to convert.

Young Lakin began teaching a Bible class. Several of his rowdy companions learned of his new ways and attended one his class meetings just to hear what he was up to. He wrote down and committed to memory a long prayer out of vanity and a desire to astonish his old friends. When the meeting at last convened, he stood up and began to pray; but before he got to the end of the first sentence, he lost his way. He ran out of the meeting in shame and confusion. "Lord, have mercy on me," he cried out, and a flood of light seemed to relieve his fears. He returned to find that his friends' mirth was gone, for they were truly saddened by Arad's embarrassment. "Let's try it again, boys!" he announced, and this time all knelt as he prayed freely and with genuine ardor. Five hours later the meeting ended with the conversion of five of his wildest companions.

When Arad reached the age of twenty-one, he resolved to go off on his own. Jonas wanted his son to stay, needing his labor, and even offered to leave him part of the homestead. Arad had other plans. "You are too thick-headed to become a preacher," his father advised. "There is a great difference between piloting a raft, and piloting souls to heaven. You are a fool to think yourself fit for such work." Despite Jonas's vowing to leave his son not a cent if he disgraced the family by entering the ministry, young Lakin had made up his mind. The prospects of losing an inheritance never gave him pause.

The Methodist ministry was not a career that a penniless and poorly educated young man could simply enter. Lakin took his first step by going into a partnership with Major Bradstreet, the blacksmith who had conducted one of the meetings, to harvest a lumber lot some eighteen miles downstream from the Forks. Unlike his father, Bradstreet encouraged Lakin to devote the whole of his spare time to studying, attending prayer and class meetings twice a week, and giving exhortations to three congregations on Sundays. Lakin received his first appointment as a local preacher in March 1835. After only a few sermons, he left to pilot a raft downstream. Upon returning, he found himself appointed to the Deposit Circuit in Delaware County by his presiding elder (the minister appointed by the bishop to oversee churches in a particular district). Methodists divided their ministers into the local ranks (the class leaders, exhorters, and lay preachers who ministered to their own local church) and the traveling or itinerant ranks (those circuit riders, missionaries, and other ministers ordained by the conference and sent by their bishop to a different circuit or congregation as needed). Lakin's probationary appointment was clearly in recognition of his potential and a major step toward formal ordination into the traveling ranks of the New York Conference, then at the center of religious enthusiasm.[2]

On his first Sunday Lakin preached at three settlements with good results. The next Sunday he was to preach at three other settlements. The first service went well, but he was especially concerned about the second, at Stockport.

He carefully wrote out a sermon in hopes of impressing his neighbors and friends in the congregation. After taking his seat next to the pulpit, he led the congregation in a hymn and then turned to pull out his sermon. But it was nowhere to be found, having apparently slipped out while riding his somewhat fiery horse. Like his prayer before his rowdy friends, Lakin could recollect nothing. So he opened his Bible at random, read the text before him, and started preaching. As soon as he was done, he pronounced a blessing, dismissed the congregation, frantically elbowed his way out the door, and galloped off towards his next preaching assignment. "If thou desirest me to proceed no further," he prayed, "signify thy will, and let thy will be done. I would be thy servant. Help me, Lord!" By the time he reached the schoolhouse at Equinunk, he knew peace and tranquility. Once again he prayed fervently for assistance. His prayer was answered in a remarkable way. Not long into his sermon, several awakened sinners cried for deliverance. The young parson stopped exhorting and turned the meeting entirely over to prayer. When some were converted he felt himself blessed as an instrument in "hastening the time when the whole world shall be filled with the glory of the Lord."

It did not take long before Lakin sensed the limitations of his poor education. He was too old to go back to school; but he could carry a Bible, concordance, and some religious works with him whenever and wherever he rode. Whether alone in the still forest or after the generous family who offered him a room had gone to bed, he would sit for hours carefully reading the texts. When his eyesight gave way for several months, he hired a woman to read for him. It was not quite Abraham Lincoln (who was a year older); still, the evidence of Lakin's self-education can be seen in the references ranging from the ancient Greeks to Spinoza that made their way into his reminiscences.

The year 1837 was important for Lakin. In July he married Miss Achsah Labar Newton, a woman of superior education, who had been converted early in her life. They met while she was teaching in the Forks. Money was tight. He spent profits from the sale of the lumber lot on books, household furniture, and expenses. When the couple needed money, he would pilot a few more rafts down the Delaware. That same year Lakin was formally received into the traveling ranks of the Methodist Episcopal Church (MEC). This meant that every year, or perhaps every other year, the bishop in the New York Conference would appoint him to a different circuit. The next two decades he and Achsah would move about southern New York State.[3] His first appointments were near his home in Delaware County: the Bloomville Circuit in 1837, then the Jeffersonville Circuit, and then to Prattville in Greene County.

The spectacular success of Methodism in nineteenth-century America can be attributed to many things, but two in particular: its organizational structure and its belief in individual freedom. The local preacher and the circuit rider were but the most numerous and most visible members of a large structure of support and connection. Circuits (several small churches served by a single minister) and larger churches were grouped into districts led by presiding elders (later known as district superintendents); districts were lumped together into conferences (called annual conferences because they met as a body once a year) led by bishops; all the annual conferences sent delegates to the General Conference of the Methodist Episcopal Church, which met quadrennially and made the final determination of church policy. Ministers in the traveling ranks could be sent by their bishop into various districts within their conference. Some criticized the structure as antidemocratic; but it was in practice pragmatic, dynamic, and flexible when and where it had to be. The hierarchical structure proved amazingly successful in promoting growth, particularly through its circuit riders; in fostering a sense of connection among all Methodists; and in giving the denomination a voice of authority on issues before the public, particularly during the 1860s and '70s.

The success of Methodism also had a great deal to do with its theology, specifically its insistence that humankind was *not* predestined to eternal damnation, as the Calvinists taught, but capable of redemption. "God willeth all men to be saved," John Wesley had written in the mid-eighteenth century. Some would accept this offer of God's grace; others would reject it. All were capable of responding on their own. This in turn implied both the individual's ability to improve himself and a responsibility to share his experience of grace with others—ideas that would echo the notion of Christian freedom crafted by the Protestant reformer Martin Luther. Lakin's life would embody these core Methodist values.

Wesley's timing had been auspicious, for the introduction of Methodism into America coincided with the colonists' drive for liberty and equality. Methodists believed that all could be saved because, in the words of the Declaration of Independence, all had been created equal. Methodists believed that all men could be free—again, as the Declaration held—or at least free from the damnation of sin. Theirs was an optimistic theology and an empowering one. Americans were entering an age of reform based on the conviction that people could do better, could improve their lives. Some Methodists, building upon Wesley's theology, were convinced that individuals even had the capacity to reach a sort of holy perfection. But the main thrust of

Methodism remained the freeing of people to do good in the world. It is no surprise that Methodists were on the forefront of the nineteenth century's reform movements.

In time Lakin, too, would devote much of his life to reform. But in the 1830s his priority, like other circuit riders, lay in freeing souls from sin. He found people in Beaver Dam "almost lifeless under freezing doctrines of election and reprobation" because of the preaching in the Dutch Reformed Old School and the Baptist churches there. Indeed, many members of those churches opposed the coming of the Methodists at all. But it was the conversion of one of the village's leading citizens, a disbeliever, that turned the corner. He confided in Lakin that a decade before he had felt "convicted of sin and desired to seek the Lord. My friends said I was a fool in entertaining such a desire. One of them gave me a book to read, which he said would make me feel all right. I read the work and my convictions left me." The book was one with which Ryland Randolph was familiar: Thomas Paine's *The Age of Reason* (first published in 1794), perhaps the most widely read antireligious work of the early republic. "In the name of the Captain of our salvation," Parson Lakin responded, "I take you as my prisoner of war." That conversion led to others. At the Prattville revival he estimated that some 350 were converted.

Lakin's rising reputation was not matched by a rising income, for his charges were among those too poor to contribute more than a mite to their pastor.[4] Achsah found it difficult to make ends meet. When Arad's wagon was worn out, he had been forced to purchase another with an on-demand note for eighty dollars. Hard currency was scarce in rural areas even before Andrew Jackson issued his 1836 Specie Circular demanding gold or silver for the purchase of public lands. To get around the shortage of currency, those in remote rural regions circulated promissory bills of credit. Lakin had given such a note to a pious Methodist who, unbeknownst to the preacher, had used it to purchase something else. The next thing Lakin knew, he had received a writ from the court demanding that he pay the promissory note in specie. Achsah proposed selling the household furniture to meet the bill. The Lakins' "providential deliverance" came from those attending one of his revivals who scraped together $130 to get them out of their fix.

Time and again Lakin structured his reminiscences by recounting the many instances in which small acts by individuals pulled him from difficult situations. Whenever things looked their worst, a path would open. Whenever he would pray, God would answer. This made sense because Lakin believed in two worlds: the visible and the invisible. Nonbelievers, such as

Ryland Randolph, knew only the first; but conversion allowed believers to glimpse the second. These worlds were not independent. God did involve Himself in our affairs, and we could advance God's plan by right thought and action. Lakin did not pretend to self-satisfied certainty, for much was hidden. "How surprised shall we be in Eternity," he would quote the German theologian Friedrich Adolf Krummacher, "when the veil shall be removed." Then we will discover all the members of the true Church, including many that we never suspected.

In 1845, the Lakins received news that he had been appointed to the Second Street Church in New York. In contrast to his charges in rural Delaware and Greene counties, this congregation had the reputation for being wealthy, fashionable, and critical. Parson Lakin was from the country, and the move filled him with concern. He need not have worried. During that year he added some 250 new members to the 700 who had greeted him. While there he received news from the Forks that Jonas had experienced religion. The younger Lakin believed that through God's grace his father had at last realized "that Voltaire and Tom Paine were quite unable to pilot him to that port where the heart of the righteous mariner pants to be, the haven of Eternal rest."[5]

Lakin served in various pulpits in the New York Conference before being appointed agent at the Five Points Mission in early 1854. Five Points, near the southern tip of Manhattan, was easily the most notorious slum in North America. Its unhealthful location, close to a poorly drained pond, was the destination for those who could afford no better, especially the poor Irish immigrants fleeing the 1840s potato famine. Five Points became infamous for disease, prostitution, unemployment, and particularly crime. In the words of the New York Ladies' Home Missionary Society, Five Points was "a synonym for ignorance the most entire, for misery the most abject, for crime of the darkest dye, for degradation so deep that human nature cannot sink below it."[6] By the time that Lakin arrived in Five Points, its murder rate was said to be the highest in the world.

Various groups had tried their hands at reforming Five Points. The Baptists, Episcopalians, Swedenborgians, and others had all established churches in the neighborhood. The Female Moral Reform Society and the Tract Society had worked there. In the 1840s several Protestant denominations operated a common mission for a few hours each week. The New York Ladies' Home Missionary Society, a Methodist group, took over in 1848. Rather than continue the frustrating and largely ineffectual volunteer efforts, the society laid plans to hire a full-time paid missionary who would live and minister there.

Left: 10. Arad Lakin painted about 1854 in New York City, probably by James Evans
(Courtesy North Alabama Conference Archive, donated by Bill and Gail Mapel)

Right: 11. Achsah Newton Lakin painted about 1854 in New York City, probably by James Evans
(Courtesy North Alabama Conference Archive, donated by Bill and Gail Mapel)

The missionary was expected to "avail himself of every providential opening for usefulness."[7]

The first was the Reverend Lewis M. Pease, who, with his wife and daughter, began his indefatigable service in 1850. Pease and the Missionary Society clashed from the beginning. The women's goals were limited almost entirely to converting sinners—in which they lumped Catholics—to Methodism. Pease quickly realized that prayers and tracts meant nothing to those without even a crust of bread. When he tried to explain the value of a sober, honest, and virtuous life, the Five Pointers replied, "We do not live this life because we love it, but because we cannot get out of it." On his own initiative Pease hired down-and-out women to sew shirts for him and even paid for the failures. He expanded the Methodist Sunday School into a nondenominational weekday school, eventually adding baking, shoe making, hat making, and basket weaving to his program. The women dismissed Pease when, at the end of his first year, the missionary could not give the name of a single convert to Methodism.[8] He would continue his work without the Missionary Society's help.

Not to be outdone, the society appealed to the bishop of New York for a new missionary and in early 1852 purchased the Old Brewery. The run-down

12. The New Mission House, where Lakin ministered to the destitute at Five Points
(*The Old Brewery, and the New Mission House at the Five Points*, 1854)

building had been erected in the 1790s, been changed to a tenement in the 1830s, and at the time was said to be home to a thousand of the poorest. On one side was a dark narrow passage known as Murderer's Alley, perhaps leading credence to the rumor that the Old Brewery had seen a murder a night for the last fifteen years.[9] The women had the Old Brewery demolished, and the next year a handsome four-story brick Five Points Mission stood in its place. Inside was a chapel, parsonage, two classrooms, and twenty apartments.

The impressive new building, costing $36,000, was but six months old when Lakin arrived in January 1854, first as the mission's agent and then as its missionary.[10] He may well have been chosen because of his insistence that conversion dwarfed all other Christian responsibilities. (A few years before in Ulster County, just southeast of his Delaware County home, Lakin had complained that the "firebrand of abolitionism" had diverted Methodists from their real purpose, freeing souls from sin. He saw no such problem in promoting another reform: temperance.) With his reputation for sticking to the Gospel and with the success he had demonstrated at the Second Street Church, the women at the Missionary Society may well have seen Lakin as the perfect choice to refocus their work in Five Points. The women wanted missionaries to be preaching and converting—not paying for poorly made shirts.

Lakin plunged into the work. In his reports, regularly published in the

New York Christian Advocate and Journal, he would list attendance at the weekday and Sabbath schools and at the Sunday morning services. He also gave statistics on those who had signed the temperance pledge. These would be followed with personal stories of redemption. "O, Mr. Lakin, is this religion?" asked a young Catholic widow whom Lakin had taken in until he could find employment for her. Sometimes the *Advocate*'s editor would follow Lakin's report with his own extensive commentary: "*Omnia vincet amor,* — love overcomes all things,—even the population at the 'Five Points'." At other times the editor would publish reports by some of the many visitors to the mission. One described how Lakin was called out to save a poor woman from the cruel rage of her drunken husband. The powerful missionary "mildly laid his hand on Peter's neck, and told him if he did not behave he should tie him up, and carry him to the Tombs," the notorious prison in Manhattan. Lakin was "a great acquisition," the visitor concluded.[11]

The women surely agreed, for Lakin's writings while at the mission were not only consistent with their goals and activities but put the women's efforts in a most favorable light. If Christianity were to make its way into the hearts of men, he argued, then it must be by an appeal to the individual's conscience. Everyone seeks happiness as a matter of instinct. But true happiness does not lie in the enjoyment of earthly possessions. God has revealed that the path to reaching happiness is rather in love—not as a sentiment or emotion, but as a principle for action. And in a bit of historical re-creation, he described how the New York Ladies' Home Missionary Society had acted on love first by establishing the Sabbath School and an employment program (Missionary Pease's efforts conveniently ignored) and then by building the new Five Points mission. In the past year alone, Lakin reported, the society had introduced new trades for women and distributed some twenty thousand garments, five hundred pairs of shoes, and three hundred pieces of bedding. Summing up, "by friendly calls, by entering into their difficulties, by supplying them with work, by the word of warning and the love of affectionate entreaty, by an unceasing interest in the welfare of their children, and by a patient bearing with the manifold infirmities incident to ignorance and poverty"—by all of these initiatives, souls had been led from sin and into the church.

The driving force behind the efforts of the New York Ladies' Home Missionary Society came from Phoebe Palmer, the most important leader of the holiness movement[12] and a strong influence on Lakin's theology. John Wesley had rejected the Calvinists' insistence on predestination, emphasizing instead the individual's ability—and responsibility—to respond to a loving God's gift. Because Wesley wanted to be sure not to fall into the heresy of think-ing humankind capable of achieving salvation, he insisted that the experi-ence of sanctification was a gift of God and that it was one's faith in Christ's atonement that allowed the Holy Spirit to regenerate the individual. This did not mean that the individual ceased sinning, for no one is capable of that. It did mean that those who took their conversion seriously would be so grate-ful and trusting as to dedicate their lives completely to Christ and to become disgusted by their former desire to sin. In dying to self, they would emerge purified. Yes, they would continue to make mistakes of judgment and commit sins of omission; but their will would not be in it, having been replaced by the Holy Spirit. Such a subtle concept was difficult enough to articulate, much less name. Wesley wrote of God's love as excluding sin and called the process variously a *second blessing, sanctification, Christian perfection*, or *perfect love*. American proponents used such terms as *entire sanctification, the baptism of the Holy Ghost*, or just *holiness*.

The holiness movement started to gather steam in the 1830s, with New York City as its center, and remained strong in the North. In 1835 Phoebe Palmer and her sister met there to form the Tuesday Meeting for the Promo-tion of Holiness. Palmer would emerge as the most powerful lay proponent of holiness through a series of devotional and personal writings expound-ing the joys of the second blessing. Palmer simplified Wesley's theology by stressing that entire sanctification was immediately available and not neces-sarily a lifelong pursuit. By 1851, while Palmer was deeply involved in the Five Points ministry, *The Way to Holiness*, which she first published in 1843, had sold twenty-four thousand copies. Southern Methodists harbored suspicions, probably because many holiness proponents were committed abolitionists; indeed, the idea of Christian perfectionism could be uncomfortable in the imperfect and brutal world of Southern slavery. Bishop Davis Wasgatt Clark—abolitionist, first president of the Freedmen's Aid Society, and the bishop who would send Lakin to Alabama after the Civil War—was a strong proponent of holiness. It is no wonder that Lakin would himself become committed to the holiness movement and spread its message in camp meetings to Alabamians both black and white.

Lakin's ministry at Five Points was by all accounts a success. His last report to the New York Ladies' Home Missionary Society was dated March 6, 1855. By May the position was listed as "to be supplied."[13] The Lakins were gone.

Gone to Indiana, of all places. By 1858 the family was in Peru, where Arad was finishing out another minister's term at the Methodist church, while

Achsah and their nineteen-year-old daughter, Mary Martha, taught school. Why Lakin left New York and what he was doing between 1855 and 1858 are questions that will probably never be answered.[14] It is all the more curious because his career as a minister in the New York Conference had been one of rising success, a fact reflected in each new appointment but especially his last, for what the Five Points Mission lacked in wealth it surpassed in prominence. Peru, by contrast, may not have been nowhere, but it was surely on the way. The winter fields in Indiana were bleak, much like the prospects of a man who had once pastored big churches and run important missions but who was now, at the age of fifty in 1860, back riding a circuit.[15]

Another man who knew the bleak fields of Indiana was about to emerge from the despair that often characterized his own life. The election of Abraham Lincoln in November 1860 gave first South Carolina and then the six other southernmost states the occasion to declare independence from the Union. In February their delegates met in Montgomery, Alabama, to create the Confederate States of America. Two months later the guns in Charleston opened fire on Fort Sumter.

When the Thirty-Ninth Indiana Infantry Regiment organized in Indianapolis at the end of August, Lakin enlisted. It was later said that he joined as a fifty-one-year-old private but that the parents of his younger colleagues insisted he serve as chaplain.[16] His reasons for enlisting are not known. It is possible that enlisting was for Lakin, as it was for many, an opportunity to reestablish direction in his life. The Thirty-Ninth Indiana would serve in the Western Theater. These Hoosiers saw their first and only action of 1861 at Upton's Hill, Kentucky, on October 12. As the regiment's chaplain, Lakin was under no obligation to carry a gun; yet he did, supposedly as an example to others. The next year the Thirty-Ninth was engaged at Shiloh (April 6–7) and the siege of Corinth (April 29–May 30). During that summer the regiment was part of Don Carlos Buell's pursuit of Braxton Bragg's Army of Tennessee through north Alabama to Nashville, and then from Louisville through Kentucky before returning to Louisville. The year ended with the Thirty-Ninth badly hurt at the Battle of Stones River. With his regiment in winter quarters near Murfreesboro, Tennessee, Chaplain Lakin returned to Indiana to preach at a funeral and to speak at a Union rally—the first evidence, beyond his enlistment, of any attachment to the Union.[17] The following April the Thirty-Ninth became a mounted infantry regiment, and in October it would be designated the Eighth Indiana Cavalry. The cavalrymen would be in Tennessee through 1863 until the Battle of Chickamauga (September 19–20) took them into northwest Georgia. After an expedition into east Tennessee, the Eighth Cavalry spent the winter on courier duty between Chattanooga and Ringgold. The summer of 1864 found the Eighth back in Alabama. After the fall of Atlanta on August 25, the regiment joined in Sherman's March through Georgia, where Chaplain Lakin was discharged from the service. He requested that he be allowed to accompany the regiment at his own expense, and the request was granted. Savannah fell to Sherman's army on December 21, and Lakin then departed for Indiana by way of New York.

During his four years with his Indiana regiment, Lakin probably engaged in the same sort of activities as hundreds of other Methodists who served as chaplains: he conducted services, buried the dead, and led his comrades in prayer. His memorialist would call him "conspicuously fearless," which Lakin frequently explained with the aphorism, "Man is immortal till his work is done."[18] One story has it that Major General George H. Thomas, perhaps at Chickamauga, called for a volunteer to carry a dispatch between enemy lines. Chaplain Lakin rode up and saluted. "General, I'll take it." Years later Lakin was given credit for filling the ranks of his depleted regiment on a recruiting mission to Indiana and for saving north Indiana from the grasp of the Peace Democrats, who opposed the war.

Unlike the meager details known of Lakin's activities during the Civil War, a great deal is known about the activities of the Methodist Episcopal Church during those four years. In 1861 the MEC was by far the largest and most influential of the Protestant denominations. It would have been an even greater presence had not the issue of slavery caused the Southern wing to secede in 1844 and to establish the following year the Methodist Episcopal Church, South (MEC South). Enthusiastic worship services, great hymns, and a hierarchical system of clergy had helped to spread the MEC into every hamlet across the North. The funds collected on the Sabbath underwrote great missionary programs, an immense publishing network, and the construction of thousands of houses of worship.

That influence only grew during the war as Methodists worked hand in glove with the Union government and its armies. The 1864 General Conference stated categorically that the "cause of our country . . . we regard as the cause of God." That same year the MEC missionary to New Orleans declared "that loyalty is a religious duty, as truly obligatory as prayer itself."[19] The phrase "Methodism is loyalty" even found its way into their *Discipline*, the extensive document that sets forth Methodist government and doctrine. The Union government reciprocated, not only in rhetoric (Lincoln declared that they would not have gotten through without the MEC's "steady influence"), but in deed. Union secretary of war Edwin Stanton (a devout Methodist) issued an order in late 1863 instructing the generals in the Western Theater to take churches from the MEC South and put them under an MEC bishop—to the fury of Southern Methodists, who supported the Confederacy as much as their counterparts in the North supported the Union. Perhaps more. "It is doing God service to kill the diabolical wretches on the battle field," wrote one Alabama Methodist minister.[20] By the war's end the two Methodist denominations were further apart than at its onset.

The editors of the Northern Methodist newspapers inflamed the tensions. Only a few days after Lee surrendered his army at Appomattox, the editor of the *New York Christian Advocate and Journal* deemed the South "a God-smitten place." Another found that the support for the Confederacy had left the MEC South "hopelessly debauched with proslaveryism and tainted with treason." The "Methodist Episcopal Church South is in ruins," began an extensive article in the Cincinnati *Western Christian Advocate*. "Its corner-stone was slavery, and it is fast meeting the fate of that political fabric which based itself upon the same precarious foundation."[21] Northern Methodists saw the Civil War as an obvious example of God working mysteriously in history. Even more, they saw victory as a sign of God's favor and a vindication of their taking up arms against sinning secessionists. Defeating the rebellious Southern armies was the first step; defeating the rebellious Southern churches was next. From this theological understanding of the war, the editors drew up plans for reuniting Methodism even before the fighting had ceased. A few actually believed that Southern Methodism would collapse on its own and the problem would take care of itself. Others suggested that, just as the Union demanded that former Confederates take loyalty oaths to the Union, Southern Methodists should be expected to take loyalty oaths to the Old Church, as they deemed it, confessing to the sins of secession and slavery. A third suggestion was to effect reunion by a formal process between the two denominations. The Methodist editors consistently underestimated the difficulties.

Southern Methodists did not surrender as the Southern armies had. They did not race to take loyalty oaths to the Northern church. And any hint of formal reunion was dashed by the rhetoric from Southern bishops and editors. Just four months after Appomattox, bishops James O. Andrew (who had sparked the 1844 split), Robert Paine, and George F. Pierce met and crafted a response to offers of reunion made by their counterparts in the North. In their "Pastoral Address" the Southern bishops expressed regret that a large portion, if not the majority, of Northern Methodists were "incurably radical." They "teach for doctrine the commandments of man," and they preach "political and ecclesiastical discord, rather than of those ends for which the church of the Lord Jesus Christ was instituted." In sum, the Southern bishops could see "no good result from even entertaining the subject of re-union with them." Other Methodist bishops would hew to the same line, insisting that slavery was not the cause of the 1844 secession, merely "the occasion" for it.[22]

Rather than holding out hope for a massive surrender or an institutional merger, Northern Methodists decided on invasion and conquest—but this time by missionaries instead of soldiers. The military metaphor was popular, useful, and even appropriate given the times. The strategy also built on the MEC's proven success in sending missionaries and circuit riders to lost souls on the frontier. This time the frontier was the unreconstructed South. Instead of converting infidels, however, the missionaries would be converting Christians. Instead of converting Americans, they would be converting Confederates, especially that great majority who had not owned slaves. These missionaries were, in the words of one historian, "the vanguard of efforts to reconstruct southern society and not coincidentally southern churches, all the while denouncing treason and slavery and proclaiming a gospel of freedom."[23]

Even the most optimistic in the North recognized that Southern society included unfamiliar elements that posed unfamiliar challenges. Most Northerners were convinced that an elite slavocracy had manipulated those virtuous nonslaveholding whites in the South first into seceding from the MEC and then from the Union. "Some of them vigorously opposed the great secession that followed the General Conference of 1844," wrote the editor of the Cincinnati *Western Christian Advocate*, "and have not yet forgotten the old church."[24] The missionaries, then, would start with the Southern Unionists who had remained loyal to both the Union and the MEC. Then there were the newly freed people, whom everyone suspected to be a great field ripe for the harvest.

This process was already under way before Appomattox. In 1864, the year after Secretary Stanton's order confiscating Southern Methodist church buildings, the MEC's Missionary Society added a third class of missions, beyond the foreign and domestic: those rebellious states in Union hands. The MEC further divided this third class of missions into five departments, each under a bishop who appointed the missionaries—a total of twenty by the end of the war.[25]

Alabama was placed in the Middle Department under the supervision of

Bishop Davis Wasgatt Clark of Ohio. Bishop Clark in turn appointed the Reverend James F. Chalfant as superintendent of the Western Georgia and Alabama District; he would reside first in Huntsville and then in Atlanta. In 1865 Arad Lakin, who reported to Chalfant, was appointed the presiding elder in Huntsville.[26] Lakin was familiar with Huntsville. He had been there while chaplain of the Eighth Indiana Cavalry and may very well have witnessed the accidental burning of the Huntsville Methodist church by a Yankee soldier. And he certainly read about Huntsville from frequent reports in the Cincinnati *Western Christian Advocate*.[27]

Lakin arrived in Huntsville in September and was holding services in the courthouse by the first of October. All were approaching a "state of starvation," he reported to Superintendent Chalfant, because of the combination of drought and the devastation wrought by the war. Only the supplies distributed by the Freedmen's Bureau kept the area from disaster. The yeoman Unionists, whom he described as the "most ignorant portion of our people," suffered the worst.[28]

Lakin wrote regularly detailing his work, observations, and predictions. Early letters voiced pleasure with Huntsville but concern with religious indifference and prejudice against Northerners. Then, in January 1866, an important letter by "Occasional" appeared in the Cincinnati *Western Christian Advocate*. Probably penned by Lakin himself, the letter was not so much a report as a statement of purpose and challenges from a discouraged MEC minister serving in Alabama. "There opens up no more important field of labor to the Methodist Episcopal Church than the territory embraced in that part of the country recently in rebellion." Only the freed people seemed to appreciate his sympathy and love for all the spiritually wounded in the South, yet giving them his attention only awakened feelings of repulsion against him by the whites. Another disheartening sign was those many Northern businessmen flooding into the South. Back at home they were solid members of the MEC; but once in the former Confederacy they abandoned all principles, making the vilest secessionists their intimate companions and abandoning the Old Church to its own fate.[29] Lakin was thus placed in a delicate position. He would attempt to reestablish the MEC by appealing primarily to white Southern Unionists in the Alabama highlands and to former slaves, particularly in the Tennessee Valley. But the newly freed black Christians longed to control their own churches while those white yeomen who had opposed secession would have nothing to do with the former slaves. Lakin was himself despised by former Confederates, whose hatred of Northerners seemed to know no bounds, and by members of the Methodist Episcopal Church, South, who saw him as a spiritual invader and arrogant apostate. Lakin would indeed reestablish the MEC in Alabama; but at the end of years of ceaseless and energetic activity that would have stopped a less determined man, the results would be, at best, mixed.

The missionary faced his first overt resistance only five months after his work began, when the trustees of the Huntsville church (MEC South) ordered the black congregation that he had been serving out of their building. The black Methodists proceeded to preach out of doors until the Cumberland Presbyterian church opened their facilities to them. Lakin was bitter. Despite their claims to the contrary, the trustees had "totally neglected the col'd people for four long years," even when they begged for someone to preach to them. Lakin then asked Superintendent Chalfant if he could assure the black Methodists that the MEC would assist them in building their own house of worship, which they did a few months later. At the same time the trustees of the Huntsville church turned out the school operated by the Freedmen's Bureau. The black Methodists appealed to the Freedmen's Bureau; and Major General Wager T. Swayne, the bureau's head in Alabama, ordered that they be reinstated and directed "the military to place them there and protect them till ousted by law." The order, the bureau, the North, and Lakin personally—all were bitterly denounced by Southern Methodists and the former Confederates. "No more authority exists for thus turning the Southern Church out of its property," lectured the *Montgomery Advertiser,* "than exists for turning the citizens of Huntsville and Montgomery out of their homes and installing negroes in them." The *Advertiser*'s editor concluded by warning that the trustees of the Huntsville church would "leave no means untried" in reversing the order. The Huntsville church then appealed to its black members, but only three attended the ten o'clock service, six at three o'clock, and twelve in the evening.[30] Lakin won no friends when he told another group of Southern Methodists that a "Church and ministry that had engaged in a war of four years to fasten slavery perpetually upon [black Christians] was not the Church & ministry of the chosen."[31]

It had not taken long for the former Confederates' initial feeling of shock and despair to wear off. Lakin reported that the white masses were looking with pleasure and pride upon the late rebellion, that every effort was being exerted to make the Lost Cause respectable, even "to create and manufacture public opinion that the south is loyal and the north disloyal."[32] Colonel John Benton Callis, head of the Freedmen's Bureau in Huntsville, reached the same conclusion: a "growing dislike and bitterness" were very apparent, and a large majority of the citizens were hostile to the freed people and were determined to exclude them "from all the civilities, rights and securities of human beings." And not just the freed people. After six months in Huntsville, Lakin applied to the local Freemasons' lodge for a transfer of his membership. The members rejected him because "he represented the M. E. Church North, which is considered here as an invasion."³³ The fact that the Huntsville Masons would later allow their rooms to be used for Klan organizational meetings may explain even more.³⁴

The interposition of white Northerners—and Lakin in particular—into the relations of black and white Southerners was an ever growing affront to the former Confederates. In May 1866 near Florence, black workers loading a wagon apparently lost some flour when they dropped a barrel. The farm owner, an elderly man "in his dotage," blamed it on their carelessness. When one of the workers responded to his curses, the old man pulled out a pistol and fired. The first bullet grazed the worker's ear, but the second found a home in the man's arm. In the ensuing melee, a crowd of freedmen gathered and laid siege to the old man's house. Someone telegraphed the Freedmen's Bureau office in Huntsville, and Colonel Callis arrived with Parson Lakin. The two called the workers together, assured them that justice would prevail, and coaxed them to return to their work.³⁵ Adding fuel to the fire, in August the freedmen in Huntsville celebrated the anniversary of Britain's end of slavery in the West Indies "with regalia, banners, marshals, music, &c." At the barbecue that followed, a white MEC minister, almost surely Lakin, "gave the negroes much good advice as to their duties, responsibilities, conduct, &c."³⁶

How these incidents were interpreted depended entirely on perspective—a point demonstrated by two conflicting articles on the flour-spilling incident in the same issue of the *Huntsville Independent*. Lakin and the Freedmen's Bureau officials saw themselves as performing a valuable service by defusing a dangerous situation, while former Confederates saw an intrusive collusion between the MEC and the Northern government to upset ancient and natural relationships. During the late summer of 1866, Lakin wrote repeatedly of the increasing bitterness among the former Confederates—a bitterness that manifested itself in bold and more defiant opposition. The deep-rooted hatred of the government and of all Union men cropped out "in a thousand nameless incidents."³⁷

As Lakin wrote, yet another organization was entering the already crowded fray. That same month a convention of Methodist ministers and laymen,

presided over by Bishop Clark, met in Cincinnati to organize the Freedmen's
Aid Society of the Methodist Episcopal Church. The Aid Society was modeled
on the government's Freedmen's Bureau (officially the Bureau of Refugees,
Freedmen, and Abandoned Lands) that Congress had created in March 1865
in order to aid in the tremendous upheavals that the Civil War had forced
on freed people and, to a lesser extent, on poor Southern whites. Through a
vast network of officials and cooperating individuals and agencies, the bureau
established schools, worked out labor disputes, and dispensed a great deal
of ordinary materials—food, clothes, and medicine—to these needy people.
The activities of the Aid Society and the bureau both overlapped and complemented each other.[38]

"Schools are essential to the highest success of our missions among the
freedmen; the teacher must go hand in hand with the preacher," declared
the editor of the Cincinnati *Western Christian Advocate*, for "the church and
the school are emblems of Christian civilization, and should be planted side
by side." Forty teachers were immediately needed in Bishop Clark's Middle
Department, which included Alabama. "Hungering and thirsting for the
means of education," the editor continued, the freed people "will not forget
the Church that comes to them with the Bible in one hand and the school
book in the other." Just three months after its organization, the Aid Society's
secretary, Richard S. Rust, returned from the South to report that twenty-five
teachers had already begun their duties in MEC churches. "The chief work
of this Society is to educate this downtrodden race," he concluded. Not long
afterward, the Reverend Rust purchased a site in Huntsville for a school that
would bear his name. Classes began at Rust Institute in early 1867 with Mary
Martha Lakin, the now twenty-seven-year-old daughter of Arad and Achsah,
as one of the two teachers.[39]

The course of reconstruction changed dramatically in 1867 as Congress
took firm control from President Johnson and the Southern legislatures. For
this the Methodist missionaries were grateful. "[I]f Congress fail we fail: if
Congress succeed we succeed," wrote one of them— again, probably Lakin.
Congress passed the First Reconstruction Act, over Johnson's veto, dividing
the former Confederacy into five military districts. Alabama was placed in
the third district until a new constitution could be written and approved by
voters, including former slaves. A second act, passed later that same month
and again over the president's veto, gave more details to the mechanism for
readmission of the states. Lakin likened this subversion of the established order to a dose of quicksilver, the nineteenth-century treatment for syphilis.[40]

Alabama would be consumed for the better part of the next two years with the political maneuverings, rhetoric, and violence associated with drafting and approving a new constitution. Despite the complex and multiple forces at work—principally former Confederates, former white Unionists, carpetbaggers, and former slaves—the Reconstruction Acts narrowed the political lines in Alabama to two: the Democrats (the former Confederates) and the Republicans (most everyone else).

The passage of the Reconstruction Acts, which enfranchised freedmen and disfranchised former Confederate officeholders, moved the state into uncharted seas. Lakin wrote often to his friend Wager Swayne, now also the state's military governor. His first observation was that the former Confederates had changed their tactics. No longer bitter, they had now "resigned themselves to their fate" not to make war on the Union government and had started to coax and flatter the freedmen into standing together in order to "save the South from utter ruin."[41] The former slaves were not persuaded. Soon after Lakin reported on a "rousing meeting" in Huntsville where they had passed resolutions "that made the ears of the rebels tingle." After a former colonel warned them that "Southern men did not want to be compelled to drive the negroes from the South," one freedmen was heard to remark, "that speach sounds very much like the old Bull Whip & Blood hounds."[42]

Lakin did not hesitate to mix church and state. In his same letter to Swayne, he recommended two Union veterans for government appointments: "They are men of strict morals, temperate, industrious and highly intelligent . . . the true loyal type." He also proffered a black Cumberland Presbyterian for the office of registrar in Huntsville.[43] (The position of registrar was critical to ensuring that only qualified voters, i.e., those loyal to the Union, were registered under the terms of the Reconstruction Acts.) Lakin wrote again later in 1867, this time complaining that the Morgan County registrar had proudly declared himself a Southern man; at the end of his letter a dozen or so others added their signatures, including veterans of the First Alabama Cavalry, US.[44] And a month later Lakin telegraphed General Swayne from Huntsville: "Withhold appointment of Probate judge for Limestone [County] till Communication arrives."[45] Politics and piety stuck together like fat on bacon.

The procedure established by Congress specified that an election would be held in early October 1867, in order to decide whether a convention would assemble to rewrite the state's constitution; on the same ballot were the nominees for the delegates to the convention in the likely event that it would be held. "The political elements are considerably agitated in Northern Ala."

wrote Lakin to Superintendent Chalfant.[46] The next day he continued in the same vein: "The spirit of rebellion is showing new sines of life and vitality, for 3 weeks I have never seen such a change for the worse in Northern Ala. and from the tone of the press I fear it is becoming general all over the South." Then, for the first time, the parson mentioned political violence. A man near Athens had been attacked by a band of ruffians and had his mouth and eyes filled with printer's ink; fortunately, others heard the struggle and saved the man's life. George E. Spencer, who a year later would become a Republican senator from Alabama, had also warned Lakin about a letter he had read that included the lines, "It may be necessary to use the assassins knife to free Ala. of Northern emisaries who are [in]siting up the blacks against the Southern friends." Within weeks Lakin had lost eight hundred dollars in a mysterious fire, the particulars of which were never known.[47]

No public figure could sit by, including Arad Lakin who, like other missionaries to the South, remained squarely in the Republican camp. The Methodist clergy were more than just Republicans, according to *Harper's Weekly*; they were "intensely radical, demanding the fullest, squarest, most uncompromised Republican reconstruction of the country." So Lakin kept a close eye on the developing political situation. He predicted that a "hot time is anticipated at the Montgomery Convention." He was referring to Alabama's first Republican convention, held during the first week of June. Carpetbaggers, scalawags, and freedmen—the basis of the Republican Party in the South—all set out for the state capital. There the party unanimously endorsed the Fourteenth Amendment and other Republican initiatives, a publicly funded education system, and racial harmony. The delegates styled themselves "the party of hope—of strength, of security, of restoration," and pledged to "build up, restore, protect all—make us one people."[48] The idea of a single people was the most absurd idea that Ryland Randolph and the other Democrats (styling themselves in this election the Conservative Union Party) could possibly imagine, for it removed the foundation of their understanding of freedom. *The* people were those former Confederates whose bonds of loyalty had been forged through four years of sacrifice. The carpetbaggers, scalawags, and freedmen who constituted the Republican Party were at best *those* people.

Alabamians voted in early October 1867. For the first time, free black men—former slaves—cast their ballots alongside free white men. The Republicans won easily. A month later the delegates assembled in Montgomery, and by early December they had finished their task. The resulting constitution (Alabama's fourth) was a moderate document. February 4–7 were the dates set for its approval or rejection; but before that could happen, former Confederates convened and decided to take advantage of a loophole. The Second Reconstruction Act required the participation of a minimum number of registered voters in the election in order for it to be considered official. When time came for the voters to decide whether to approve the new constitution, men gathered at the polls purportedly to challenge illegal voters—but actually to intimidate as many as they could into *not* voting. When the votes were tallied, the constitution had been approved; but the minimum threshold of registered voters had not gone to the polls. The boycott was successful. The constitution failed on a technicality. The state waited anxiously to see what Congress was going to do about it.

Meanwhile, Huntsville's presiding elder was consumed with building up the MEC in Alabama. Lakin's monthly reports to Superintendent Chalfant in Atlanta, which were often published in national Methodist newspapers, provide a gauge of his work in the state and a means of seeing who was joining the MEC churches. In the spring of 1867, for example, he had reported 886 members (of whom 330 were white) and twenty ministers.[49] He also reported that, during the end of April and first part of May, he had traveled by horseback on a four week's tour through six counties—in all, over four hundred miles on horseback, during which he preached fourteen sermons, organized four circuits, and received 150 new members and four ministers into the Old Church. On June 6 the missionary left on another four weeks' tour toward Tuscaloosa. The sense of his reports is one of constant motion. These tours were no different than those that Methodist circuit riders had been making since Bishop Francis Asbury established the itinerant ranks. But most circuit riders were young and unattached; Lakin was fifty-seven, with a wife and daughter still at home.

The tours usually passed through the mountainous region south of the Tennessee River, the heart of Southern Unionism in Alabama. The land was sparsely populated, the roads rough, the rivers deep and without bridges. The people lived in log houses and often suffered from a poor diet: corn pone mixed with cold water and a little salt served with bacon. They drank corn and rye coffee, without sugar, and often from a gourd. They burned fat pine for light. And they remained loyal to the Union. "Their sons, fathers, and brothers, rather than fight against the old flag," reported Lakin, "have been murdered in cold blood, have lain in the mountains, hunted with blood-hounds, and their wives and daughters tortured to compel them to reveal their hiding-places." The Unionists had not only opposed Alabama's secession in 1861, they had opposed the Southern Methodists' secession in 1844. These Southern Unionists would travel from five to twenty miles to hear a loyal minister. From Lakin they would learn of church and state interests, for loyalty to one was loyalty to the other.

Here, in these mountainous regions, lived not only some of Lakin's closest friends but also some of his bitterest enemies, especially those who opposed his attempts to put white and black into the same Methodist Episcopal Church. Typical was a letter from Robin W. Minor. This resident of Walker County complained that "Thare is aheap of Radical preachers Calling themselvese the mother Methidiste church. The are Causing a grate deal of truble. The are going aboute throo this Cuntry trying to distroy all othor churchis of ther order and establish a prolitical church. . . . put a stop to this or give us the powor to Exclude them from amonge us. . . . for god sak and humanity sak nevor give the negro his Equal Ritse with the wite Rase . . . and give us some advise and how to act with those Radical Preachors and how to treete them."[50] Other opposition came from more predictable quarters: the clergy of the MEC South. Lakin reported that one of his members, Edward Jones (presumably a freedman), had been working for two months to build a small church in Paint Rock, east of Huntsville in Jackson County. He had done the work principally with his own hands, living on bread and water. He spent five dollars of his own money for nails and received twenty dollars more from Lakin. Then some ministers from the MEC South came to take possession of the church building and the congregation. But this time "Edward carried too many guns for them, and they left the field."[51]

Despite the setbacks, the missionary was having enough success to be noticed. Rumor had it that Alabama would soon emerge from its status as a missionary conference to become the eighth and final MEC annual conference established in the South. On the seventeenth of October, 1867, the fold gathered at Talladega College (recently organized by the American Missionary Society to educate the freed people). "I now convoke the Alabama Annual Conference," Bishop Clark announced. The new conference then proceeded to the business of ordaining ministers and recognizing local preachers. A correspondent to the Cincinnati *Western Christian Advocate* noted that the ministers were mostly Unionists from rural districts who had suffered greatly during the war for their loyalty; now that they had connected with the Old Church, they were suffering almost as much. The new conference claimed 3,300 members in forty-five churches. As the driving figure in the formation of the new conference, the Reverend Lakin was given several important

positions: conference secretary, president of the conference missionary society, alternate delegate to the next general conference, and presiding elder
of the Montgomery District. The appointment of Lakin to Montgomery and
another presiding elder to Demopolis signaled an intention to extend further
the MEC'S ministry to Alabama's black population. The appointment, however, would have other far-reaching and unintended consequences.[52]

In late June 1868 Congress passed the Fourth Reconstruction Act, recognizing Alabama's referendum and elections and putting an end to the Democrats' boycott. A new Republican governor took office and Congress seated a
new delegation from Alabama. Republican probate judges and local officials
turned the established order on its head. "Politically our people are more discouraged than ever," concluded one of the old guard in a masterpiece of un-
derstatement.[53] New men held old offices, and new men held new offices. The
revolution was especially evident in the realm of education. The Republicans
who had written the 1867 constitution insisted that Alabama have a free public education system modeled on the Massachusetts system. The newly elected
superintendent of education, Noah B. Cloud, presided over the state board of
education, which also served as the University of Alabama's board of regents.

The regents, who began meeting in July, immediately announced their determination to work with the churches, especially in providing schools for the
freed people. They passed resolutions thanking Congress, the Commissioner
of the Freedmen's Bureau, and the many primarily religious organizations,
such as the MEC's Freedmen's Aid Society, which had established schools
in the state. The regents then invited the superintendents of those societies
to sit with them and to advise them. Beginning in late July they asked that
each day's opening session begin with a prayer by the local MEC presiding
elder, Arad Lakin. On August 6 they elected him president of the University
of Alabama.[54]

The parson was not a popular choice. When the Talladega *Alabama Reporter*, a Democratic mouthpiece, learned of the regents' choice, the editor did
not hesitate to describe him as "a thorough nigger-radical" who has "done as
much as any other 'new comer,' to poison the minds of the negroes towards
their former owners." He had been living and "missionating among the blacks
and mean whites in North Alabama" until moving to Montgomery where he
allowed blacks to visit his home "on terms of perfect social familiarity." His
daughter, who had taught at a school for freed people, had been seen escorted
by a "buck negro" on the streets of Huntsville. "As to his literary capacity we
know nothing." Nor were the former Confederates the only ones questioning

Lakin's appointment. "What can a native Union man do, expect, or calculate on in the future?" wrote future Republican governor David Peter Lewis to then Republican governor William Hugh Smith. "The Carpet-baggers have already landed everything that is Republican," thereby destroying the chance of building up the party in Alabama. "The political offices, the University, Schools all carpet-bagged!" He ended with a flourish: "Can the native white Union men make any movement that will relieve themselves from the odium that stink in the nostrils of humanity? I want to hear from you." Lewis did not leave his objections private, but penned another letter to the *Huntsville Advocate*. "Why should a man be taken by the shoulders and thrust into the Presidency of a University, who was never before in his life, in the presence of Apollo or the Muses?" he asked. "And why should a man be required to teach Greek and Latin, who does not understand the plain elements of his native tongue? . . . I must confess that I am not partisan enough, *entirely* to sanction and defend these acts as a party necessity."[55]

Explanations for Lakin's appointment were never given. The regents' decision had nothing to do with his academic qualifications, which were none. Certainly their decision had something to do with Lakin's being a Republican and being a Methodist minister; after all, their next choice would be another Republican minister. (The first two presidents of the University of Alabama had also been ministers.) The regents' decision may also have been driven by the need to reestablish moral leadership in a state sadly lacking in it. Arad Lakin was expected to supply that leadership.

※※※

On that last Friday in August, President Lakin and Superintendent of Education Cloud walked out to the university and were rebuffed by Professor Wyman. Lakin left that evening and Cloud on Saturday. Randolph published the *Independent Monitor* on Tuesday morning, and on page two was the cartoon showing the two men hanging from an oak tree. The caption singled out Lakin: "The genus carpet-bagger is a man with a lank head of dry hair, a lank stomach and long legs, club knees and splay feet, dried legs and lank jaws, with eyes like a fish and mouth like a shark. Add to this a habit of sneaking and dodging about in unknown places—habiting with negroes in dark dens and back streets—a look like a hound and the smell of a polecat." Both Lakin and Cloud "would make first rate *hemp-stretchers*," Randolph continued in another column that directed them to heed the cartoon's warning.

The cartoon was probably Lakin's first direct encounter with the Ku Klux

Klan, yet he had certainly heard of the organization. The newspapers had given the Klan extensive coverage that spring and summer, but the parson had also heard from the mountains of north Alabama near Tuscumbia that the Devil had appeared on Earth. His eyes were said to be as large as dinner plates and as red as burning coals. Out of his mouth spat fire and sometimes water. Children were afraid to hunt berries or to leave the safety of their fenced yards, even in the middle of the day. Women milked their cows before sundown; and after sundown the door was bolted until morning.[56] Lakin was not about to back down before former Confederates in costume, and they were not about to back down either. In fact, Lakin had become one of the Klan's chief targets.

)(X)(

Perhaps it was Lakin's election as the university's president; perhaps it was Randolph's cartoon; perhaps it was the approaching election—at any rate, the Democrats began targeting the Methodist Episcopal Church as never before. The *Mobile Register*'s editor charged that "at this very hour the carpetbag missionaries of the Radical Bible have arrayed the blacks into actual and scarcely repressible hostility to their own masters"; indeed, "in sagacity and cunning they out-Machiavelli Machiavelli." The editor of the Cincinnati *Western Christian Advocate* alerted readers to new threats against the Old Church under such headlines as "Reign of Terror in the South" and reprinted letters from Aid Society teachers. One correspondent, who may have been the Lakins' daughter, claimed that the Tuscumbia Klan had lynched three black members of the MEC church there, were looking for the old preacher, and had a list of twenty-one more that they intended to dangle from ropes. Another teacher wrote that "the K. K. K. approach our home with rope and revolver in hand, and demand the inmates of the house who have dared to teach niggers. Leading Southern ministers are stirring up the rabble to commit deeds of darkness."[57]

About two weeks before the 1868 presidential election, some ninety-five Klansmen passed by the Lakins' Huntsville home, blowing their whistles but making no overt action. But such was not the case on Halloween, the last Saturday night before the Tuesday vote. The Republicans were holding a mass meeting in the Huntsville courthouse square when they were surrounded by about 150 disguised and armed men. Undisguised footmen followed, and some of the strongest were placed at the four gates to the tall iron fence with sharp pickets that surrounded the square. Gunfire started at the north gate.

Lakin, who lived about a block from the square, had walked up to see the commotion. "The Ku-Klux," he recollected, "by order of the cyclops, wheeled into line of battle with the adroitness of veteran cavalry." When the undisguised man who had started the firing was wounded in the head, the cyclops ordered the firing stopped. The column then wheeled into line and rode off. The Republicans suffered worse. A freedman was instantly killed and two others severely wounded. Silas Thurlow, Limestone County's probate judge, was wounded in the bowels and died three days later. He had been a member of Lakin's church and a dear friend. The military arrested four armed Klansmen with their disguises and turned them over to the civil authorities, who then let them loose.[58]

The intimidation did not change the vote. On election day, November 3, U. S. Grant and the Republicans were victorious, even in Alabama. But the intimidation continued and even seemed to increase toward MEC ministers.

Just a week later Lakin was seated by the large bay window at the front his house writing. Known as the Saroni House, the Lakins shared it with several other prominent Republicans. At seven o'clock he got up for supper, leaving the lamp on and the thin curtains drawn. After supper, about eight, they heard the snapping of three caps and sixteen buckshot passed through the shutters, the windows, and the curtains, lodging in the wall above their heads. Black men arrived within a few minutes to post guard, and the (false) report that "old Parson Lakin was killed" was circulating within a half hour. A few days later a friend warned Lakin that he was targeted for assassination. So he fled to the mountains of Winston County for two months, pursued by two Klansmen. His family remained in their Huntsville home, where Klansmen intimidated them. The *Huntsville Democrat* tried to have it both ways: although "the occupants of the house are obnoxious to the community," their presence "furnishes no excuse for such outrageous lawless conduct."[59]

An observer at one of the annual meetings of the Alabama Conference confessed "to strange sensations" when the secretary, Lakin, read out the roll: Of one, "[a]ssassinated by the Ku-Klux immediately after the session of the last Conference." Of another, "beaten nearly to death, and had to fly from the country to save his life."[60] The list was long. It included the Reverend Moses B. Sullivan, who was staying at the home of Henry Stephens in Madison County.[61] "When I raised up in bed," recounted Sullivan, "I saw it was surrounded by men in disguise, faces masked, and persons covered with black gowns, having pistols in their hands pointed toward my body." Holding Stephens and his daughter personally responsible if anything were revealed,

13. Union troops wearing disguises confiscated from Klansmen arrested after raiding the Huntsville courthouse. On the back of another print of this photograph, an inscription in the handwriting of Investigating Officer Lafayette E. Campbell, reads: "Photographs of Uniforms etc. taken by Lt. L. E. Campbell, 33rd Inf. On the night of the 31st October 1868. These were worn by Ku Klux on night of ~~the night of~~." (Carte de visite by Robinson & Murphy, Huntsville, 1869, in private hands)

the Klansmen took Sullivan with them. After a couple hundred yards, they stopped and convened a trial of sorts, charging the minister with favoring negro equality, of being paid by the US government to preach to the negroes, of having been disloyal to the Confederacy during the war, and of associating with Southern Tories (the common term for Alabama Unionists). "He is head leader of the Northern Methodist Church," noted one who thought it best just to kill him. They eventually decided on forty licks with a club. "I gave him that for you," said the assailant, "now this one [is] for *me*," and hit him one last time over the shoulders. One of the strokes broke Sullivan's skull and others left him hemorrhaging in his bowels and lungs. They left with a further warning that he should leave for his home at daylight, cease the quarterly meetings, and begin preaching for the Methodist Episcopal Church, South. The next day the preacher reached home, thereafter a chronic invalid. He sent a note to the editor of the *Atlanta Christian Advocate*: "I cannot stay at home. They have their pickets out for me. Will I have protection? I cannot think of appealing to the Governor of our State, believing it would be useless. I can only appeal to our noble President for protection. In the Government of the United States can we in North Alabama get protection?"

The attacks continued throughout 1869. One Saturday night George Taylor, a local black preacher, was taken from his bed by a band of men with white sacks over their heads and black gowns. They whipped his back, pistol-whipped his head, and then punctured his body and legs with a knife. Then they gave him until Tuesday to leave—which he did. The Reverend Johnson of Fayetteville, another local preacher, was shot dead in the pulpit. The Reverend Isaac W. Dorman of Wetumpka, whipped after Sunday services, took the hint and left. And on several occasions, Lakin, too, was fired upon.[62] In none of these cases were the perpetrators brought to justice.

During the fall of 1870, when traveling from DeKalb County to Guntersville in Marshall County, Lakin left his horse on the riverbank and boarded a boat down the Tennessee River. As he and Captain Spiller sat chatting on the deck, two pistol volleys were fired a couple hundred yards from the boat. The next day he learned that forty-odd disguised men had crossed the bridge a little above Guntersville and, finding only his horse, resolved to shear its mane and tail. They then left word that "old Parson Lakin ought to be very thankful that he had lost nothing but his horse's mane and tail, for if he had not been upon Captain Spiller's boat he would have had his damned old radical neck broken."[63]

That same autumn Lakin held a revival at the Gum Grove campground in the mountainous and remote regions of Blount County. On Saturday night three men with Bowie knives searched the congregation for Lakin while the congregation sang and the seekers came forward. Being very warm and worn out from his preaching, he had fortunately retired to a private house a hundred yards away. The three men vowed that they would cut out his "damned old radical throat." Once again a personal friend came to warn him of an impending attack on Monday evening. Lakin called a council of the preachers, selecting one to lead the service while he stayed in his private quarters. As the first preacher was ending and approaching the altar, a whistle was heard and about forty armed men in white pants surrounded the arbor and stood guard while three men with revolvers searched for the old parson. The alarmed congregation snuffed the candles and skedaddled. Presently some dozen men came up to a few who had decided to stay. "You believe that when you die you will go to Lakin?" a Klansman asked a woman. "If he ever undertakes to preach here again he will land in hell before he gets it done. Just let him try it." Then they fired a volley and with a terrible (Rebel) yell, went off. With perhaps a thousand unsympathetic witnesses, it was not hard to get federal indictments against at least seven of the armed men.[64]

This particular camp meeting was remembered for more than just the appearance of armed men. Early that Sunday morning a woman gave birth to a stillborn child who was "a perfect representation and fac-simile of a disguised Ku-Klux." The child's scarlet red eyes and mouth were about a third smaller than ordinary, while the head itself was about three times normal size; projecting from the forehead an inch and a half were two "gristly horns." The mother, a Mrs. Horton, was a delicate and pious member of the church, and her husband, Benjamin, had been forced into joining the Klan but had since renounced it. The Klansmen had already whipped him once for abandoning them. Eight or ten days later they whipped him again, this time for exhibiting the Klan-faced child. That the child looked like a Klansman was no coincidence to these unlettered mountaineers at Gum Grove. They blamed the malformation on the Klan's having ridden by the Horton home every Wednesday and Thursday night for months and thereby frightening the pregnant Mrs. Horton.[65]

This chronicle of the Methodists' troubles with the Klan reads like a testimonial, for in fact it was. Beginning on June 13, 1871, Lakin testified in Washington, DC, for two days before a Congressional committee charged with investigating Klan activities in the South. His testimony was direct and specific, at times a deeply moving catalogue—complete with affidavits—of outrages against those loyal to the Old Church and the Old Union. His was the most extensive, the most damaging, and the most controversial. Predictably, Lakin's opponents countered his statements at every turn. The contrast

14. Arad Lakin about the time of his testimony to Congress
(Courtesy Ann O'Hara)

between the two speaks to the unbridgeable gulf separating Democrat from Republican in the postwar South.

Democratic governor Robert Lindsay, for example, testified that Lakin's reputation was that of a "very shrewd, sagacious, cunning man," a zealot who "looks at everything through a jaundiced eye, with a magnifying eye; small events that would not be noticed by other men his imagination and fancy work into terrorism." Asked about the bitterness between the two Methodist denominations, the governor replied, "In my county the Northern Church belongs to the republican party and the Southern Church to the democratic party." The MEC missionaries, he explained, had been sent south in order to seduce the freed people away from the Southern church and to inspire hatred toward the white people of the South, in part by planting in blacks' minds that the Democrats wanted to put them back into slavery. In sum, Lakin's efforts "to raise antagonism in communities; to advance the church at the expense of social peace, to advance Christianity at the expense of harmony between the two races that existed in the South" were reprehensible. The Reverend Lakin was simply an un-Christian man.[66]

James Holt Clanton, friend of Ryland Randolph and head of the Democratic Party in Alabama, called Lakin "a man of very bad character, . . . notorious there as a mischief-maker and a stirrer up of strife." When asked about the Klan, of which he was the reputed leader in the state, he replied that he did not know of any general organization in Alabama but it may have been isolated to a few localities.[67]

Nicholas Davis, another lawyer from Huntsville, had served in the Confederate Congress and commanded a battalion. After the war he refused to take the loyalty oath. Davis testified that Lakin was a near neighbor in Huntsville who had incited the freedmen to rise up against the white Southern people. But Lakin's real goal, according to Davis, was political office, having made himself a candidate for the US Senate soon after arriving in Alabama. "I tell you that old fellow is a hell of an old rascal," concluded Davis. "He is a humbug; a liar and a slanderer; that's what he is, and he ain't nothing else."[68]

For each of the Alabama Democrats who testified to Lakin's vile character, an Alabama Republican testified that he was a saint—or close enough. Especially compelling were the remarks of the unlettered. George Taylor, the black local preacher who had been beaten by the Klan, stated that the white people in the old Southern Methodist Church, those who formerly owned slaves, would have nothing to do with Lakin because the MEC "was the church that was started for a Union society to elect Mr. Grant." He signed his affidavit with his mark.[69]

William Shepard, a poor white farmer and Unionist from Blount County, spoke of being persecuted constantly by the Klan. Shepard had nothing but praise for the old parson, whom he claimed to know well. "I have ever regarded him as a gentleman and a Christian, and not only a gentlemen and a Christian, but a very energetic man." Even more, "I defy any man living, since my acquaintance with him, to point to one spot on him now, sir, as to his moral character." Shepard had seen two of his churches burned. "We have been careful to call it Old Church," rather than Methodist Episcopal Church, "because we want this North and South to die out." Lakin wanted to erase other distinctions as well. His witness to black Alabamians was most often condemned, but he continued to speak out against those who would limit God's grace to the elect. Lakin deeply offended an old fellow by speaking for universal atonement, a good Methodist doctrine rejected by Calvinist churches. "Well, sir," said Lakin, "if you have lived to be sixty years old or upward, and never knew that the promise of God applied to both female and male alike, I don't want to undertake to enlighten you." But the real problem was always the charge that he promoted "negro equality and everything else offensive."[70]

Not all the Republicans supported Lakin. The most troubling opposition came from Joseph H. Speed, a scholar and former Whig who had served as a member of the 1867 constitutional convention and who in 1872 would be elected the state's superintendent of education. Speed objected to Lakin as an example of the improper and incompetent officers that the first board of regents had selected. Yes, Lakin was sometimes reckless and careless with his statements. But the real problem was that he "was known to be a man who fraternized with the negroes." Lakin would sit with black men and women at the same table, and "there was that sort of social equality going on and carried much further than abolition ever went." That trumped all. "Southern white people, as everybody knows, who knows anything of them, will not visit socially, as equals, men who fraternize with the blacks and treat them as equals."[71]

Perhaps the most balanced account came from Major General Samuel W. Crawford, then in command of the Northern Alabama military district. He cast Lakin as a divisive figure. Members of his own denomination spoke well of him, believed him of good standing; but those on the other side simply detested the man. "I think these church people have a more intense hatred to each other than any other classes." The matter did not end there, because the parson was known as both a Republican and an effective speaker to the freed people. The two—religion and politics—could not be separated. "I think, to come down to the absolute facts, that he has had a very hard, rough time of it."[72]

The testimony before the Joint Select Committee ended, and the witnesses went back to their workaday lives. The testimony had revealed the animosity between Democrats and Republicans—certainly—but it had also suggested the divisions within the Republican Party as well as within the Alabama Conference of the Methodist Episcopal Church. The white members of the Old Church were opposed to worshiping as equals alongside black members, and the black members wished to have more of a say in their own churches—a problem that was beyond Lakin's abilities and, in fact, would take another century to solve.

The Civil War had encouraged Northern Methodists to broaden their understanding of the church. Just months after Appomattox, the North-West Indiana Conference, for example, called upon Methodists to "carry the tidings of a free salvation to all classes, white or black, rich and poor—thank God, we need not add bound or free." This did not mean that former slaves could enter the ranks in their present condition. They needed immediate help, and this help was administered through the Missionary Society, the Freedmen's Aid Society, and other organizations. The idea of worshiping separately was not considered, or perhaps ignored, by those framing policy. Several of the Northern bishops had no understanding of the racial and cultural accretions of centuries. Bishop Clark, for example, began as a rather conservative anti-slavery man. But in 1865 he joined other bishops in signing what was known as the Erie Platform, which acknowledged God's hand in destroying the evil of slavery and announced the MEC's intention to "occupy" the Southern states. (The Southern bishops met a few months later to denounce the Erie Platform and all attempts at unification.) Bishop Clark went on to become the first president of the Aid Society and the bishop overseeing Lakin's mission to Alabama. The Reverend Gilbert Haven, the former editor of the *Boston Zion Herald*, became the Alabama Conference's new bishop in 1873. He had been a confirmed abolitionist and radical (for his time) integrationist who would eventually advocate miscegenation. His biographer put it gingerly: Southern Unionists "did not generally share Bishop Haven's sentiments concerning the wickedness of all separations among Christians of the same faith on any grounds of descent or color." Lakin found him "a great man in many ways but utterly impractical and impossible in his views of race relations and administration."[73]

White animosity to worshiping alongside black Christians was widespread in Alabama. Those Tories from regions that had never known slaves were, in fact, among the bitterest opponents of a biracial church. A single example will suffice. In 1874 a short entry in the *Mobile Register* reported that near Arkadelphia in remote Walker County,

Twenty-seven members of the Northern Union Methodist Church abandoned their faith and order, both religiously and politically, and joined the Missionary Baptist Church, and were baptized by Rev. L. Williams, of Jasper. They were all Republicans, but when they abandoned their denomination they also abandoned their Radicalism. Now they declare themselves Democrats, and will support the Democratic State ticket. The reason for this change was because their presiding elder, one Lakin, while on his grand rounds preferred staying with his negro brethren in preference to the white members of his church. This man Lakin is nothing more than the scum of the Union Methodist Church of New York, sent down here, I presume, to regenerate the

negroes in religion and politics. When preaching to his God-loving
social equality brethren, his text is the Civil Rights bill. Long may he
live on earth to kiss the negro children and fondle them on his paternal
and patriarchal knee.[74]

Lakin faced different challenges from black members of the MEC. Within
a year of his moving to Alabama, the editor of the Mobile *Nationalist*, a Republican newspaper with a large black readership, warned the missionaries
of the MEC that they were pursuing an unwise course. "It is well known that
in the large cities of the North the colored people almost unanimously prefer
to worship by themselves and listen to the ministrations of ministers of their
own race." The circumstances in the South after the war meant that the same
desire for autonomy was felt even more powerfully in churches. This was particularly the case among the Methodists, for the Methodist Episcopal Church
was not competing just with the MEC South but with the two black Methodist denominations, the African Methodist Episcopal (AME) and the African
Methodist Episcopal Zion (AME Zion). The editor predicted that neither of
the white Methodist denominations could reasonably hope to maintain a significant number of black members.[75] The *Nationalist*'s editor, a white man in
sympathy with the MEC, was mistaken, for the Old Church did retain black
members, especially in north Alabama where Lakin's ministry was centered.
But the editor had put his finger squarely on the religious impulse of the freed
people of Alabama: They accepted assistance, but not direction.

The MEC had already broached the subject of separate conferences for
white and black Methodists before the war had even ended. The reasons offered were hardly surprising: the relics of the former state of master and slave
would create friction if black and white were to occupy the same pews, the
same churches, and the same conferences; black Methodists would prefer the
all-black AME or AME Zion churches; and whites would refuse to worship
beside their former slaves. At the 1868 General Conference, Alabama's delegate, the Reverend J. W. Talley (Lakin was the alternate), presented a resolution that Alabama be allowed to organize on the basis of race; but the
resolution was buried in committee. It would take eight more years before
the General Conference finally relented and allowed Alabama to form racially separate conferences if a majority of both the races agreed.[76] Only four
months later, in October 1876, black Alabama Methodists met at a remote
camp ground in Randolph County to establish the Central Alabama Conference. Its secretary: Arad Lakin, who decided to cast his lot with the new black

conference. He and Achsah continued to live in Huntsville, but in the black section of town. On several occasions he served as the Central Alabama Conference's delegate to the General Conference.[77]

҂X҂X҂X

What might account for the course that Arad Lakin took in his life, for the decades he spent going from church to church, for his lack of fear, for his drive? Christian freedom.

Christian freedom, like the people's freedom that Ryland Randolph embraced, had ancient origins. But there the similarities ended. Where Randolph defended a freedom restricted to his own people, Lakin's freedom was offered to all. Where the people's freedom was an inheritance to be defended, Christian freedom was a gift. Most strikingly, the people's freedom seemed natural and obvious, whereas Christian freedom was filled with paradox.

Lakin first confronted those paradoxes at that revival meeting back in the Forks. "Whosoever shall seek to save his life shall lose it," the preacher read, "and whosoever shall lose his life shall preserve it." Martin Luther built on this and other biblical passages when he wrote the classic statement, *On the Freedom of a Christian*, in 1520. There he makes an extraordinary statement: "We are free, subject to no one; we are servants, subject to all." Christian freedom, in other words, involves severing certain bonds—to self and fortune—and appropriating new bonds—to serve others. Christians are no longer slaves to sin; instead, they are bound to follow God's will. In one stroke Luther turned on its head conventional notions of freedom as some sort of right to do as one pleases, as an inheritance to be defended, as the easy life. Freedom is instead about doing something unexpected, about giving up oneself in order to free oneself, about coming to grips with sin and obligations.

Sin is not a popular notion these days, for it conjures up visions of sanctimonious church ladies with wagging fingers judging matters that are entirely personal. Fair enough. The notion of sin rests on the premise that some standards—in particular right and wrong, good and evil—stand above personal whim or social convention. Christians believe that humankind is hopelessly mired in sin; or as Luther put it more emphatically, we are slaves to sin. But in a gesture of pure grace, God sweeps sin away. The believer responds by serving God through others. We are free, but free to serve—a paradox, a mystery, a profound truth at odds with our common sense.

Arad Lakin's life perfectly exemplified Luther's explanation of Christian freedom. The young man had thought himself free as a bird, without significant restraints, until he was forced to confront the triviality of his own life. This was hardly the cause for immediate celebration, but rather a deeply disturbing event. Yet his anxiety turned to joy upon finding himself freed from sins by a loving God. Instead of a servant to sin, he became a servant to God, renouncing his former ways and entering the ministry. That he chose the Methodist ministry is significant. All Protestants agree that God's gift of salvation is itself entirely undeserved on our part. Methodists stand somewhat apart, particularly from the Calvinists, in stressing the believers' freedom, responsibilities, and capability for improvement. The Reverend Lakin's appointment to serve the Irish in the Five Points slum was entirely within the Methodist tradition. From New York City to Tuscaloosa, the parson brought the word of freedom from sin and even, following Phoebe Palmer, freedom from the desire to sin. In Alabama he started churches, missions, camp meetings, and two conferences. The community of believers included all.

Lakin's efforts were typical of the reformist impulse that swept nineteenth-century America.[78] The Second Great Awakening was a time in which many came to believe that the country could be turned in a new moral direction. The goal was not merely to change the individual's behavior, but to change the individual's motivation. It was not enough to live differently; the individual must *want* to live differently. The resulting Christian nation would serve as a city on a hill, as a model for the world. Temperance, one of Lakin's causes, was an obvious example of Christian engagement. The other great cause was antislavery. Christian reformers were at the forefront of calling for physical and spiritual freedom for black Americans. The enormity of slavery may seem in and of itself to explain their zeal, but Christians could easily have retreated from the world. Instead, first Quakers and then other abolitionists were driven by their sense of Christian responsibility, by their sense of gratitude for God's grace and their attendant obligation to respond by serving—by their Christian freedom, in other words.

That the end of slavery came with a sword and not a Bible did not change Christians' sense of obligation. The missionaries' energy certainly flowed as much from their belief in Christian equality as Christian freedom. ("There is neither Jew nor Gentile, there is neither slave nor free, there is neither male nor female"—Galatians 3:28.) When Lakin tried to extend that holy community to include black and white, former slave and former master, former Confederate and former Unionist, he met with mixed results. The old parson would ultimately bow to reality and establish racially divided churches and conferences; for Christians, including Lakin, never claimed to be entirely free of sin in this world. Regeneration is of the soul and is due to God's saving grace. Man was born in chains—to sin—but can be freed to free others.

)()()(

As the issues that had so bitterly divided the South for so many years settled down, as people began to fall back into established roles, Lakin's name would still crop up occasionally. In 1880 the editor of the *Tuscaloosa Gazette* reported that Lakin had been in the City of Oaks preaching for nine hours one Sunday. Then the editor sarcastically asked whether Lakin had really come to find those keys to the university that Professor Wyman had denied him a dozen years before. The same editor had earlier reminded his readers how the University of Alabama had once fallen "into the hands of the rapacious carpet-bagger, and became part of the spoils of the dominant political faction."[79] Lakin and Cloud's walk to the campus, memorialized by a crude woodcut, had entered the world of myth.

The old parson's ministry was drawing to a close. He was well into his seventies and had led a vigorous life. But he was not done, for as he often said, "Man is immortal till his work is done." In 1870 his only daughter, Mary, married Captain John Wigel Raines, a Union veteran who had been badly wounded at Second Bull Run. Raines came to Huntsville as a clerk for the Freedmen's Bureau and then transferred first to the Internal Revenue Service and then to the US Marshal's office. For a time the Lakin and Raines families lived together in Huntsville (briefly in a home belonging to the younger C. C. Clay, cousin of Katharine Randolph). In 1885, the year of Achsah's death from pneumonia as well as the year that a new Democratic administration dismissed Republican government officials, they all moved to Rockport, Missouri. Why the family chose Missouri is unknown. Once there Lakin was sent by the Central Missouri Conference to establish a mission to the black residents in Kansas. He accepted and was appointed first to a church and then a circuit in the black conference.[80]

Arad S. Lakin died in early 1890. His son-in-law and granddaughter returned the body to Huntsville for burial in Maple Hill Cemetery. No announcement was to be found in the Democratic press, but the Republican newspapers carried several notices. Individuals had been assessing his contributions even before the obituary notices appeared. The editor of the New Orleans *Southwestern Christian Advocate* put him among those who came south "when the vigor and prime of their manhood was upon them" in order to save the flock from the wolves.[81] He had died in the freedom of a Christian:

absolved from the guilt of excessive self-interest, grateful, and vigorously bound to serving others.

A funeral service was held at Lakeside, a black church that Lakin had helped to found. After the congregation sang *Servant of God, Well Done* and the scripture was read, the presiding elder discussed the man he had known for twenty-three years, a man whose distinguishing features were listed as simplicity, strength, and directness. The newspaper reported that the immense congregation had a last look at his "familiar face, still bearing that strong and manly appearance, though in the embrace of death. Then strong arms, impelled by grateful hearts of the people among and for whom he had labored and suffered bore the corpse out of the church, and a large procession proceeded to the cemetery where the remains of the distinguished divine were laid to rest beside his departed wife, the grave being decorated with flowers by loving hands and grateful hearts."[82]

THREE

Scalawag

Only the educated are free.
—Epictetus

Unlike Ryland Randolph and Arad Lakin, Noah Bartlett Cloud did not write his own reminiscences. Like those two, however, he did reach a moment that turned his life in an entirely new direction.

Cloud was born in early 1809 in Edgefield District, on the southwestern edge of South Carolina, just north of Augusta, Georgia. Edgefield District was known as a point of departure for Southerners moving west, especially after Alabama was granted statehood in 1819. The young Cloud would have seen people passing through on their way westward in search of their main chance. But he stayed put until the age of twenty-four, when he entered Philadelphia's prestigious Jefferson Medical College. He graduated in 1835 alongside Alabamian J. Marion Sims, who would become known as a renowned pioneer in gynecological surgery. That same year Dr. Cloud married Mary Barton, also of Edgefield, and, with a partner, opened a pharmacy across the Savannah River in Augusta.[1]

The young physician headed west in 1838 to practice medicine in east Alabama, a vast region that had just been opened to white settlement after the Creeks had been forced out. At Planter's Retreat he made a home along with Mary, his father, and eventually two of his three brothers. The next summer Dr. Cloud was visiting a friend who lived on Uchee Creek in northeast Russell

County and noticed the superior cotton that grew there. In that simple observation he discovered his lifelong cause—agricultural and educational reform—and embarked on a path.

His friend's cotton grew better because it grew in more fertile soil. This was hardly a novel observation. Farmers had known for thousands of years that superior soil produced superior crops, as they knew that planting the same crops every year wore out the soil. But the problem had become acute for Americans, and for Southerners in particular. With a seemingly endless frontier, it was simply more profitable to keep clearing new land and start again than to improve old land. Their practice was cheap in terms of financial capital, but expensive in terms of social capital. "Why is it," Cloud once asked rhetorically, "that you cannot converse five minutes with scarcely any planter without encountering the oft repeated story—'My land is wearing out; I must hunt new rich land in the far West?'" And off he would go. "All this sacrifice to get new land to recommence the same routine of desolation upon the soil, and to die in an uncomfortable wilderness!"[2]

This constant westward movement left Southerners rootless. Families would leave established social networks in the East only to arrive as strangers in the West. The new country was filled with men on the make. Typical was the western Black Belt near Greensboro, Alabama, where Ryland Randolph's family had their plantations. One resident there wrote back to his father, "Do you forget that I am in a wilderness, cut off from all mankind. . . ?" A few years later little had changed; after being away for six months, he returned to Greensboro and recognized no one, for the population was so transient.[3] Another young man on the make wrote back to his father in Virginia that there was "little or no society . . . the people are from all quarters & care no more for each other than dogs do, except [if] it is to cheat you." No one noticed a stranger, for they were all strangers; so to overcome their separation, they greeted each other with "friend." But why develop a real friendship with someone you might never see again? Besides, that so-called friend could easily be a confidence man or criminal on the lam. "Beset with scoundrels," he concluded, and "no confidence in one another, all is suspicion & distrust."[4]

Then just when things were starting to fall into place, new lands opened up farther west, families would sell out and move, and the cycle would start all over again. Traditional communities were impossible to sustain where friendships were fleeting, where reputations were not earned but declared, where rapacious young men were consumed with making money, where most stayed only a few months and few stayed more than a few years. Too much was left undone. To further their own self-interest, individuals began to cooperate in constructing voluntary communities for limited goals. They would call a public meeting to build a church, to start a school, to bring in a railroad, or to promote temperance. Temporary, flexible, and focused, these voluntary communities could accommodate a constantly shifting population. They were not, however, the same sort of communities that took generations of mutually supporting families to establish.

Observant individuals like Dr. Cloud were aware of how disruptive this pattern was. On this subject he was not as eloquent as some of his correspondents, who would link desolate landscapes to desolate communities. In the 1850s one writer began by acknowledging that Southerners' opportunities were without parallel in history. Living in a favored region, owning their own property, and producing the greatest commercial staple ever known—cotton—the planters' path "was open and sure to the accumulation of wealth, the attainment of liberal and refined education, and the enjoyment of the fullest measure of happiness springing from the comforts of life." Cotton had covered the ocean with the white sails of merchant navies, strengthened the bonds of fellowship among nations, and diffused the beneficent influences of civilization and religion. Yet the South was a picture of desolation. Unsightly gullies, deserted homesteads, and barren hillsides covered the landscape—and all because its restless and dissatisfied population would use up the soil and then head westward searching for cheap and fertile new lands in order to start the destruction anew. The "old homesteads descending from father to son and receiving the embellishments of successive generations" were not to be found because of the Southerners' haste to be rich. Under this system "no nation can permanently prosper, and nothing but the unparalleled fertility of the soil; the vast extent of unoccupied territory, and consequent low price of land; and the cheapness of slave labor, has enabled the South to sustain herself so long."[5]

When Dr. Cloud viewed his friend's superior field of cotton, he surely did not immediately recognize how improving the soil could revolutionize Southern society.[6] But he did recognize that he could apply the scientific methods he had learned in medical school to make his own poor land as rich as his friend's. He began by preparing manure from his stock lot and stalls for an experiment. The other planters all ridiculed his plans, predicting that *"manure would burn Cotton up!"* He looked at agricultural papers, but they said little about cotton and not a word about manuring the land. With public opinion arrayed against him, the doctor only planted a small patch his first year. The unexpected result: "a perfect triumph." Recognizing that a single successful experiment could have been the result of a singular circumstance, the next year he selected three acres of extremely poor land to continue his experiment. He precisely calculated and recorded the exact quantity of manure he applied, the dates that it was applied, the width of the rows and the distance apart of the stalks, and the most efficient labor methods of preparing the soil. He had some failures, which he addressed. But the results were staggering: 9,040 pounds of cotton taken from the three poor acres! "It was a triumph that exceeded my most sanguine expectations."[7]

In 1842 or '43 Cloud sold Planter's Retreat and purchased three hundred acres north of Tuskegee in Macon County. With the labor of six slaves, he built his elegant but unpretentious plantation home in the Greek Revival style.[8] At LaPlace, as he called it, Cloud pitched into his program to create a practical and productive system of cotton production that would stop the ruinous cycle of buy, exploit, sell, and move on.

Also in 1842 he began writing articles on his agricultural experiments with the fervor of a convert. His first known contribution was "South American Evergreen Grass," an essay published in the *Cultivator*, the organ of the New York Agricultural Society. Two months later he wrote the first of three extensive articles, "The Improved Culture of Cotton," for the same journal. In these he exposed the ruinous system by which the cotton plant was then being grown, explained the principles on which he based his improvements, and provided a detailed explanation of what quickly became known as the Cloud System. By improving the soil with compost heavy in manure and then carefully managing the plants at certain points in their growing cycle, he predicted that "it is perfectly practicable to produce the 2,000,000 bags—the cotton crop of the United States—with *one-third* the capital engaged under the present system of culture." These essays were no mere letters penned by a successful planter but instead carefully documented reports complete with drawings of more efficient hoe designs, recommended quantities of compost, and prescribed distances between beds. While soil improvement lay at the core of his program, he also made recommendations on leaving land fallow, rotating crops, terracing, and using labor most efficiently. By 1850 the Cloud System had made the doctor's name, as one historian put it, "synonymous with agricultural reform."[9]

As an incentive to read the first essay, the *Cultivator* had printed the phrase "Gathered 5,989 lbs. per Acre" under the title. The hook worked. Cloud's articles caught the attention of other agricultural journals and newspapers that

15. LaPlace, Noah B. Cloud's plantation home in Macon County, since renamed Cloud Nine
(Courtesy author.)

would extract and republish the pieces.[10] The most important journal to re-publish an essay by Cloud was the *Southern Cultivator*, just established in Cloud's former home of Augusta, Georgia.[11] Cloud wrote the journal a let-ter, which the editors also published, thanking and then gently chastising them for giving his piece a new title, "How to Make a Large Cotton Crop." Merely increasing the size of the crop was not his object, he insisted; rather, he wanted to impose a new scientific and enlightened policy that would cur-tail the wasteful and expensive features of the old system. Educated planters began to look upon the *Southern Cultivator* and other exemplars of the ag-ricultural press as harbingers of a great national movement. Their primary object, according to Cloud, "is improvement, their views are liberal, and their motives patriotic." Instead of continuing in the same methods, hidebound by habit, the educated planter should look dispassionately at the evidence before making a decision, recognizing that science has improved the destiny of man in the past half century "more than all the *brute force* of the previous fifty centuries of the world's age."[12] It was a call for reform that he would make again and again.

And not just in print, for Dr. Cloud was becoming deeply involved in—in-deed, "addicted to," according to one agricultural historian—the convention movement.[13] Conventions were among the most formal expressions of nine-teenth-century voluntary association. There, like-minded individuals would share information and gather support for initiatives. Conventions were held to promote education, to press for political reforms, and, in Cloud's case, to revolutionize agricultural techniques. When in 1845 the price of cotton reached a nickel a pound (having been seventeen cents a pound a decade be-fore), Alabama's legislature even got involved, calling for two conventions to address the problem. The delegates met and decided, to the surprise of no one, that Southerners were growing too much cotton and failing to add value to what they did grow. The delegates called for cutting production and for building spinning mills instead of shipping the lint to Liverpool. All of these were the sorts of conclusions and solutions that had been bandied about for years. It only got interesting when the delegates went further to call for invest-ments in manufacturing and mining. That, in turn, required investments in education. They had in mind conducting a geological survey of Alabama and creating a state society to promote scientific agriculture. Dr. Cloud expanded the proposal in the *Southern Cultivator* by calling for the establishment of "a large and an efficient *Southern Planters' Agricultural Society or Association, for the promotion and Advancement of Agricultural Science*," not just for Ala-bama but for the entire South.[14]

During the early 1850s, major planters' conventions seemed to occur yearly. Dr. Cloud strongly backed what came to be known as the Florida Plan, which called for state associations to own extensive warehouses in the South-ern ports where all the cotton would be collected; the associations could then use their leverage to negotiate better prices than individual planters and their factors. (The Populists would float a similar proposal at the end of the cen-tury.) From other quarters came calls for regulated prices, quotas, and still more conventions. At an important three-day meeting held in Montgomery in May 1853, Dr. Cloud helped to establish what was formally deemed the Agricultural Association of the Slaveholding States, an organization he had first proposed in 1847. The first day ended with an important speech by Mi-chael Tuomey, Alabama's state geologist and University of Alabama professor, calling for every school to have its own professor of scientific agriculture and every state to have its own agricultural college. Although the subject of slav-ery had not been mentioned in the promotional literature, the subject was on everyone's lips and particularly on the lips of future secessionist but then senator Robert Toombs of Georgia, whose speech on the third day "electrified the assembled multitude." The Montgomery convention of 1853 ended with a significant commitment to scientific agriculture.[15]

The next meeting of the Agricultural Association convened only seven months later in Columbia, South Carolina. Dr. Cloud served as secretary, as he had at Montgomery, and reported to the *Southern Cultivator* on the six-day convention's decisions. The only resolution he mentioned was a motion to create and substantially endow a Southern Central Agricultural University, whose importance he noted by using italics. Under the control of the association, its immediate purpose was to "provide the best means of instruction in all the sciences and learning pertaining to agriculture and its kindred arts," particularly in stimulating planters to adopt improved systems of agriculture and promoting rational systems of diversifying labor.[16]

Nothing came of it. The Columbia meeting was the last held by the Agricultural Association of the Slaveholding States, as it merged with the commercial conventions. Beginning in 1851 Cloud was a delegate, and often the secretary, at a series of conventions designed to promote the commercial and industrial interests in the Deep South. By the 1858 convention in Montgomery, these were firmly in the hands of the disunionists. Delegates included the fire-eaters Williams Lowndes Yancey from Alabama, Robert Barnwell Rhett from South Carolina, and Edmund Ruffin from Virginia. Ruffin and Cloud were the foremost scientific agriculturalists of their age and had been in correspondence. Cloud called on Ruffin as soon as the latter had taken his room in the Exchange Hotel. On the first day a resolution was introduced to reopen the African slave trade, and much of the next two days were consumed with its merits. Yancey spoke for secession and for reopening the trade. "And in conversation, out of the Convention," wrote Ruffin, "I have not yet heard a dissenting voice to the measure." As these commercial conventions increasingly became forums for secession, they took over the Agricultural Association's interests in commercial independence and direct trade.[17]

The promotion of scientific agriculture was left to the state and local societies, where Dr. Cloud enjoyed considerable success. He had chaired a meeting in the Montgomery statehouse to look into creating a state agricultural society, but it was not until January 1855 that the Alabama Agricultural Society was formally established. The following month the legislature supported the society with a bill of incorporation and $10,000 appropriation for a state fair. "It is earnestly hoped," began an editorial in the *Montgomery Advertiser and State Gazette*, "that every Alabamian will make it a personal matter, and contribute his mite to render our first Fair a credit to the State, and a sure index to the industrial and mechanical resources of the State." That October people eagerly flocked to the thirty-acre plot in Montgomery to see the usual carnival side shows and to attend the theaters. (In 1860 they would watch John Wilkes Booth and listen to presidential candidate Stephen A. Douglas.) Fairgoers also came to see the exhibits, many housed in the Industrial Palace, whose ambitious name was at odds with its shabby construction. There they could see for themselves the state's best agricultural products, suitably marked with blue ribbons. The whole was described in immense detail in articles probably written by Cloud himself, who won prizes for his sheep and swine.[18] These fairs entertained, gave politicians a ready audience, and proved that farmers and planters could do better. Even more, the fairs were examples of cooperation and community building in a region that needed both.

"By such associational compact," urged Dr. Cloud, the experienced and intelligent devotees of science will secure "a strong bond of union in the active cooperation and concentrated energy of such elements." Theirs was a patriotic—nay, almost sacred—charge: to light up "every cottage and hamlet, and mansion, too, in this free and widely extending Republic, by the brilliant effusions of minds richly stored with science and practice, and the experience of systematic and enlightened agriculture." In other words, the practical information that the scientific agriculturalists had acquired needed to be taught, especially to the yeoman farmers. This was to be accomplished through the agricultural press, but also through state, county, and neighborhood agricultural societies all working together toward a common goal. The result: "a most formidable array of energy, efficiency and devotion would be combined in the one determined effort to accomplish a great national enterprize."[19]

Buried in Dr. Cloud's passionate oratory, his articles calling for a tidal wave of dedicated souls who would sweep ignorance aside and usher in an age of great national enlightenment—buried in all that was the deep-rooted anxiety of a Whig.

The Whig political party had emerged in the 1830s in response to Andrew Jackson's reformation of the party of Jefferson.[20] Many of those who had voted for Jackson were alarmed at the way the new market orientation was displacing traditional structures. Instead of the household economies that had been the mainstay of American life for generations, it was the railroads, steamboats, industries, and commercial establishments that were gaining firm control. These innovations brought great benefits, without question. But some people—clever, manipulative, and conspiratorial people—were getting rich

16. The first Alabama State Fair
(*Harper's Weekly* 1858 November 27; courtesy Birmingham Public Library)

in ways that made no sense, in ways that confused and alarmed the Jacksonians. Why was it that the same crop of cotton that brought twenty cents a pound one year brought ten cents the next? What exactly was the Liverpool market anyway? This new economy was expanding as if there were no limits. But there *were* limits; there had to be limits, not just to money but to freedom. The Jacksonian Democrat wanted to be rid of all this, to return to the natural order, to hasten the day of reckoning.

Most features of the market economy that the Jacksonians deplored, the Whigs celebrated. A network of rail and steamboat lines and an economy based on large banks and paper money may have created unfamiliar large and anonymous bureaucracies, but they could also be tools for liberating the individual from a comforting yet stifling dependence on the past, on the inherited habits and customs that kept people from building more fulfilling lives. Whatever social situations an individual was born into, Whigs believed that they could be surmounted by disciplined individual effort. Whigs were optimistic because they were convinced that we can do better.

Unfortunately, the solitary individual was weak when standing before the power of tradition and the majority. Thus Whigs promoted voluntary cooperation as a means of doing together what could not be done separately. Joining agricultural societies was a perfect example. Planters shared their experiences and insights with each other, to the benefit of all. Voluntary association could only go so far, so Whigs supported an active government that would promote railroads, keep the banking system running smoothly and predictably, and create schools and universities—all means of encouraging individuals to rise above their lot. Of these, education was crucial, for it freed individuals from ignorance, the cruelest of masters. Whigs believed, in other words, in giving people the tools that would simultaneously create both freedom and society in this individualistic country. Whiggery was thus more than any political or economic platform; Whiggery was a new way of looking at a new world.

The Jacksonian Democrats vigorously opposed the Whigs on every count. An active government, they believed, was a tool of greedy plutocrats to increase their own wealth at the expense of the people. Democrats could see the advantages of railroads and steamboats, but banks and paper money became the symbol of all that was askew. As they saw it, banks could not create wealth, merely redistribute it to those clever enough to know how to use the system. After all, the foundation of wealth was in labor, not in investments or loans or speculation. Money had weight and jingled in your pocket. Money could not be burned with a match. It would not blow away in the wind. If the special interests centered in the Whig Party (Jacksonians looked upon the Whigs as if they were a separate class) could be held in check, then the people would once again return to their natural state of sovereignty. So President Jackson "slew" the Bank of the United States and attempted to return the country to silver and gold currency.

Jacksonian Democrats were not only alarmed at an active government. They dismissed Whig efforts at voluntary cooperation and moral reform as meddlesome or at best irrelevant. And in the South the presence of black slaves added another problem. Everyone could see that the black men who toiled ceaselessly in the fields were enslaved—totally, legally, and racially enslaved. But the white farmers who continued the same timeworn, inefficient, and wasteful methods of wearing out the soil and moving on were also, in a different sense, slaves: slaves to habit, ignorance, and low expectations. But unlike the field hands who had little control over their own destinies, the white farmers *could* change theirs. Dr. Cloud was one of many Whigs, such as the first owners of the *Southern Cultivator*, who were pushing them to do so.[21]

In short, Whigs and Jacksonian Democrats talked past each other. Whigs feared the undisciplined masses, while Jacksonians feared concentrated wealth and power. Whigs praised the self-made man; Jacksonians praised the natural man. Whigs asked Americans to reform; Jacksonians asked to be left alone. In the words of a Whig editor, the difference between Whigs and Democrats was "that the former dealt with man *as he should be*, while the latter appealed to him *as he is*."[22]

Dr. Cloud was a committed Whig. His first political involvement came in 1840 when he served as a delegate from Russell County to the first state Whig convention, meeting in Tuscaloosa.[23] His active participation in planters' conventions and other voluntary associations, willingness to share the results of his agricultural experiments, and commitment to education in general and not just agricultural education—these were all expressions of the Whiggish belief in cooperative reform.[24] Cloud himself tried his hand at explaining this theme in another three-part essay he wrote for the *Southern Cultivator*. He began by reiterating what he considered the most basic truth, "that man is endowed with an innate or intuitive sense of inquiry" that prompted him to seek his own personal advantage. It is to this "living, insatiate and inextinguishable principle of the human mind that we are indebted for all the advancement which we at present enjoy in our moral, civic and social relations." More than this, in this age of progressive improvement, new inventions were decreasing the manual labor that once consumed the day. The science of agriculture consisted first of a determined will followed by the "combined assistance of reason, diligence and industry, guided by the light of science and experience." The result of the "judicious practice of this system of Improvement," he insisted, was not merely better crops, but "all the terrestrial happiness allotted here to man."[25] Here was the essence of Whiggery: using self-interest to promote the public's interest.

One of the proposals on which delegates to the planters' conventions consistently agreed was the need to publish their own journal. It was certainly the next step for Dr. Cloud, who had been writing articles for quite awhile, and it was certainly the next step in enlisting the public in his great cause. On the first day of 1853, he introduced the *American Cotton Planter*. The first issue began with a thirteen-page address to the Historical Society of Alabama by Isaac Croom, a prominent planter from near Greensboro who would serve as the first president of the Alabama Agricultural Society. His address, titled "A Memoir on the subject of the Cotton-plant, its History, Influence on Commerce, Politics, and the Welfare of the Human Race, and its Probable Destiny as the Great Product of the Southern United States" (short titles were not the rage), was followed by more practical articles, such as the use of guano and method of hillside ditching, a call for county agricultural societies, an essay touting railroads, letters by planters and by the industrialist Daniel Pratt, and the entire Constitution of the Alabama State Agricultural Society.

In that first issue Dr. Cloud also wrote an introduction that served both as a prospectus and as a summary of his reform program. He was at pains to set aside any rivalry with other like-minded agricultural journals. The *American Cotton Planter*, in other words, did not intend to eliminate competition but to cooperate with those "co-laborers in the great work of reform and improvement in the industrial pursuits of our common country." And although the journal's title singled out cotton, its scope encompassed the perfection of the entire art of obtaining sustenance from the earth. With that out of the way, the new editor returned to his old theme. He denied that the South's problem was too much cotton; rather, the problem was that planters produced too little grain, too little bacon, too few mules, and no wool—in other words, no diversification. The immediate consequence of single-crop farms was that Southerners spent their profits from cotton on imported goods that could readily be made at home. The long-term consequences were much worse and evident to anyone who compared the prosperous farms of New England with the worn-out farms of the South. The New England farms had a balance and efficiency that Southern farms lacked. Moreover, Southerners could not even process their own cotton but had to send it to the mills of Liverpool to be spun into cloth and sewn into garments. The South needed to value manufacturing and the mechanical arts as much as the agricultural arts. "We can spin, and we can weave, as well as other people, and we can give to cotton its greatest value at home here, where it is grown." In a prescient observation, he noted that the South, and particularly Alabama, had inexhaustible supplies of iron ore and coal, the building materials of industrialization.[26]

Even this did not complete his case, for the South possessed one advantage over all others: "the best labor, because the surest and safest *and always at hand.*" Dr. Cloud had made the point more explicit in his announcement published thirteen months earlier. One of the purposes of the *American Cotton Planter* "will be vigilantly to sustain the institution of slavery as it exists in the cotton States, and to demonstrate that it not only contributes to the success of cotton planting, but that it is indeed an essential element of that prosperity."[27] For all the talk of worn-out lands and the need for economic diversity, it was slavery that defined the South.

Dr. Cloud and his family seemed always to have owned slaves. He received four slaves through his marriage in 1843. By 1850 the couple together owned eight slaves; his father, who lived next door, owned at least two dozen.[28] Dr. Cloud realized the economic benefits of slave ownership. What complaints he had about the institution focused on the part it played in Southerners' inherited and wasteful farming techniques.

In his journal Dr. Cloud reprinted apologias for the South's bound labor force. "Moral Benefits of Slavery," written by William S. Price of Marengo County, was standard stuff: God sanctioned slavery in various contexts, including civilizing the Hebrews by enslaving them to the Egyptians; slavery continued to be the surest and speediest method of civilizing the heathen; slavery would not cease "so long as there are heathens, or until the world is brought to the light and liberty of knowledge." In the meantime we should guard against interfering with the ways of Providence. Other articles pressed the same point from different angles. "Standing by reason of our 'peculiar institution,' alone among the family of nations," wrote another correspondent, "it becomes us to compel the respect and admiration of the world, not less by our material wealth, than by the liberal education, scientific attainments, and literary eminence of our people." Still another article, "The Influence of Slavery upon the Progress of Civilization," (deemed commendable) was followed immediately by "Re-opening the African Slave Trade" (deemed deplorable).[29] Cloud was aware that slave labor was inherently inefficient, but he seemed obtuse regarding its ethical dimensions. That he remained close to the planter mainstream before the war may explain much of the vehemence against him when he joined the Republicans after the war.

Cloud's *American Cotton Planter* had been in print exactly one year when Stephen A. Douglas, then-chair of the US Senate Committee on Territories, reported a bill that would allow the question of slavery in the territories to be left to the settlers. (That Southerners so coveted the territories was a tragic confirmation of Dr. Cloud's failed efforts to wean them away from their wasteful practice of wearing out lands in the East and then moving to exploit new lands in the West.) Douglas had acted in order to secure the votes of Southern politicians for his transcontinental railroad. Popular sovereignty, as he deemed it, embodied his belief that if (white) people voted to have slavery, that was fine; and if they voted against slavery, that too was fine. So very democratic, and so morally indifferent. President Franklin Pierce signed the Kansas-Nebraska Bill into law at the end of May 1854, plunging the country into a series of confrontations that would eventually lead to the firing on Fort Sumter. Their party by this time gone, most Northern Whigs gravitated to a new political party, the Republican, which combined the traditional Whig platform of moral reform and an active government with a commitment to stop the extension of slavery. Southern Whigs tried various unsuccessful options for compromise, while Southern Democrats would eventually take the South out of the Union.[30]

These were puzzling times for Dr. Cloud, especially when he became a co-owner of the state's leading Democratic newspaper. The situation arose as a direct result of the *American Cotton Planter*'s success. Dr. Cloud had only five hundred subscribers when he began publishing in 1853, but soon had ten thousand subscribers. His journal had become a resounding success, which brought him a considerable amount of money. In October 1856 Cloud purchased with others the *Montgomery Advertiser and State Gazette*, whose presses also printed the *American Cotton Planter*. A month after purchasing the *Advertiser*, Cloud purchased another journal, the *Soil of the South*, published in Columbus, Georgia. The first issue of the *American Cotton Planter and Soil of the South* was dated December 1856. Much of this was going on during the 1856 presidential election, the first in which Republicans were on the ballot, and during the bitter arguments over what to do about Bleeding Kansas, where a guerilla war was waging over the future of slavery in the territories. By late 1859, after constant griping and threatened duels from Democrats, Dr. Cloud sold his entire interest in the *Advertiser*.[31]

Part of Dr. Cloud's decision to disengage himself from the *Advertiser* surely grew from his realization that the newspaper's controversies could only detract from his extraordinary reputation as a scientific agriculturalist. In 1858 he was featured in *Harper's Weekly* along with a piece on the Alabama fair. Prominent foreign visitors sought him out.[32] The *American Cotton Planter and Soil of the South* was arguably the most successful journal of its type, and its cause seemed to be gaining wide acceptance.

It was not scientific agriculture but the possibility of disunion that seemed to be on everyone's mind as the 1860 presidential election approached. The Alabama Baptist Association met in Tuskegee, just down the road from LaPlace, and unanimously adopted the secessionist resolution of the Reverend Basil Manly, former president of the University of Alabama who would serve as chaplain first to Alabama's secession convention and then to the Confederate Congress.[33] Dr. Cloud, however, was a Unionist. He served as a vice president in the Montgomery Bell and Everett Club. Its members were Southern Whigs pledged to support Constitutional Union Party nominees John Bell and Edward Everett, in hopes of finding a middle ground that would avoid secession.[34] Meanwhile, Dr. Cloud continued his work for agricultural reform,

17. Noah Bartlett Cloud (*Harper's Weekly* 1858 November 27)

published the *American Cotton Planter,* and served as a delegate to yet another convention of southern planters in Macon, Georgia.[35]

Bell and Everett lost the election, and Lincoln won. The Southern states se-
ceded, and cannon opened fire on Fort Sumter. Americans and Confederates
eagerly joined to fight

But not Dr. Cloud. He ceased publishing the *American Cotton Planter* and
seemed to have stayed in Montgomery for the first year and a half of the war.[36]
Despite not having practiced medicine in decades, by December 1862 he had
nonetheless been appointed surgeon and was soon one of three members of
the board of examining surgeons in Savannah, Georgia.[37] He may have been
on duty in Savannah when Arad Lakin and Sherman's army reached there
two years later; and in another odd conjunction, Dr. Cloud's son, also named
Noah B., served as a private in James Holt Clanton's artillery company. Nothing before, during, or after the war points to any commitment by Dr. Cloud to
the Confederate cause: he was a prewar Unionist, his military career was far
from the front and (unlike Ryland Randolph's) never discussed later, and he
would join the Republican Party.

Even as soldiers returned after Appomattox, daunted by the task of rebuilding their broken lives, Dr. Cloud seemed to have been invigorated. He entered politics at the first opportunity, in August 1865, running unsuccessfully from Macon County for the state constitutional convention that would revoke Alabama's secession as a first step in President Johnson's reconstruction plan. Later that fall Cloud would be nominated for state superintendent of schools, but the legislature appointed a different candidate.[38]

By October he was the secretary of the Alabama State Agricultural Society's executive council, planning for yet another planters' convention. When the entire society convened the next month in the statehouse, it became clear that little had changed in the minds of too many. One of the first orders of business was to select as president the former governor, Andrew B. Moore, who had led Alabama out of the Union. To an unreceptive audience Cloud delivered a speech pushing once again for enriching the soil, this time in order "to enable both whites and blacks to sustain themselves. . . . We must act towards the black man in his new relations with manly forbearance, do our whole duty to him as a fellow man, and not stick at matters of prejudice in determining what shall be done for his welfare." But the next speaker severely attacked the Freedmen's Bureau and proposed a plan for regulating labor, "utterly repudiating all Yankee interference, all Yankee systems and all Yankee theories in the management of the negro race." George W. Stone, the law partner of James Holt Clanton (who served on the executive committee with Cloud), also spoke to the convention. He believed that African slavery was sanctioned by the laws of both Heaven and Earth, although the black people were now legally equal to the white. He also spoke against ratifying the Thirteenth Amendment (abolishing slavery) as the opening wedge that would magnify and perpetuate the Freedmen's Bureau out of all proportion. And with that, the direction of the convention was set. The legislature followed suit a month later, when it passed "An Act to Regulate Contracts with Freedmen and to Enforce the Same." Commonly known as black codes, these laws passed by several Southern legislatures punished unemployed freedmen as vagrants and apprenticed orphaned black children to white masters. Governor Robert M. Patton vetoed the measures as class legislation, and his veto was sustained.[39] *didn't last long* 🙂

While the convention was meeting, Dr. Cloud announced plans to resume publication of the *American Cotton Planter*, which he did, this time as a semi-monthly. He would also attempt to revive interest in the annual state fair and agricultural society. But the war had changed too many things, as he soon realized.[40]

The first direct evidence came in an important letter that he penned in December 1867 to his old friends at the *Southern Cultivator*. Addressing "the new order of things," Cloud called for the balanced agricultural policy that he had been promoting for twenty-five years: producing food and other necessities first, with only the surplus devoted to market crops. Cloud's remarks to this point represented merely an extension of positions he had long held. The real departure came when he addressed the interests of the freed people. Once he had called for a more efficient use of slaves, but he now claimed that reliance on bound labor had consumed and impoverished the once beautiful and rich Southern lands more than all other causes combined. Indeed, he had no regrets that "the country is relieved of the evil of slave labor" and even celebrated the fact that now "every man in the country [is] the master of his own labor." The South now had a unique opportunity that "places the freedman in a position to favorably exert his productive capacity, and in which position the landlord establishes a relationship that secures the confidence in the laborer—promotes his intelligence, and makes him safe in a good and competent living for himself and family." Nor did he leave it at that. "We owe these people a debt of more than gratitude," he continued. "They served our fathers and our mothers faithfully, and they served us and our children with an extraordinary fidelity, up to the day of emancipation, in the bringing about of which they exerted no voluntary agency whatever. Our first duty, then, in the matter of productive labor, is to them." He urged large landowners to divide their estate into lots to be leased to the families of their former slaves; to erect comfortable houses, outbuildings, and gardens; and then to sign long-term leases conditioned on their implementing modern systems of agriculture. With such a material base and with free schools, a contented freed people would grow in intelligence and good citizenship. In sum, the combination of free labor and a balanced agriculture would benefit all—planters and freedmen alike—by creating "incalculable prosperity." His was an extraordinary departure for someone who had heretofore voiced no obligations to black Southerners.[41]

That same month, December 1867, Dr. Cloud acknowledged being an active member of the Republican Party and their nominee for the superintendent of education. The Democrats could not have been more shaken. A man who for years had rubbed shoulders with Yancey and Clanton, who had even

owned the state's chief Democratic newspaper, was now "a full-blown Radical" who had thrown in his lot with "adventurers, new comers, [Freedmen's]
Bureau officials, carpet baggers, loyal leaguers, &c.," in the words of *Mobile
Register* editor John Forsyth.[42] Cloud's timing was propitious; his Democratic
opponents would say opportunistic. When he published his letter, the Fourteenth Amendment, granting former slaves citizenship, had been proposed
but not yet ratified, and the decisive 1867 Alabama Constitutional Convention was in full swing. There had been hints that he would cast his lot with the
Republicans, but only hints. Likewise regarding his decision to broaden his
interest from agricultural reform to improving general education: only hints.

A decade before, during the 1850s, the legislature had granted an act of incorporation to Dr. Cloud and others for LaPlace Institute, one of countless local schools that Americans created by voluntary association. He also helped to
write a report to Judson Female Institute's trustees on instruction at the Baptist school in Marion. His most public role in education had been his series of
articles published in the *American Cotton Planter* in 1858 and 1859 urging the
legislature to create an agricultural college and experimental plantation.[43] Dr.
Cloud dropped his proposal when a bill was introduced in Congress providing that over six million acres of public lands be used to endow an agricultural
and mechanical college in each state. He was profoundly shocked when all
Southern Congressmen, except for two Georgians, voted against it on strictly
political grounds. Noting that the size of the cotton crop had remained essentially unchanged in ten years, although the size of the slave population had
increased about 50 percent, he insisted that the South needed such colleges
more than ever. Not only would the colleges adapt science and theory to practical uses on the farms, they would also send out five hundred young men
each year to demonstrate these methods to their fellow citizens. Such was not
to be, at least not in 1859. Dr. Cloud was bitter, and he did not forget.

Creating an agricultural and mechanical college was but one expression
of a larger program of educational reform during the 1850s. In 1854 Alabama
took tentative steps to create a free school system modeled on the one developed in the late 1830s by the Whig reformer Horace Mann for the state of
Massachusetts. The general assembly appointed a superintendent of schools,
who presided over three commissioners in each county, who in turn super-
vised three trustees in each township. Despite repeated attempts to abolish
the superintendency, the commissioners, and even the system itself (Alabama
spent a meager $1.33 on each pupil its first year), it all managed to keep going.[44]

In 1856, two years into Alabama's first experiments with public education, the state's leading reformers established the Alabama Educational Association. Dr. Cloud was not in attendance, but the association expressed his views. The keynote address came from Landon Garland, president of the University of Alabama. The mission of public education and colleges, he insisted, was not to impart professional knowledge; that was the role of the special schools of law, medicine, divinity, and the agricultural and mechanical arts (Dr. Cloud's special concern). Rather, the role of public education and colleges was to prepare the individual morally and to teach the individual needed skills that would allow him to succeed in this competitive new world. The well-educated individual who succeeded in this new world also contributed to it—ideally as a minister, teacher, statesman, or physician—thereby tempering the ambition and greed that was threatening the great American experiment in self-government. The scientific and technological achievements that Dr. Cloud touted as a means of ending the cycle of buying, exploiting, selling, and moving had too often been used for selfish ends in the rapacious pursuit of lucre. The right sort of schools, the reformers insisted, should bring light to benighted souls and prepare young people for responsible citizenship. The classroom, like the church and family, would become the means of freedom, the means of personal and social salvation. In Dr. Cloud's own words, "Intelligence is the great sovereign cure."[45]

The war interrupted these initiatives as public schooling was suspended. Alabama's first state constitution after the war, adopted in September 1865, made no mention of education. The position of state superintendent of schools was not eliminated, but the failure to require an annual report suggests that the state took little or no responsibility for educating its children. The Republicans demanded that the state's school system be reestablished and this time on an efficient and well-functioning basis. More than that the Republicans built much of their message on free schools, available to all—rich and poor, black and white—that would create friendship and mutual regard, while displacing ignorance and passion.[46] The Democrats detested such proposals.

Precisely what led Cloud in the end to join the Republican Party and to run for superintendent of education will never be known. Certainly several factors—his Whig background and apparent lack of enthusiasm for secession, his failure to gain support for agricultural colleges and new economic policies, perhaps even his failure to win election as superintendent of schools in 1865—contributed.[47] He may also have seen in the Democrats a backward-looking party committed to outmoded social and economic institutions that the war should have destroyed or, in fact, did. The Republicans, by contrast, were intent on introducing a modern economic and educational system to a state that had been held back by those unwilling to try to do better.

At the same February 1868 election to ratify the new constitution, Dr. Cloud easily won the most votes for the position of superintendent of education. But because of the Democrats' boycott, he also waited until June 25, when Congress passed the Fourth Reconstruction Act, to learn that the constitution was in effect and that he was in office.[48] This new constitution changed the superintendent and board of education from appointed to elected positions. They began meeting in July, tackling the daunting task of creating a modern educational system in post-war Alabama. They faced four hurdles: ensuring finances during a time of unprecedented economic upheaval, hiring competent teachers and administrators, educating the freed people, and dealing with Democrats opposed to a system of free education.

The problem of finances alone was enough to overwhelm them. Alabama's new constitution gave the board of education legislative authority and specifically charged it with establishing in every township or other school district at least one school that children and youths between the ages of five and twenty-one could attend entirely free. The funding was to come from the standard leasing of the sixteenth section of every township and from an additional "one-fifth of the aggregate annual income of the state." The general assembly was given the authority to levy taxes on railroads, insurance companies, and other corporations to be devoted exclusively to education. (Education had been, of course, a paramount Whig concern.) The members of the board established some ten or eleven normal schools, distributed throughout the state, as part of their long-range plan to raise the level of teaching. They defined and detailed the duties of the superintendent of education, thus making it difficult to disguise the inactivity that had characterized the tenure of former superintendents. The contrast with the earlier regime was evident in Superintendent Cloud's first annual report. The previous administration, he noted, had failed to disperse to many counties the appropriations for the previous two years, a sum totaling over $254,000. Believing the state to be bound in good faith to do so, the new Republican legislature proceeded to appropriate the sum over the next year and a half. This decision, however, gave the Democrats an opening to charge Cloud with financial malfeasance, a charge that would register deeply with white Alabamians facing higher taxes for the first time.[49]

Adding to Democratic fury, the board of education worked hand in glove with private agencies associated with abolitionism and the Republican administration in Washington. At its July 28 meeting, the members explicitly thanked Congress and O. O. Howard, commissioner of the Freedmen's Bureau. They also thanked those private organizations that had maintained schools for Alabama's freed people: the American Missionary Society, the Pittsburg Freedmen's Aid Commission, the Freedmen's Aid Society of the Methodist Episcopal Church, and the Westchester Aid Society of Pennsylvania. The board then invited the aid societies' superintendents and the Freedmen's Bureau superintendent, Reverend R. D. Harper, to offer assistance and advice. Capping it off, the board passed a resolution of cooperation that directed the superintendent to work with the Freedmen's Bureau and the Christian aid societies.

If all this were not already enough, the board passed an act titled "To Provide Separate Schools." While the title of the act appeared to be a victory for segregation, its true effect was to put into law the requirement that the freed people be given schools at taxpayers' expense. Buried within the fine print was a provision that black and white children could attend the same schools "by the unanimous consent of the parents or guardians of such children." In an attempt to add a new transparency and responsibility to its deliberations, the board published the minutes of its meetings under separate cover. Some of the board members defended their actions, and the Republican press proudly published letters alongside the new regulations. They went out of their way to address the financial problems, noting that the state owed the school system three million dollars. They also insisted that the schools would be separated by race and free "without a dollar's expense to any pupil between the ages of five and twenty-one."[50] Creating a free public school system open to both races would remain a difficult, perhaps impossible, task for Superintendent Cloud and the board of education. At every turn—operating a school system without sufficient funds, soliciting help from Republican and Northern agencies, providing free education to the freed people—the Democrats opposed the actions of the new board of education.

In contrast to the state's public school system, distributed throughout the state's villages and towns, the University of Alabama represented a single and tangible object.

The university that Cloud and the board of regents oversaw had moved far from its beginnings a mere thirty-seven years earlier.[51] Little was left of its original campus, which had been arranged in the shape of the Greek letter Π in order to reflect the balance and harmony of nature and of the democratic ideals and timeless truths that lay at the heart of the university's mission: to prepare young men for service to state, society, and church. This was accomplished by disciplining students' moral and mental faculties through study of the Greek and Latin languages and civilizations, by providing them with sound religious and moral teaching, and by drilling them in logic. Mathematics and natural philosophy (as science was then called) were studied primarily as demonstrations of the reasonableness of God's creation. Students were encouraged to develop their rhetorical skills in debates and public orations given in the Rotunda, which lay at the center of the Π. The curriculum was optimistic, progressive, and emphatically democratic.

The first faculty had been led by a minister and included Professor of Classics Henry Tutwiler, product of the University of Virginia and later founder of the Greene Springs School. Things began to change in 1838 with the arrival of Frederick Augustus Porter Barnard. Over the next fourteen years as professor of chemistry and natural history, he made critical advances in the daguerreotype, established the state's first Phi Beta Kappa chapter, helped to correct the border between Florida and Alabama, and introduced engineering to the university's curriculum, of critical importance on the southwestern frontier where bridges were needed to cross its many rivers and where citizens were desperate for railroads. The discovery of massive coal deposits, a renewed push for railroads in the 1850s, and the adoption of the military system (with its heavy emphasis on engineering) in 1860 validated the wisdom of Barnard's innovations.[52]

Meanwhile others, such as Dr. Cloud and Isaac Croom, were calling for the development of scientific agriculture. The state geologist, Michael Tuomey, taught scientific agriculture to the university's students and in 1847 called for an agricultural college, probably linked to the university. It would take a Republican Congress to pass the 1862 Morrill Act creating agricultural colleges. With the state in dire financial straits and specifically prohibited from using the Morrill Act funds for construction,[53] Governor Robert M. Patton in 1866 recommended making the agricultural college part of the state university, as Georgia had done. But the proposal languished until the Republican board of regents took over in the summer of 1868—just as construction of the university's new building neared completion and the Democratic press, led by Ryland Randolph, reached new levels of abuse.[54]

At the end of the first week in August, word filtered out that the superintendent and regents had chosen four professors, three from Ohio, along with several in reserve. They had also nominated three individuals for the presidency: the Reverend Arad Lakin, the Reverend R. D. Harper, and Professor

18. The University of Alabama during the 1850s
(Courtesy Hoole Special Collections Library, University of Alabama)

William Stokes Wyman, who had been introduced a few days earlier as "the alternate President of the University." Wyman won on the fourth ballot but resigned two days later. Then on August 6, Lakin was immediately and unanimously elected president of the University of Alabama.[55]

This could not have come at a more divisive or difficult time. Alabama in 1868 was in the midst of a political revolution, and education itself was undergoing its own revolution. Even as the university was faced with having to rebuild its torched campus, the curriculum was moving from the study of classical works to one that emphasized engineering and other technical fields. Choosing a new faculty had everything to do with choosing the future of Alabama's economy. And it had just as much to do with choosing Alabama's past. The faculty, as keepers of the state's heritage, would be assessing responsibility for secession and the war's dead before transmitting those judgments to the next generation—a subject that was publicly debated in controversies over school textbooks.[56]

Everyone had a stake: For Ryland Randolph and his ilk, reopening the university under Democratic control was about maintaining the autonomy—and thus freedom—of Southern whites. For Arad Lakin, reopening the university was about reestablishing moral leadership. For Noah B. Cloud, it was about at last having the opportunity to create a modern institution devoted to freeing individuals from the shackles of the past. And for the freedman Shandy Jones, reopening the University of Alabama could represent the ultimate opportunity for his descendants to decide their own futures.

)X(X(X(

The caption to Ryland Randolph's cartoon, published four days after President Lakin and Superintendent Cloud had been rebuffed, reserved its harshest language for Cloud.

> Our scallawag is the local leper of the community. Unlike the carpet-bagger, he is native, which is so much the worse. Once he was respected in his circle; his head was level, and he would look his neighbor in the face. Now, possessed of the itch of office and the salt rheum of Radicalism, he is a mangy dog, slinking through the alleys, haunting the Governor's office, defiling with tobacco juice the steps of the Capitol, stretching his lazy carcass in the sun on the Square, or the benches of the Mayor's Court.
>
> He waiteth for the troubling of the political waters, to the end that he may step in and be healed of the itch by the ointment of office. For office he "bums" as a toper "bums" for the satisfying dram. For office, yet in prospective, he hath bartered respectability; hath abandoned business, and ceased to labor with his hands, but employs his feet kicking out boot-heels against lamp-post and corner-curb, while discussing the question of office.

The caption's language may have been typical for the *Independent Monitor*, but it was not original. Randolph had lifted it directly from an earlier issue of the state's main Democratic newspaper, the *Montgomery Advertiser*.[57]

)X(X(X(

The Democrats quickly published their own version of the struggles over the university's leadership. Much hinged on an open letter that Professor Wyman penned in an effort to combat "many erroneous reports." The board of trustees, he began, met in June and devised a plan to reopen the university in October. The trustees' first choice for president had been former Professor Henry Tutwiler; their second, current Professor Wyman, assumed the office when the former declined. Soon afterward the new constitution came into effect (through the illegal devices of the Republican Congress), and the board of regents took over. Wyman met with them in Montgomery and presented his report. The regents had other plans. They swept aside the trustees' appointments and installed their own officers. Three of the regents, native Southerners, had voted against replacing the faculty; and Superintendent Cloud, Wyman admitted, "manifested an anxious design that nothing detrimental to the interests of the University should be done." When the Reverend Lakin arrived at the campus to assume the presidency, Wyman refused to deliver him the keys "under advice of counsel." If he had acted otherwise, he would have proven "false to all the people of Alabama, who must regard the University as the centre and focus of the education system of the State." He signed his letter "W. S. Wyman, President of the University."[58] Wyman's account of incompetence and extralegal appropriation became the basis for the Democrats' assaults on the Republican efforts to reopen the university. Ryland Randolph led the way through his pointed editorials and political cartoons on the pages of the *Independent Monitor*.

It took a year, but the regents finally lost their patience. They proposed removing the University of Alabama from Tuscaloosa. Their reasons were straightforward enough: Where once the people of Tuscaloosa had been proud of their university, they "have abundantly shown that they do not want it there any longer." Other locations served by the railroad (several years off for Tuscaloosa) were more suitable. The present buildings could be sold for other purposes (a doubtful proposition given the military nature of its architecture). And most importantly, other towns were ready to contribute enough money to make the move cost effective. They were looking for a location "where the largest contribution may be obtained towards defraying the expenses; where the hostile feelings of the community will not be continually exhibited towards the institution and its professors, and where the institution will be welcomed and cherished as the Alabama University ought to be." Selma, Montgomery, and especially Elyton (soon to become Birmingham) were mentioned.[59] In one move the regents had turned Randolph's blasts against him.

The *Monitor*'s editor fumed. Over five consecutive issues, he laid out his case and condemned the regents for considering such a move. Elyton had a bright future, he admitted. At the center of the mineral district, two railroad lines would soon converge there and a "Pittsburg of the South" (Birmingham) would spring up. But the people of Elyton, Randolph predicted, were too noble and unselfish to get involved in a bidding war. Moreover, new elections would replace the money changers, office brokers, and sellers of justice with honest men who would only return the university to its proper place in Tuscaloosa.[60]

In the end, of course, the University of Alabama stayed put. But in 1872 the Methodist Episcopal Church, South, presented the state with the East Alabama Male College in Auburn. Renamed the Agricultural and Mechanical College of Alabama, it became the state's land-grant institution. The measure certainly got the strong support of Dr. Cloud, who was then in the legislature. What influence he had on the decision is unknown, but the new school was close to his old homestead at LaPlace.

If the regents' motivation in threatening to move the university had been to embarrass or somehow turn the tables on Randolph, it did not work. A pattern had by now developed: the regents would appoint a new faculty and president, Randolph and the Democrats would harass them publicly in the newspapers (and sometimes privately), few if any students would register, the faculty would quit, and the process would start again. After Lakin formally resigned in December 1868, the regents chose a new faculty and unanimously elected the Reverend R. D. Harper as the new president. Like Lakin, Harper was a minister from the hated Northern branch of Methodism; even worse, he was then serving as Alabama's superintendent of schools for the Freedmen's Bureau. Randolph warned that the "disreputable Harper is destined to soon turn gray through 'sudden fears,' if he ventures to occupy the respectable mansion of the President of the University. . . . Lakin's chances of security would have been infinitely better." The editor again unleashed threats and woodcuts. President Harper was gone by March, his place temporarily assumed by another carpetbagger, who opened the university in April to about twenty students. Randolph reported the ceremonies with his acid-tipped pen. When the superintendent of education (cleverly labeled "N. B. Nubibus," or "in the clouds") observed undisguised Klansmen among the visitors, his knees knocked and voice trembled, according to Randolph. The university would be controlled by no political party, Dr. Cloud proclaimed, and everyone would have a right to an education there. When this "greatest burlesque upon an institution of learning" ended, Randolph wrote that he "gazed upon the still unremoved *debris* of the old University, burnt to the ground by Yankee vandalism" and felt "a firmly seated feeling of revenge in our heart."[61]

Perhaps because the *Montgomery Advertiser* lacked the invective of Randolph's *Independent Monitor*, its analysis of the problems faced by the Republicans was more perceptive, although no less partisan. In order for

Superintendent Cloud and the board of regents to reestablish the university, the editor argued, they would have to "cast all Radical politics to the winds, and select a President and Faculty from among men most popular and honored . . . for sound Southern principles." The fact is that the "planters, merchants, professional men, and the great body of property owners in Alabama" will send their sons to the many other fine Southern institutions that are "free from the offensive and mischievous ideas of Radical party teachings." Former Confederates have become reconciled to the Union but will ever remain true "to the cherished sentiments and memories of the past, to the sensibilities which lie buried in the graves of their sons and brothers, and to the great cause for which they fought and bled, and have suffered so terribly. Depend on it, that these people will never permit their children to be educated by Optimists, Fanatics, or Radical politicians of any kind or degree."[62]

It was a telling passage. A few years before, only a few voices, such as Dr. Cloud's, had challenged Southerners to improve their lands, to give people reasons to stay, and thereby to stop the westward exodus that left worn-out fields and worn-out villages in its wake. The soils were still worn out, but the people were not. Former Confederates were now committed to each other in cast-iron bonds of loyalty. A short phrase used by the *Advertiser*'s editor put the transition in perspective: "in the affections and confidence of our people"—using the term to refer to former Confederates, but not to the slaves who had once been "our people."

The Republicans had no intentions of structuring their society on "cherished sentiments and memories" of "our people's" lost cause. They looked forward instead to Alabama's entering the American mainstream. They looked forward to a society where tools for effecting freedom—beginning with education—were available to all, which was why a free public school system was the Republicans' first order of business. "Republicanism and the *Journal* want intelligence, free schools, and perfect equality to all men—rich and poor alike," proudly summarized the editor of the *Advertiser*'s rival, the Montgomery *Alabama State Journal*. "Dr. Cloud has struggled against innumerable obstacles, natural and peculiar, and in the face of all this, we see school houses rearing in the wilderness, and thousands of children plodding their way school-ward—children, who, heretofore have been bound hand and foot in the shackles of slavery and ignorance." One of the board members, Gustavus Adolphus Smith, wrote an open letter defending the system whereby no child could be barred from an education on account of race or financial need. This was a great principle and "all will realize the rich fruitions of our glorious work in the march of progress." Needless to say, the *Journal*'s editor also went on record declaring that the "credit of putting our University in complete working order, is due principally to our able and energetic Superintendent of Education."[63]

Smith resigned from his position on the board of education at the end of 1869 to take up his appointment as Collector of Internal Revenue for the New Mexico Territory. (His son would join him later the next year after shooting Ryland Randolph and escaping from the Tuscaloosa jail.) At the same time Superintendent Cloud issued his report praising the education section of the 1867 state constitution. "Dr. Cloud is an industrious and honest official," assessed the *Journal*, and reiterated his pledge "to exert the power of government for the promotion of education." By contrast, the result of the Democrats' hostility to educating the masses during all their years in power was thirty-seven thousand white adult Alabamians who could not read.[64]

During the summer of 1870 the regents announced yet another new faculty, again comprised of Republicans. This one, too, failed when only ten students enrolled, four of them sons of faculty. The Republicans would have to face the voters again in November with nothing to show for all their efforts to reopen the university. At their state convention, held August 30 in Selma, Dr. Cloud easily won the nomination again, although the names of Arad Lakin and several others were also advanced.[65]

At the Democratic State Convention, James Holt Clanton, chair of the executive committee, nominated Randolph's old commander, friend, and editorial counterpart at the *Montgomery Mail*, Joseph Hodgson "amid great excitement" for superintendent of education. The Democrats in Alabama, Clanton proclaimed in his nominating speech, "owed more to Hodgson than any other living man," and if the convention failed to name him their nominee, "the Radicals would glory over the defeat of Hodgson in the Convention, more than over any other man." Colonel Hodgson won the nomination easily and then addressed the delegates. After promising to kick out Cloud along with his Republican board, he posed a question: "Will you stand by me in defying even the authorities at Washington against mixing our children with negroes in school? (Repeated cries of yes! yes!) Again gentlemen I thank you for this honor."[66] That the Republicans wanted to integrate the schools was not the only campaign charge. Colonel Hodgson also accused the board of having adopted textbooks with a Northern slant, especially the history books (particularly odious to the man who had coined the word *carpetbagger*). And, of course, he blamed the Republicans for fiscal mismanagement.

7

All of these charges—integrated schools, slanted textbooks, and financial fraud—were closely tied. The Republicans, for example, had decided that the freed people deserved a proper share of the education budget. Colonel Hodgson and his Democratic critics countered that Superintendent Cloud and the board were using the funds for political gain because the funds had been appropriated to cover the money not distributed during years in which the state had had no black teachers or black students. They would further charge that it was all part of a scheme to direct money to certain private schools, such as those run by the MEC's Freedmen's Aid Society.[67] The claims were not without foundation, but neither were they without interpretation. The board had decided from the beginning to work closely with the aid societies in joint enterprises. It all boiled down to unmitigated resistance to every Republican effort to establish a working modern system of public education for both blacks and whites.

The Democrats were also at pains to point out Dr. Cloud's hypocrisy. He had not only been a slaveholder before the war, they noted, but a cruel one at that. He had been a secessionist, they charged, who was so concerned with preserving the institution of slavery that he advocated a prescribed servile uniform. And he had advocated removing all free blacks and absolutelu forbidding their preaching.[68]

As the Democratic press leveled accusation after accusation, the Republicans responded. Some denied financial mismanagement. Three appointed auditors who looked at the board's books in detail declared them in good shape, and Superintendent Cloud himself responded in print to Colonel Hodgson. But such tactics probably worked to the Democrats' advantage because they reminded white voters that their taxes had increased substantially under Republican administrations now that the former basis of taxation—slavery—was gone. The Republicans were on stronger grounds when they appealed to higher ideals. The public letter by "Instructress" was exemplary. The pseudonym of a teacher who had taught under both the old and new systems, she lauded Dr. Cloud's efforts. The creed of the Democratic Party, she insisted, had been "to enact laws to forbid the colored race from learning to read and write, as if thus effectually to fasten upon him and his barbarian progeny the manacles of ignorance and degradation" in a new form of slavery. The creed of the Republican Party, by contrast, was "to extend to these benighted men the lamp of enlightenment." The new system under Superintendent Cloud "established upwards of seven thousand common schools throughout the State for the education of all colors, classes and condition of the youth of the state." The teachers were paid, and the students did not have to pay. In sum, "Dr. Cloud has acted under the generous inspiration of the teachings of our Savior, *that all men should improve their talents*."[69]

Other Republicans predicted that the Democrats intended to shut down public education completely. The editor of the *State Journal* observed that if Colonel Hodgson had his way and returned to the antebellum system of local control and local funding (which allowed dishonest local trustees to divide the spoils amongst themselves and allowed no redress for the hardworking teachers), then black children could not receive any education and poor white children only an inadequate one. Dr. Cloud's statewide system of common schools, by contrast, guaranteed all children free access. The Republican vision of education was, quoting British reformer George Peabody, "a debt due from present to future generations" and grew out of a larger understanding of government itself: "the association of mankind together in political communities for their development and perfecting of humanity to its highest attainment in life."[70]

State Supreme Court judge Thomas M. Peters, a former Whig, continued the theme in a public letter. "Ignorance is misrule, it is confusion, it is sin, it is death and hell," he began; and "our safety, as a free people, requires that we ceaselessly war against it with a Carthagenian zeal." Because the ignorant and bad will contaminate the good if all are not educated, "I therefore feel that I serve my God, my country and my fellow men when I do anything that advances the great cause of universal education."[71]

In early November, the Democrats did well, putting their nominee in the governor's office, taking control of the lower house of the general assembly, and sending three Congressmen to Washington, DC, to balance Alabama's three Republican Congressmen. Colonel Hodgson also defeated Dr. Cloud. When the colonel came to assume the office, the outgoing superintendent took a cue from his reception by Dr. Wyman at the university: he refused to leave, charging Hodgson with having violated the dueling law. It was all to no effect. "Napoleon Bonaparte Cloud" is no longer in office, Ryland Randolph announced with glee.[72]

The new superintendent revived the old idea of supplementing public funds with local, private ones. The general assembly provided that counties elect their own local superintendents of education and appointed a commission to look into the financial affairs of the state superintendent of education's office. The commission's report criticized Dr. Cloud's financial management, despite noting that he had acted with the consent of the attorney general.

Superintendent Hodgson imposed his own significant economizing measures. In July 1871 some Democrats began calling for a constitutional amendment to abolish the board of education now that they were in power. Nothing came of the threat, for the Democracy had its own man in charge. The Republicans, of course, declared that the school system had already collapsed under Hodgson. While extreme statements—some wanting to abolish the system, others claiming it was already gone—were bantered back and forth, huge numbers of students were enrolling in the public schools. In 1873 Hodgson's successor as superintendent made his annual report, noting that a want of money had "led to the suspension of the free public schools throughout the State."[73]

)X()X()X(

Ryland Randolph fought to preserve the freedom of his own self-governing people. Arad Lakin embodied the freedom of a Christian in devoting his life to sharing the joy of God's forgiveness. Noah Cloud took a different path to freedom, which grew from the intellectual and moral convictions of a Whig.[74]

Nineteenth-century Americans confronted unprecedented change. In this Age of Progress, as they called it, undreamt possibilities were revolutionizing everyday life. Goods moved along canals, people along rails, and messages flashed instantly under the ocean by telegraph. Americans purchased manufactured items in their local general stores that only a few years before had been considered luxuries. Sophisticated methods of acquiring wealth started to replace the traditional reliance on farming, and complex methods of handling that wealth started to replace the direct exchange of silver and gold.

Perhaps in reaction, perhaps as a cause, a new understanding of the individual and society was also emerging. Alexis de Tocqueville termed it individualism, the belief that people could live fulfilling lives by withdrawing from the larger society and creating their own destinies. Individualists were not hermits; rather, they focused their attention on family and close friends. Nor did they necessarily move to the frontier; for their withdrawal was psychological, not physical. But they did follow their own inner compass. Those most comfortable with this commercial and transportation revolution and its accompanying individualism were the Whigs. Struck by the possibilities for individual achievement, Whigs would march hand in hand with Methodists in championing many of the same great reform movements of the nineteenth century: among them, temperance, the asylum movement, free public education, and antislavery.[75]

But if Whigs celebrated the good that well-intentioned individuals could accomplish, they were dismayed at the damage that unfettered individuals could do. Whigs thus regarded as worse than naive Ryland Randolph's blind and blithe faith that the people should just be left alone. Even if they did not turn to crime, those without structures and boundaries were at best unaware of their own enslavement. The uneducated were slaves to ignorance; the unyielding, slaves to habit and convention; and the undisciplined, slaves to the charms of the crowd. Merely doing what one wants is no synonym for freedom, the Whigs insisted, but a barrier that makes true freedom all the harder to create.

Because Whigs realized just how compelling the absence of constraints could be, they pushed for schools for freedom, in Tocqueville's phrasing, to train individuals in the art of living responsibly—and thus freely. Such schools included juries to teach participation in civic affairs, churches to teach transcendent values, and educational institutions to combat ignorance. The result was an enlarging network of such artificial communities as colleges, hospitals, charitable organizations, and local governments—all sorts of institutions that gave citizens experience in governing themselves, both collectively and individually. These schools for freedom had other benefits. They enlarged the individual's sense of what he could accomplish. They built confidence. And voluntary associations in particular, such as the Masons, created habits of sociability to overcome the destructive selfishness implicit in the American experiment. Although they were individualistic, Whigs such as Dr. Cloud were also—ironically—the greatest supporters of collective endeavors, for they realized how much more could be done together than alone.

Whiggish freedom, then, was no inalienable right that merely needed defending; freedom was rather an ideal to be sought, an ongoing project of self-improvement. Whiggish freedom was ordered, purposeful, complex, and placed in our own hands. Whiggish freedom was about empowering individuals to rise above their own limitations. But make no mistake: Whigs could lapse at any moment. They could become self-satisfied. They could take the easy road of letting others decide. They could become distracted by trivial pursuits and lose sight of the greater good. Whigs could never rest easy. But when it worked, Whiggish freedom was a direct path to success.

Dr. Cloud was squarely in this tradition. In a region where over 90 percent of the economy came from farming, scientific agriculture meant liberation from centuries of self-destructive techniques. The worn-out fields and abandoned farmhouses across the South were signs of a social and intellectual poverty as much as an economic poverty. Staying on the land and improving it, however, would break the terrible cycle of move, exploit, sell, and move again that had made community building so challenging. By sharing farming techniques at the conventions and fairs in which Cloud was so energetically engaged, individuals could learn ways to escape the timeworn habits that held them back. Even more important, sharing with others at these events created feelings of gratitude and obligation, the building blocks of community.

When the Civil War radically changed Alabama's political and economic direction, Dr. Cloud moved from agricultural education into general education with the same spirit. Working alongside his state board of education, he created Alabama's first genuine public school system. Just as Arad Lakin was a missionary preaching freedom from the shackles of sin, Cloud was a missionary preaching freedom from the shackles of ignorance. With a good education and a generous spirit, the individual would then be prepared to face an uncertain future. Here was the essence of Whiggish freedom: a ceaseless task of self-creation resting on the conviction that we can do better.

✕✕✕

Dr. Cloud had been defeated in his attempt to remain as superintendent of education, but he did not leave politics. In August 1872 he announced himself a candidate for the state House of Representatives. He won his seat, representing Montgomery, but was easily defeated for speaker (although he would serve on many occasions as temporary speaker). Dr. Cloud introduced a number of bills, many related to his long-standing interest in reform: industrial exhibitions, temperance, and education. He was also among the Southern white Republicans who supported the Civil Rights Bill when it was reintroduced in Congress in 1873.[76]

In July 1875 Dr. Cloud returned to editing, this time of the agricultural department of the *Alabama State Journal*, Montgomery's Republican newspaper. He had no new insights: too much cotton was not the problem, but rather the inefficient use of land and the failure to diversify. In the evening of November 5, Noah Bartlett Cloud died of a "congestive chill." He had been working on an article on grafting fruit trees. His funeral was held the next day, a Saturday, with Masonic ceremonies. He was buried in Montgomery's Oakwood Cemetery. The newspapers reported that his wife, two daughters, and five sons mourned his passing, along with a large circle of friends and acquaintances. He reportedly left his estate to the Baptist Orphanage to provide for the children of Confederate dead.[77]

FOUR

Freedman

They are near enough to see its charms, but too far off to enjoy them;
and before they have fully tasted its delights, they die.
—Alexis de Tocqueville

Unlike the three other characters portrayed in *A Prospective Scene*, Shandy Wesley Jones was a slave when in late 1816 he took his first breath in Huntsville, Alabama.[1] He would have spent the next half century as a field hand or laborer, and his name would have been quickly forgotten, had he not been freed nine days before his fourth birthday. The two brothers who freed him along with his mulatto mother and two sisters did not give their reasons, but surely it had something to do with the fact that one of the brothers was almost certainly Shandy's father.[2] Jones was thus probably three-quarters white, and his photograph presents a man who could have passed for white. He would use his pale complexion and free status to his advantage. That, along with what few details of Jones's life remain, suggests a deliberate man who took careful measure at every turn. His life also suggests a man who was never at peace.

In 1837, just before his twenty-first birthday, Jones was living in Tuscaloosa. There he married Evalina Love on December 4, the only non-white marriage recorded in Tuscaloosa's official ledger from before the Civil War. Family tradition holds that Evalina's family included at least some Indian blood. Evalina, like her husband, was both fair skinned and free, her mother having been born a free mulatto.³ It was important that Jones marry a free woman if he were to bestow his own freedom on his children, for the status of the mother determined the status of the children.

Industrious young men on the make were flooding into the City of Oaks during the 1820s and '30s because of the opportunities created when the frontier town was selected as the seat of government. The ramshackle river port needed to be an elegant city. Fortunately, they had at hand an English-born architect, William Nichols, who had already proven his worth by designing the North Carolina state capitol. Tuscaloosa presented Nichols with a virtual *tabula rasa* on which to erect elegant structures that would express in stone and brick the state's aspirations.

An intense building program commenced, and artisans came in search of work. Many of these artisans were free blacks like Jones. In 1830, during the early phase of the building, the census recorded twenty-two free blacks living in Tuscaloosa. A decade later the number had increased to sixty. The most prominent and successful was Solomon Perteet, a plasterer who had come to Tuscaloosa because of the demand for ornamental work in the many public buildings and elegant homes then being erected. Perteet made a significant amount of money in real estate, enough to absorb a $17,000 loss in the 1840s by standing security for an unscrupulous white man.⁴ Not all the free blacks were artisans, of course. Ned Berry, for example, was a teamster. Jones's father-in-law, Zadock Love, made his living farming and dabbling in real estate.

And James Abbott was a barber. The many legislators and petitioners who came to Tuscaloosa while the general assembly was in session needed their beards shaved and hair trimmed, which could make barbering a lucrative endeavor. Barbershops in the South were frequently owned and managed by free blacks. Roughly half the barbers in Mobile and Richmond, for example, were black men. Barbering required little in the way of capital investment and was not onerous work. A successful barber was a deferential barber, adept at pleasing his white customers with a good cut, small talk, and flattery. More than that, a good barber listened and learned. He might overhear, for example, when a valuable piece of real estate had to be sold at a low price. Abbott had arrived in Tuscaloosa by 1829 and during the 1830s had a stand at the same intersection as the *Independent Monitor*'s office.⁵

Although no mention was made of Shandy Jones, he could well have been an apprentice in Abbott's shop. It seems more than coincidental that in 1837 Abbott stopped advertising his barbershop and Shandy Jones and Evalina Love were married, since Jones may have taken over from Abbott by then.

Owning his own shop would have given Jones the financial security to begin his family. Nothing is known about the couple for the next decade other than the names of their many children. Then, in late 1848, just as Tuscaloosa was beginning a long decline after the legislature removed the seat of government to Montgomery, a letter from Jones appeared in the *African Repository and Colonial Journal*, devoted to colonization. Much as Arad Lakin had found his calling in the ministry and Noah B. Cloud had found his in scientific agriculture, Jones found his calling in championing the freedom of black Americans to govern themselves in Africa.

Decades before, such luminaries as Henry Clay, Daniel Webster, and John Randolph (a distant relative of Ryland Randolph) had established the Society for the Colonization of Free People of Color of America (familiarly the American Colonization Society) in order to assist black Americans in moving to their ancestral homeland. In 1821 the society founded Liberia, on the west coast of Africa, and began transporting free blacks there. Some backed colonization as a reform movement that would provide black Americans with their own homeland and bring Christianity to the Dark Continent. Others saw colonization as a means of ridding the country of the black race altogether. Still others saw colonization as a means of preserving slavery by exporting what they deemed as the pernicious and influential example of free blacks. The idea thus appealed to a broad range of Americans—black and white, slave and slaveholder, Christian and freethinker—who disagreed among themselves about all sorts of things except one: all were convinced that whites and blacks could not live in the same land as social equals.

The situation in Alabama typified colonization's eclectic appeal. When a state society dedicated to colonization was founded in 1830, for example, its officers included the governor and other successful slaveholders. The Perry County branch, founded that same year, included as a charter member Andrew B. Moore, the lawyer and planter who as governor would take the state out of the Union three decades later. Prominent educator and antislavery advocate Henry Tutwiler was a member, as was John Hartwell Cocke. A reformer who had worked to build the University of Virginia, improve agriculture, and promote temperance, Cocke in 1841 established a plantation a few miles west of Greensboro, not far from Ryland Randolph's family, as an ill-fated experiment in preparing slaves to emigrate to Liberia.[6] Communication among slaves was extensive, and it is entirely possible that Shandy Jones heard about Cocke's experiment even though the participating slaves were all pledged to secrecy.

The state's foremost—white Alabamians would say most notorious—proponent of colonization was James Gillespie Birney. After an excellent education, first at Transylvania College and then at the College of New Jersey (Princeton), Birney returned to his native Kentucky to practice law. But in 1818 he purchased a plantation and slaves in Madison County, Alabama, and moved there. After hearing an agent from the American Colonization Society on a tour of southern states, Birney helped to establish a Huntsville chapter of the society in 1830. Shandy Jones may first have heard of colonization when the same agent who lured Birney had spoken a few months earlier in Tuscaloosa. Or Jones could have heard of the movement from reading any of Birney's several articles published in the Colonization Society's mouthpiece, the *African Repository*, and reprinted in the Tuscaloosa *Alabama State Intelligencer*. There Birney described colonization as a "noble benevolence" that would lift all bars to their fellowmen's "enjoyment of life, liberty, and the pursuit of happiness—in the land of their fathers." (Three years later, Birney would read a Christian critique of the tenets of colonization, renounce the organization, and embrace immediate abolition. He moved back to Kentucky and in 1844 ran unsuccessfully for the presidency as head of the antislavery Liberty Party, taking enough votes in New York State from Henry Clay to put James K. Polk in the White House.) Colonization must have been a powerful message to Alabama's free blacks, chafing under a belligerent white population. The Colonization Society's agent reported that in Huntsville many free blacks had been contemplating removal to Liberia for some time and had even raised money to hire one of their own to go there in anticipation of migration. Suspicious whites, fearful that it was all a cover for plotting insurrection, frustrated their work.[7]

Aside from Tutwiler, Cocke, and Birney, practically no Alabamians were prepared to give up their slaves in order to send them to Africa. Free blacks were another matter, for they were living proof that black people could be free and successful. The overwhelming mass of white Alabamians, from governors to poor white farmers, saw in colonization a chance to rid the state of their example. Whites suspected them of spreading the cause of liberation through the churches and barbershops—the haunts of Shandy Jones. In the aftermath of Nat Turner's bloody 1831 rebellion, in which over fifty whites had been murdered, getting the free blacks out of Alabama was thought a significant step toward ensuring the perpetuation of slavery. In the state House of Representatives, a committee was formed to look into that very option; but nothing came of it. Each time white nerves were frayed, the call to get rid of the free blacks resounded.

The colonization movement itself died down in Alabama after Birney left for Kentucky, and by 1846 Alabama was one of four Southern states without a state society. That same year the Reverend John B. Pinney, another agent for the American Colonization Society and former governor of Liberia, came to Tuscaloosa in hopes of reviving the idea. He delivered lectures in the churches, was "cordially received & hospitably entertained," and collected over $100 for the cause—principally from elite slaveholders.[8]

Pinney's visit, seventeen years after the first society agent visited Tuscaloosa, along with the 1847 establishment of the Republic of Liberia, may have been the catalysts that at last prompted Shandy Jones to write his June 1848 letter to the *African Repository*. It was not his first letter to the society, but it was the first published under his own name. Others would follow, elevating Jones to become Alabama's leading non-white proponent of colonization. He began his letter by acknowledging that, after the Christian religion, African colonization was the subject that lay nearest his heart. He was most anxious to acquire the latest issues of the *African Repository* that he had not yet received, for he wanted to read in it the message of colonization to "our people" (perhaps inadvertently using the evasive and patronizing term that white masters had used to refer to their slaves). Jones was allowed to travel and reported having met with a great many other free persons with whom he always raised the subject of emigration to Liberia. Enough were receptive, even the superstitious and prejudiced, that Jones predicted that he could easily raise a company of a hundred or more willing to leave. Then particular problems would arise, usually business details that needed settling. The main setback, however, was that each waited for his friends to make the first move. "My word for it," wrote Jones, "whenever there is a start made in Alabama, the whole body of free people will join in a solid phalanx." At the end of his letter, he announced his intention to travel through north Alabama and perhaps into Tennessee, where he had some business to conduct and would use the opportunity to talk with some of his family there. Six weeks later Jones reported that on a short tour to the adjoining county he brought up the topic of Liberia with some free black people. They agree "that it is the best thing they can do for themselves; but they are poor and seem disposed to defer going, until they can get something ahead, to commence life upon in a new and distant clime." He was considering more trips to spread the message.[9]

Jones continued his correspondence with the *African Repository.* Almost a year later he wrote of the excitement that the publication of his letters had created in Tuscaloosa. Their contents had been exaggerated, he reported, and used against the cause of colonization by those fearful of losing their slaves. The postmaster turned out to be his worst enemy because he owned a man who was also a barber and wanted Jones's customers. And it was business that held him from leaving for Liberia. His poor heart was heavy with the thought of having to spend ten years more in this country, so he was making extra efforts in hopes that "I Start for the Land of Promis (to the collord man) next spring."[10]

A few months later Jones was writing again of some twenty-five free blacks in the Tuscaloosa area anxious to leave for Liberia as soon as possible. But he was sorry to report of the many more who refused to emigrate until someone they knew personally had gone to Liberia and reported back. As for Jones, "I am certain to go next Spring if life & health last."[11] The next spring came, however, and he had not left.

That September of 1850 he was probably the author of a letter urging Congress to fund the construction of large steamers to ply between the United States and Liberia. If the proposal were carried out, he claimed, "I candidly believe that in ten years from the date of the first trip there will not be a free man of color left in the southern or slave-holding States." The author himself asked that his name not be printed because he was winding up his business with the intention of emigrating to Liberia the coming spring.[12] But again, spring came and went with Jones still living in the City of Oaks.

At the end of 1851 he reported that the Alabama State Colonization Society had been reestablished. This new organization included Tuscaloosa entrepreneur Robert Jemison, a large slaveholder, proponent of industrialization, and a man who dealt extensively with free black artisans and businessmen. Because most Alabamians believed that the national society was a crypto-abolitionist organization, the state society refused to associate with any but similar organizations in the Southwest devoted solely to ridding the state of free blacks. "The object of the Society," as its constitution explicitly stated, "is to promote the emigration of free colored people from the State of Alabama to Africa"—and not slaves. An accompanying address reiterated the dangers of slave insurrection that free blacks raised.[13]

Jones saw the reestablished state society as an opportunity. Support for colonization was rapidly growing in Alabama, he wrote. "I doubt not that the day is not distant when there will be an uprising of the free people of color—not only in Alabama—not only in the much persecuted South, where it is said by the fanatics that we are sorely opprest, and inhumanly treated, but in the liberal and philanthropic North. We are treated about as well here," he continued, "as the same class of persons in the North," at least those who behave themselves and conduct themselves as they should. When asked if he would go to Liberia, Jones without hesitation answered yes. But then came the inevitable waffling: "We would most certainly go now, if we had our little matters closed, but those of us who want to go to Liberia are men who have been striving to do something for ourselves, and consequently have more or less business to close up." Perhaps in the spring or fall. "The day is coming, and I trust is not far distant, when every free person of color in this country will esteem it a privilege to be sent to Liberia." There we will "make us a great nation of our own, build our own cities and towns, make our own laws, col-lect our own revenues, command our own vessels, army and navy, elect our own governors and law makers, have our own schools and colleges, our own lawyers and doctors, in a word . . . be men."[14]

His letter to the *African Repository* written during the spring of 1852 brimmed with optimism. "I am still more than Ever Encouraged to believe that we will have a large and Inteligent company from Alabama in the fall or spring at farthest." But it would be his last letter for four years. "You doubtless think that I am Slow In making up my mind about going to Liberia but such is not the Case for my mind have been for years Settled upon the Question," he confessed to the editors in November 1856. He still could not tie up the loose ends that hindered his going. So he bided his time, committed to his belief that "Liberia is the country Emphattically the Country for the Colored Race and the only Country upon this Green Earth where they may or can Enjoy Social and Political Liberty which is the dearest of Earthly Blessings."[15]

Jones's letter was but one expression of rising tensions during the 1850s. In 1852 the nation was reading *Uncle Tom's Cabin*, a book in which the freed slaves journey to Liberia.[16] And the next year a series of a dozen or so let-ters were published in the *Mobile Herald and Tribune* on the problem of free blacks that seemed to be directed at Jones himself. "An Old Methodist" began the series by bringing up the recurring question of how the relationship be-tween master and slave could be improved to their mutual benefit. Having observed certain blacks "in the (so called) state of freedom" in both North and South, he concluded that having slaves and free people of color in the same community was a source of evil. In particular, black churches on the Sabbath were "the rallying points around which black hypocrites and villains caucus and arrange their plans of rascality for the ensuing week." In the same issue, "Citizen" added black barbershops as sources of abolitionist and incendiary circulars. A couple of weeks later, "An Old Methodist" expanded that point. Churches were filled with many righteous people with pure motives. But at the barbershops, the crowds were smaller and more select, "made up, for the most part of suitable materials out of which to form special and corresponding committees. Colored gentlemen meet at the barber shop—compare notes—keep the keeper of the shop as the central repository of facts, figures, intentions, and who it is most likely can be used." There the schemes are devised that are then broadcast on Sunday in the churches. This, he insisted, was the means by which the worst of the slave problems had occurred. Another correspondent completed the syllogism: "[T]he sooner the negro Churches of our city are closed, the better." In June came proof: an insurrection in New Orleans. The ringleaders were said to have confessed their plans to seize the arsenals, gunsmith shops, and arms depots; attack the powder magazine and army barracks; and then set fire to the city as a signal for the slaves to revolt. Nothing came of it. The readers of these letters in the *Mobile Herald and Tribune* probably learned little or nothing new, but that was not the point. The point was to be vigilant, ever vigilant.[17]

Shandy Jones represented the worst of white fears, for not only was he a free black barber, not only was he financially successful and a family man, but he was a minister. During this time he was almost certainly a Methodist, as his middle name and later career suggested, and may even have been quasi ordained by a local church. One planter described him as "a man of some education," who would conduct ceremonies for slave couples who wanted to be married "by a preacher of their own color." In one instance ten couples assembled on the porch of the overseer's house, where the Reverend Jones officiated. They then commenced a wedding feast consisting of an appetizer of Kentucky-brewed Dexter whisky followed by barbecue, cakes, and pies.[18]

The behavior of Shandy Jones and the other free blacks in Tuscaloosa—and the rest of the South for that matter—was tightly controlled. The town's bylaws and ordinances required free blacks living within city limits not only to produce papers and testimonials of good character, but to pay the enormous sum of $200 and to obtain a guardian. Special penalties were levied against those who sold alcoholic beverages or kept disorderly houses of entertainment. Although the law did not restrict where free blacks could live, they did reside close together in the western part of town. (The three most prominent black families in Tuscaloosa—Perteet, Jones, and Berry—were enumerated consecutively by the 1850 census taker.) And they seemed to have cooperated with each other. In 1831 Perteet, for example, purchased the thirty-four-year-old Ned Berry, a teamster, and then allowed him to purchase his own freedom over the next year.[19]

Berry found his way into a piece of Southwestern humor that provides a close look into white attitudes toward the free blacks: "Relief for Ireland! or, John Brown's Bad Luck with His Pickled Beef," written by John Gorman Barr and published in the New York journal *Porter's Spirit of the Times*.[20] The story is set in the spring of 1848, as the potato famine ravaged Ireland. Brown, a gullible Irish shoemaker, solicits donations for a couple of barrels of pickled beef to send to his countrymen. The young men of Tuscaloosa tire of Brown's solicitations and resolve to hide the barrels. When the inebriated Brown discovers the apparent theft, his dozen tricksters call out to "SARCH the Free Niggers! That's the lick! Sarch their houses, . . . by ransacking every *Free nigger den* in and about the town. Now the thing is, not to give the free nigger thieves time to take the plunder to the woods or to bury it, but pounce at once on Ned Berry, Jim Jones, and the rest of the gang, and surprise 'em." The company head west into the suburbs of "free-niggerdom." They never get to Ned Berry's home, but they do find Jim Jones and interrogate him mercilessly. The poor man denies all, and Brown tears apart the floor and loft of his rickety shanty looking for the missing barrels. Apart from demonstrating the contempt that the young white men show for the free blacks, Barr's story underscores how they were made the scapegoats for any disturbances to the natural order.

The same year that Barr published his tale, 1857, a correspondent wrote to the *Independent Monitor* complaining about Tuscaloosa's free blacks. The editor during those years, W. H. Fowler, introduced the letter by noting that some of these were people of good character who had earned a strong hold upon the public's sympathies. The mass of free blacks, however, were unreliable, mischievous, "and dangerous to the interests of the slaveholding community." The correspondent's letter, and probably Barr's tale, made sense against the backdrop of friction over such national issues as slavery in the territories, the Dred Scott decision, and the rising Republican Party. If the Union should ever dissolve, the correspondent predicted, the South will have "hugging to her bosom" the free blacks that it has allowed to reside within her borders. These are "so many fire-brands, fit weapons for her own destruction." Because so many can read, "they secretly poison the ears of our slaves with the incendiary publications of abolitionism." The remedy lay with the general assembly: "Let it pass such laws as will remove them from the State or sell them back into servitude."[21]

Tuscaloosa did not wait on the legislature. On August 8, 1859, Tuscaloosa's aldermen passed an ordinance requiring all free blacks within the city to register with the mayor, to post security of $100, and to stay in after ten at night without a special pass from the mayor. That same day the aldermen passed similar restrictions on slaves within the city limits.[22] Exactly one week later, Shandy Jones received his pass.

> The bearer, Shandy Jones, a free man of Color, has my permission to go at large after 10 o'clock at night. He has also permission to attend Divine Worship and Class Meetings where slaves assemble for the purpose, as also any of the female members of his family.
> R. Blair
> Mayor of Tuscaloosa
> Aug 15, 1859.[23]

Two months later John Brown launched his raid on Harper's Ferry, Virginia. Instead of provoking a slave insurrection, he provoked legislators in the Alabama statehouse to do exactly as the correspondent to the *Independent Monitor* had suggested: to introduce bills that would remove all free persons of color from the state. Those who did not leave before the first day of January 1861 would be required to select their own masters. Tuscaloosa's Robert Jemison immediately introduced an amendment exempting Solomon Perteet and Horace King, the famed bridge builder. Such exemptions by Jemison and others signaled divisions among the citizenry. The *Mobile Register*, for example, noted that no free blacks had actually been known to interfere with the institution of slavery; besides, the bill would cruelly divide families without any of them having committed a crime. The editor of the *Montgomery Mail*, however, saw the bill as a chance to drive the free blacks ("useless—vermin—a nuisance") into the arms of the abolitionists and thereby with one stroke dispense of the one while punishing the other.[24] Nothing came of the measure. The following year, after Alabama had left the Union and joined the Confederacy, it was reintroduced. In the state senate, Robert Jemison once again added amendments excepting prominent free blacks, this time including Shandy Jones. The amended bill died.[25]

The process that began with touting the advantages of colonizing Liberia

19. A barbershop in Richmond, Virginia (*Illustrated London News* 1861 March 9)

and ended with attempts to force free blacks to leave spoke to the fears and anxiety that their presence provoked among white Southerners. Shandy Jones and others like him—successful men attending to business, raising families, owning their own homes—presented problems for those who believed that servitude was the natural condition of the black race. Perhaps worse. Because successful free blacks offered examples and hope to their bound brethren, they could only be agents of insurrection.

Meanwhile, Jones dreamed of liberty in Liberia and continued with his business. At the start of the 1850s he reported real estate holdings of $500, but by its end that figure had risen to $7,000; ten years after that Jones was counted as one of the richest black men in Alabama.[26] He lived with his wife and many children in a two-story home on the southwest corner of Cotton and Brown streets, just across from the old capitol. He purchased Dossie Roberts, who worked in his barbershop. Like Solomon Perteet's Ned Berry, Roberts was allowed to purchase his own freedom. Jones also posted bond for a black family trying to recover its freedom. He was wealthy enough to loan money to the humorist John Gorman Barr, whose tale "Relief for Ireland!" recounted the ruin of Ned Berry's home.[27]

Jones achieved that remarkable level of prosperity by charging twenty-five cents a haircut—and by listening.[28] His barbershop had the best possible location, adjacent to Washington Hall, the hotel that served as Tuscaloosa's unofficial political and social center. In Shandy Jones's barbershop, the men could loaf and swap stories. One young man, presumably a student, wrote an amusing letter to his mother reporting that he had happily "formed the acquaintance of a scientific celebrity here called *Shandy Jones*," who from "scientific investigation" had determined that his moustache and goatee had a ways yet to grow. Jones's solicitude of his white clients extended to giving some fifteen or twenty of them a room over his barbershop to use for private card games.²⁹ In return he probably learned a great deal about where to invest money in real estate. On the eve of the Civil War, Shandy Jones had achieved more than any black man in Alabama could reasonably expect. But cutting the hair of free and wealthy white men, while telling them what they wanted to hear, could be demeaning.

Following Alabama's secession white Tuscaloosans quickly aligned themselves with the new Confederate government. At the presidential inauguration in Montgomery, the Reverend Basil Manly, former president of the University of Alabama and father of the Tuscaloosa Baptist Church's pastor, gave Jefferson Davis the oath of office while a contingent of university cadets stood at attention. Crowds cheered as the Warrior Guards left the City of Oaks by steamboat to join the Greensboro Guards as part of the storied Fifth Alabama. Shandy Jones, like the town in which he lived, would remain out of the limelight during the four-year conflict, for free blacks were specifically exempted from Confederate military service until 1864.³⁰

The 1865 invasion of Tuscaloosa and fall of the Confederacy presented the newly freed people with unprecedented opportunities to make decisions. Some walked off the plantations to explore beyond the next hill, and the next hill after that; others immediatetly began looking to reunite divided families. Some returned to the plantations; others ended up in towns, where they found the protection of occupying federal troops and the chance for jobs. The Reverend Basil Manly observed in July that a thousand freed people had come to Tuscaloosa since the war's end, which was "daily filled with idle vagrant negroes."³¹

Whites assumed that with a few minor accommodations, their former slaves would return to the fields and resume life pretty much as it had been. Those who were unwilling could perhaps be sent back with vagrancy laws and enforced apprenticeships. But such was not to be. Black workers demanded to enter into negotiations. Planters drew up legal contracts stipulating that they would furnish the necessities—food, clothing, a house, fuel, medical attention, and a portion of the crop—in return for their former slaves' labor. Constructing these contracts was anything but smooth, and today they seem heavily weighted in the planters' favor. From the workers' perspective, however, these contracts represented a tacit recognition of their right to bargain. Other freed people began opening small businesses in the towns.

While labor problems were being worked out, these newly freed Americans were desperate for their children to begin receiving an education. "The great want of wants now existing in this State," declared the first issue of the Mobile *Nationalist*, "is that of free schools." The editor of the state's premier newspaper for the freed people was less concerned with education as a means of personal economic self-interest than as a tool of social improvement. Both the black population and the poor white population needed access to free schools, he argued, because both were unlettered. But uneducated whites also needed schools in order to temper their oppressive spirit toward black people. As long as ignorance prevailed, the spirit of violence would prevail; but with a free public education, enlightened principles would foster "reciprocity and friendly co-operation as well as mutual regard for each other's rights." In so many words, the editor was pleading for integrated schools. When children associate at school, when they follow the same academic subjects, become familiar with the same ideas, and play sports together, then "feelings of mutual friendship become stronger and stronger, and thus a generation is brought upon the stage of life unified by ties of the most enduring character." The editor concluded by declaring that the state needed to create an education system for all her youth, irrespective of color, and with dispatch.[32]

A year after Appomattox, Tuscaloosa was still without schools for its black children. One white congregation allowed black Christians to hold religious services in the basement of its church, but they were not allowed to open a school in it. Without a new state constitution and functioning board of education, the void would be filled by the Christian aid societies and the federal Freedmen's Bureau. Declared Bureau Assistant Commissioner Wager Swayne, "to open a school has been to have it filled." Another Alabamian reported that the freed people "have scarcely a leisure moment that you cannot see them with a book in their hand learning to read." The subject of education consumed many correspondents to the *Nationalist*. What the freed people need and desire is "to teach them to *take care of themselves*." "Let the negro learn all he can," wrote another. "Ignorance is the parent of vice. Intelligence is the hand maid of prosperity."[33]

Even after Dr. Cloud established public schools, black children faced enormous difficulties. In June 1869, the state superintendent wrote to Hampton S. Whitfield, superintendent of education for Tuscaloosa County, complaining that the county had reported forty-four schools for whites but only two for blacks, this in a county with over two thousand black children. Whitfield's reply, published in the newspapers, argued that the discrepancy was a consequence of the system's inadequate funding. White patrons had agreed to pay the teachers after the state funding, which was less than half of what he had been promised, ran out. Because black patrons were unable to come up with additional money, he had been unable to hire teachers. Whitfield's solution was to shut down the schools, both black and white, for a year while the system could be placed on a firm financial basis.[34]

Hand in hand with the push for schools came the push for churches. Christian faith had long been part of antebellum black life; and the first leaders, including Shandy Jones, had honed their skills in the pulpit. Whites had, of course, carefully scrutinized black worship services, but that could not prevent slaves and free blacks alike from coming to their own understanding of the Civil War and God's role in it.[35] The central fact of that understanding was that some four million slaves had been freed. Why had God waited so long to deliver black Americans from their bondage? Why had God chosen this particular moment? These were questions without answers. But that God had once again intervened to change the course of human history could scarcely be denied. And like the drowning of Pharaoh's army in the Red Sea, God had plans for the white Southerners who had enslaved black Americans.

From this theological perspective of deliverance and judgment, black Christians developed a practical plan of religious reconstruction. They would establish their own churches with their own ministers, apart from the white Southern churches that had willingly supported the sins of slavery and secession. And they would accept help and even join the Northern denominations that had stood with the Northern armies. Here, the hierarchical Methodist churches had financial and administrative advantages. Pastor Lakin enjoyed great respect and success among black Alabamians, but missionaries sent south from the black Methodist denominations did even better. In a ten-year span after the war, the African Methodist Episcopal (AME) Church gained some 250,000 members in the South, and the AME Zion about half that number. The extraordinary gains by these two denominations came at the expense of the MEC South, which dropped from 208,000 black members in 1860 to 49,000 members in 1866—and kept dropping.

Black Methodists in Tuscaloosa were part of this push for independence.

In May 1866 the Louisiana Conference of the AME Zion opened its second session in Mobile. It was an important conference for Shandy Jones, who served as the conference's secretary (the same position that Lakin filled in the MEC's Alabama Conference and Central Alabama Conference), became fully ordained there, and then was sent out to three churches in the Tuscaloosa district.[36] The Tuscaloosa delegates claimed that some six hundred black Methodists in Tuscaloosa needed a church, and two hundred Sunday school children needed a school building. They were allowed to hold religious services in the basement of one of the white churches. Jones returned from Mobile to help in founding Hunter's Chapel AME Zion, the first black church in Tuscaloosa, and its school.[37]

The black members of the Tuscaloosa Baptist Church were also anxious to have their own congregation but seemed to be getting nowhere. Prince Morell traveled to Mobile in 1866 for ordination by representatives from New Orleans. When he returned, the black congregants met with the Reverend Charles Manly, Tuscaloosa Baptist Church's white pastor, who chastised them for their "unscriptural and disorderly way of procuring a sort of quasi ordination for Prince." The patronizing Manly left the black members to think about what he had said, and they promptly sent him a note declaring their withdrawal from the church. The next year Morrell would be assaulted while attending a worship office.[38]

The pent-up ambition of Jones and the other black Tuscaloosans to improve their lives was bursting forth. The freed people had started their own schools, churches, and voluntary associations.[39] Soon enough they would be deep into politics, but that would have to wait on events far away. In the nation's capital the Republican Congress grew exasperated with President Andrew Johnson's lenient plan for reconstruction and proceeded to impose its own Radical version. In early 1867 the Republicans placed Alabama once again under military rule until another constitution could be drafted and approved in a referendum with black men voting. Congress also stipulated that Alabama ratify the Fourteenth Amendment, which extended federal citizenship to former slaves, forbade states from restricting individual rights, and mandated due process.

This was just what black Alabamians wanted and needed. The second Convention of Colored People, which convened in Mobile on May, 4, 1867, was the focus of their hopes and expectations. In a key address by three prominent black leaders, the freed people claimed "exactly *the same rights, privileges, and immunities as are enjoyed by white men*—we ask nothing more and will be content with nothing less." They particularly wanted to end all legal distinctions based on race by striking the word "white" from laws. The delegates pledged themselves to the Republican Party in return for its long record, recounted in detail, of opposing slavery and supporting black voting and new state constitutions. They ended their convention by calling upon Republicans to demand that the state create a system of common schools open to all. "In a republic education is especially necessary as the ignorant are always liable to be led astray by the acts of the demagogue." Many of the delegates also attended the first statewide Republican convention, which met the next month in Montgomery. This was the convention that endorsed the Fourteenth Amendment and other Congressional initiatives, called for public education and racial harmony, and then pledged to "make us one people."[40]

Alabamians began registering to vote during that summer. In Greensboro a black registrar was murdered. In Tuscaloosa a white registrar resigned after deeming his black counterpart "unacceptable." Black and white Alabamians went to the polls in early October to elect delegates to the constitutional convention, and the election went resoundingly for the party of Lincoln. Of the one hundred delegates, ninety-six were Republicans, including sixteen black Alabamians. The convention produced a moderate document that provided for free public schools. Although the black delegates were successful in stopping any overt language establishing segregation, most Alabamians understood the new constitution to uphold segregated schools. This lack of explicit language would nonetheless be used against Dr. Cloud.[41]

While the Democrats resolved to boycott the February 1868 referendum, Shandy Jones sought the Republican nomination for the US Congress from the Fourth District. Black Tuscaloosans supported him against his opponent, a white Freedmen's Bureau agent and Union army major who also sought the nomination. Yet, Jones dropped out—perhaps from lack of funds, perhaps to avoid splitting the party, or possibly for some other combination of reasons. Jones was not going to Washington, DC, but he was going to Montgomery, for he had been elected to the state House of Representatives.[42] He could not take office, however, until Congress decided to do something about the Democratic boycott.

The strain of uncertainty mounted during the spring and summer of 1868. In Washington, the US Senate sat in judgment of the impeached president. In Alabama, citizens waited to learn whether they had a new constitution and new elected officials. They also heard reports of something called the Ku Klux Klan. "If attacked," the *Nationalist* warned its black readers, "it is your right and your duty to defend yourself."[43] And in Tuscaloosa, Ryland Randolph kept up his diatribes. Shandy Jones had other problems. Dossie Roberts, whom Jones had once owned and had apparently taught the barbering trade, returned from Mobile to set up his own rival barbershop.

Dossie Roberts was heavyset, dark complected, according to Randolph, and balanced his head with large brass earrings. His demeanor was described as at times pompous. He used his words in measured terms, although more often in the wrong than the right contexts. Roberts returned to Tuscaloosa just as Jones was challenging the Democrats and Randolph was looking for ways to retaliate. Roberts saw his opportunity and took it, establishing a "Caucassion Barber Shop" in an upstairs room directly opposite Jones's barbershop. Roberts advertising himself in the *Independent Monitor* as the "White Folks' Barber." Randolph praised the ingratiating Roberts. "His will soon be the only shop of the kind here," he cackled, "if the Ku-klux ghosts remain hereabout."[44] The editor then chastised white men for patronizing the barbershop of that insolent "Gorilla Shandy Jones," rather than Roberts, the "Ku-Klux Barber." The result, according to the self-congratulatory Randolph, was that Roberts "secured nearly all the respectable tonsorial business."[45]

From Ryland Randolph's perspective, Dossie Roberts's path to financial success lay in returning to the servile role proper to black men. When Randolph returned to Tuscaloosa after his Selma trial, Roberts was chosen the driver of the carriage and horses to bring the petticoat hero back in his triumphal return. "I can even now see Dossie," recalled Randolph years later, "sitting away up on the driver's seat, and bedecked in a handsome new black suit of clothes with elegant gauntlets reaching to his elbows. . . . he was certainly the proudest-looking negro I ever saw, not even excepting Soulouque, the big black negro emperor of Hayti, whom I saw reviewing his negro army." For Roberts, and for too many of fragile character, the path to success lay in malleable convictions: after Randolph left Tuscaloosa, Roberts would become a Republican.[46]

Yet it might also be argued that Dossie Roberts made choices allowing him to survive, even thrive, in uncharted waters. He was both clever and opportunistic, a trickster who would not hesitate to turn on those who had once been on his side. Nor did Roberts mind playing the fool if it got him ahead. But who really was the fool? Ambitious slaves had always played their masters for fools, as seen in the Uncle Remus tales recorded by Joel Chandler Harris. Whatever it took, Dossie Roberts would gain his economic independence—his own brand of freedom—in a way that Ryland Randolph could never fathom.[47]

20. Shandy Wesley Jones (Courtesy Ophelia Taylor Pinkard)

In the spring of 1868, with his mind beset with problems—the state's political future, the emergence of the Klan, competition from Dossie Roberts—Jones turned his mind once again to the prospects of being rid of his woes elsewhere. The American Colonization Society resumed its activities after the war, offering in Alabama newspapers shelter, subsistence, and five to seven acres of land during emigrants' first six months in Liberia. In a letter published in the *African Repository*, Jones asked if transportation were available for the several families in Tuscaloosa who were ready to go to Liberia as soon as possible. "I am still of the opinion that Africa is the black man's only hope in this world," he noted with more than a tinge of sadness, for there is not "a shadow of hope for equal rights and justice in this land, and therefore no inducement for a colored man who loves freedom and its train of blessings to continue here." Once again he pledged that he was ready and willing to cast his lot with those struggling in Liberia for Africa's "moral redemption" in order that the children will have "an earthly heritage for succeeding generations."[48]

All of Jones's decades of efforts came to naught. No evidence survives of Tuscaloosans ever emigrating to Africa. From the hindsight of another century, it seems easy to expect persecuted and downtrodden people to pull up stakes and leave. But life is never that neat. Like Gulliver on the beach, thousands of threads held them in place. America was their home, their families' home, and their friends' home. In the end imagined redemption elsewhere can be far more soothing than the real pain involved in realizing that redemption.

At last the Republican Congress validated the referendum and the elections. Alabama had a new constitution and new state and local officeholders. Noah B. Cloud took his place as superintendent of education; and Shandy Jones took his seat, along with twenty-six other black men, in the state House of Representatives.

Jones would not stand out during this or any other legislative session. In addition to a few local bills, his only important action was to sponsor legislation, which passed, to consolidate the North East and South West Railroad with the Wills Valley Railroad.[49] His lack of political stature should not in any way diminish the significance of this moment. Jones was among those first black men to serve in the Alabama General Assembly, only three years after the passage of the Thirteenth Amendment had ended slavery.

)(X)(

In a speech delivered in the Tuscaloosa courthouse only a month before President Lakin and Superintendent Cloud arrived to take control of the University of Alabama, Jones argued that he "did not see why white people should object to having their children at school with colored children, provided the parents of the latter had no objection to the arrangement." He should have been "Ku-Kluxed" right there, the *Monitor*'s editor fumed, and "negro ambition squelched in its incipiency." Now Jones was engaged in trying to pass social equality laws in the bogus legislature, "and is about to send his half-grown stinking pickaninny *to the State University!*" According to family tradition, one of Jones's sons, William Henry Jones, had served three years in the Confederate navy and thus would have been the perfect person to integrate the University of Alabama.[50]

Although the silhouette of Jones does not appear in Randolph's woodcut, the caption to *A Prospective Scene* puts him there nonetheless: "P.S. It will be seen, that there is room left on the limb for the suspension of any bad Grant negro who may be found at the propitious moment." Jones was "undoubtedly the greatest rascal amongst the negroes of Tuscaloosa," according to Randolph, who predicted that the "ambitious darkey" would without doubt "rise as high as Haman."[51]

The idea that Shandy Jones would send his son to the university was not as outlandish as it appears. Consider: Political events were moving in unpredictable directions at a dizzying rate, Dr. Cloud and others were tentatively broaching the subject of biracial education, the Reverend Lakin had just established the biracial Alabama Conference of the MEC, the Jones family had wealth and some were light-skinned enough to pass for white, and young William Henry Jones was a Confederate veteran. Then there were Ryland Randolph's repeated references to Jones's expectations that he would enroll his son there. In one edition of the *Monitor*, Randolph had penned a satiric play that included Shandy Jones's son as a University of Alabama student. In another scurrilous column Randolph described the new professor of natural philosophy, J. DeForest Richards, who "celebrated himself, soon after his arrival, by embracing the stinking buck gorilla—Shandy Jones—on the streets. It seems that these two were bed fellows, when in Montgomery together."[52] Two weeks later an equally scurrilous cartoon appeared in the *Monitor* depicting the meeting.

One line of the caption is telling: "The young gorilla, to be seen climbing the barber's pole, is a son of the old gorilla Jones — said to be an applicant for admission into the new State University." In the end a black member of the board of regents, Peyton Finley, introduced a resolution in July 1871 to create a separate black university, and it was accepted.[53] Jones's son would never attend the University of Alabama; not until midway through the next century would the first black student enroll.

)()()(

Shandy Jones and Ryland Randolph continued their quarrels for the brief time they overlapped in the legislature. Jones spoke against Randolph's bill to declare all Civil War marriages illegal, but little else happened. The next elections were scheduled for November 1870. Randolph attempted to embarrass "the ambitious nigger barber" by publishing a letter by Jones asking to distribute Republican ballots (the standard practice of the day) to a white Democrat. "Our cause is the cause of the People 'Truly,'" Jones had written, "especially the laboring portion of them & as it is the cause of Justice and right for which we are contending we may confidently expect God[']s blessing upon our efforts." Randolph then called for Jones to be given the taste of a good hickory stick and to be banished from the town. Randolph's comments provoked the Republican Montgomery *Alabama State Journal* to publish a defense in the form of a long editorial. After condemning Randolph and the

21. Shandy Jones greeting Vermont-native Professor J. DeForest Richards, with carpetbag, on the streets of Tuscaloosa; Jones hopes that his son, shown straddling the barber pole, will soon attend the University of Alabama (Tuskaloosa *Independent Monitor* 1869 April 6)

"large number of ignorant, strongly prejudiced and easily excitable men" who supported him, the *Journal* editor put the incident in larger terms: "Violence and persecution may force Republicans to seek other homes," he admitted, "but the spirit of violence and persecution will not cease. . . . Once get the idea into a man's head that murder is excusable for any cause, and he will continue to kill for the very tiger-like lust of destruction." Such arguments hardly mattered. The same issue of the *Monitor* that complained of Jones's distributing ballots also included the official vote results. Jones had lost his bid for reelection.[54]

Family tradition claims that Jones again retreated into despair and disillusionment. After all, he had lost the election after struggling for a half-century to expand his own freedom and to establish the freedom of black Southerners. The family also has it that the Klan drove him into hiding south of town, where Evalina brought him provisions. Perhaps the Democratic boycott of his barbershop simply took too heavy a financial toll. Added to all that, his son-in-law died. Whatever the cause or confluence of causes, Shandy Jones left behind the City of Oaks, the town where for decades he had barbered, invested in real estate, raised his family, preached, and most recently represented in the legislature. After packing up the household, Evalina and most of the other children joined him in Mobile. In what must have seemed a tragic coda, his wife of over thirty-three years and the mother of their fourteen children died shortly afterward.[55]

Mobile held promise because a new federal appointment to the position of collector for the port opened up a number of other federal positions for black Republicans in the US Customs House. Collector for the port was the most important federal job in Alabama as a source of patronage.[56] Details of Jones's time in Mobile during the 1870s are simply unknown. From time to time he would return to his old hometown, usually for political events.[57] Some of his children continued to live in Tuscaloosa, where his son ran the barbershop. At some point Jones remarried, this time to a woman named Lucinda, reputed to have been white with two children. Jones was still ordained. Beginning in 1883, he was listed as the minister for Mobile's Little Zion Church on the northwest corner of Church and Bayou streets.[58]

✕✕✕✕

If any of the four figures in *A Prospective Scene* had reason to dedicate his life to freedom, it was Shandy Jones. He did not have to spend his days toiling in a cotton field. He instead had a much easier time as a barber and, in fact, prospered financially and raised a family in which he took pride. But nothing could change the stigma dictated by the color of his skin and the status of his mother—matters over which he had utterly no control. Jones had received his freedom as an arbitrary decision by his master/father. The possibility of its arbitrary cancellation must have hung over his head. He lived in a precarious nether world, unable to vote, unable even to leave his own home at night without a pass from the mayor. The legislature from time to time tried to exclude free blacks from the state. As a barber he had to ingratiate himself to his white customers. Even when he preached, white observers would listen to make sure that he read the scriptural passages recognizing the master-slave relationship. He worked within the system, even buying family members to prevent their being sold off.

It is small wonder that Shandy Jones looked to escape the conditions imposed by his birth. Liberty in Liberia: here was a cause worth his energies. In Africa former slaves could run their own country, make their own laws, elect

their own government, and build their own schools. There a man could govern himself, come and go as he wished without a pass. Yes, colonization was
impractical and ignored the fact that these black people were Americans and
not Africans. Still, it represented hope. And Jones was a man who could not
live without hope, as his long and vigorous support for the scheme reveals, a
man dissatisfied with the limitations under which he toiled, a generous man
willing to help his own people.

Even after Appomattox, Jones supported emigration to Liberia. When that
path at last was gone, he joined in working tirelessly for the Republican Party.
He saw in the Republicans an understanding of freedom that meshed easily
with the experiences and aspirations of black Southerners. They found in the
words of Lincoln the promises denied for generations to them as an *unfree*
people. They would place their faith in the federal government to protect the
Constitutional rights that were now theirs.

The first Convention of Colored People met in Mobile during November
1865, just as word was being received that the Thirteenth Amendment, forever
ending slavery, had at last been ratified. Amid testimonials that drew tears,
the fifty-six delegates, most of them ministers, added their names to a series
of resolutions. The first stated that "our freedom is the gift of God, and that
we are under the highest obligations to Him so to improve our n[e]w privilege
that his gift shall not be in vain." Other resolutions included a determination
to labor faithfully for just wages and the recognition that "our new condition
of freedom not only presents new motive to industry, but also imposes new
obligations upon us to cultivate all the virtues of good citizenship."[59] Jones
and his colleagues recognized that the end of slavery did not end their task.
The freed people, unprepared for their liberty, were too much at the mercy of
circumstances. (The ancient Romans had a term to describe the freed people's
situation: *libertines*, slaves set loose without proper preparation.) So Jones and
other black leaders were especially concerned with creating schools, establishing contracts, and taking the first steps toward responsible citizenship.

This was all commendable and even extraordinary. Emancipation had
freed black Americans *from* being bought and sold; what they had been freed
to, however, was unclear. ("Life, liberty, and the pursuit of happiness" is not
much advice.) The particular meaning that they would impart to freedom
was unclear because their former condition as slaves had narrowed their
sense of possibilities. Worshiping in their own churches, learning to read and
write, getting a job, perhaps even running for office—these were the sorts

of practical goals and privileges that needed immediate attention. After that, what? The people's freedom that Randolph and the former Confederates espoused was obviously repugnant to black Southerners. Many were drawn to Christian freedom in gratitude and because of the obvious parallels with the Hebrew exodus. Whiggish freedom's emphasis upon self-control was simply asking too much from those who had spent their lives under controlling masters who did not want their slaves acting and thinking for themselves. At least the Bill of Rights, while new to those who for centuries had been defined by color and not as individuals, seemed to be impartial. But protection of those rights from angry former Confederates depended on a government eight hundred miles away, a government that would lose interest in the ensuing decades.

In the end the freed people were left with hope and not enough else. "They are near enough to see its charms, but too far off to enjoy them," wrote Tocqueville of white Americans and equality. He could as easily been referring to black Americans and freedom. Unshackled into a belligerent world and without adequate preparation, "before they have fully tasted its delights, they die."[60] Jones had once sought liberty in Liberia. Things were better now, but he would never rest secure. What had been given, could be taken away. Shandy Jones knew both the joys and dangers in Emancipation; not in his lifetime, nor his children's, would they ever be able to build their own cities and towns, make their own laws. But they could find strength in the freedom that comes through hope, from the faith that the cares of this world are not final, from the conviction that release will come sometime, somewhere.[61]

※※※

In late 1885 or early 1886, the old man's health began to fail.[62] On the last day of January, a Saturday, Jones sent for some of his fellow presiding elders. "I am so glad that the Good Lord has given me power to speak again," he greeted them, "for I wanted to state how I stood before I died!" He then asked that a couple of hymns be sung. When the fourteenth chapter of Saint John's Gospel was read, Jones clapped his hands together and cried out, "Yes, yes; our Father has many mansions for his servants." He cried out so loud and so often that he was asked to be quiet. They all then said a prayer, and Jones admitted that his time was short. He lay there confined to his room until 1 A.M. on Thursday, February 4, when he laid his head back in his chair and died. At the funeral, held at his Little Zion Church, the AME Zion bishop preached on

Revelations 14:13 and then read a poem of his own composition. But one of those in the congregation had in his mind another poem:

> Of one that walked on earth and had his head in heaven;
>> Whose stature is a man's
> He is crowned in the glorious land![63]

Shandy Jones, who could not find peace in Alabama, had at last found peace elsewhere.

Epilogue

Two men walking down a dusty Tuscaloosa street in 1868 may seem an unlikely scene to search for freedom. But we should not really be surprised, for Americans have always been searching for freedom. Our most perceptive observer, Alexis de Tocqueville, insisted that what set Americans apart was their commitment to equality—the rejection of a traditional social hierarchy. Yet equality has never rallied Americans the way that freedom has. Patriots famously cried out, "Give me Liberty or give me Death!" The US mint puts *Liberty* on coins, not *Equality*. Our four freedoms stand against dictators' tyrannies.

While Americans have always agreed that freedom comes first, we have rarely agreed about its meaning. In colonial America, tidewater Virginians identified freedom with dominion over oneself and others; while backcountry frontiersmen rejected law and order as threats to their natural liberty.[1] The first ten amendments to the Constitution put into law an understanding of freedom as universal human rights protected by law. In a scant four years during the 1860s, perhaps 750,000 Americans died fighting over the meaning of freedom. Both Union and Confederate armies marched to "The Battle Cry of Freedom," although each side sang different lyrics. This gave President Abraham Lincoln pause. "The world has never had a good definition of the word *liberty*," he observed in 1864, "and the American people, just now, are much in want of one. We all declare for liberty; but in using the same *word*, we do not all mean the same *thing*."[2]

The arguments over the meaning of freedom were not settled at Appomattox. In many ways those arguments grew sharper. Ryland Randolph raged at a world spiraling out of control and longed for a golden age when the people lived easily and securely with those like them. He and other former Confederates thus set about to recover the freedom that they believed had been taken from them. The Reverend Lakin came south to extend to others Christian freedom: the joyful sense of release from sin and its accompanying responsibilities that he had first experienced as a young man. Dr. Cloud turned from agricultural reform to educational reform, convinced that Southerners needed to be freed from the ignorance that had ultimately caused their destitution. His Whiggish concept of freedom rested upon the conviction that individuals, with effort, could transcend their own limitations, that they could be freed to do better. And the freedman Shandy Jones entered politics in order to give his people the sort of hope for self-government denied them during their centuries in America.

All declared for liberty, noted Lincoln, but in using the same word they did not mean the same thing. This is because different understandings of freedom emerge from different experiences and world views. Some notions of freedom worked better together in the new social and economic order that was emerging after the war—as Lakin, Cloud, and, to a lesser extent, Jones certainly demonstrated. But in the end, whether it be freedom from, or freedom to—whether it be the people's freedom, or Whiggish freedom, or any other sort of freedom—all are means of realizing one's essential nature. Individuals believe themselves free when they can express their character through their actions. Freedom explains who we are or who we want to be.[3]

Although ultimately every individual's experiences are unique—at some point people simply are what they are—and every person's idea of freedom is different, we can see categories and patterns in the lives of these four individuals who came together that afternoon in the City of Oaks. Ryland Randolph's quest for certainty—the result of his nomadic youth and the social upheaval following the South's loss—was a crisis that many of his contemporaries faced. The religious revivals that swept America turned perhaps millions of young people in a completely new direction, just as it had Arad Lakin. Dr. Cloud's perception that scientific agriculture could be the means of establishing communities expressed the same notions that Whigs applied to other reform efforts. And while emigration to Liberia had limited appeal, four million black people living in a region committed to slavery all shared with the Liberian emigrants a desperate hope for self-government.

The matter is hardly exhausted by looking at the 1860s. These four persons also represent even broader strains in American life. Yes, Randolph, Lakin, Cloud, and Jones were products of their time; but in more basic ways they were more like us than apart from us. Their understandings of freedom give us clues to our own understandings of freedom.

Christians, like Arad Lakin, still believe that conversion frees them from a life of sin to shoulder a life of service. If taken seriously, this is a demanding sort of freedom; and the zeal that it inspires in believers continues to inspire awe. Yet with each passing day, an increasingly secular modern world seems to dismiss evangelical Christians as out of touch and their faith as mere superstition. The future of Christian freedom seems particularly at risk, not only because it grows directly out of Christian faith, but because its paradoxical nature is patently at odds with common sense. How can servants be free? Does personal liberty lie in taking on the cares of others? For those who have not already experienced grace, Christian freedom cannot be entirely comprehended.

The advantages of the universal education that Noah B. Cloud championed are no longer questioned, and his Whiggish freedom remains a recipe for personal success. But for too many, the unending quest for self-perfection asks too much. Whigs are constantly at war with themselves, mastering their own passions while fending off the temptations of the world. Complacency is their path to disaster. Creating one's own freedom is hard work. And Whiggish freedom seems to contradict our founding documents, which assure us that happiness—or at least its pursuit—is a natural right, the very stuff for which we were created and thus entitled. Few take the long and relentlessly demanding Whiggish path to freedom.

Shandy Jones found a type of freedom in hope. If we are trapped and without options, then we can at least find freedom in hope; for without hope, no one can go on. Politicians, advertisers, and state lotteries cleverly appeal to our hopes. But unmet hopes are frustrating. Jones died unfulfilled, at least in this world. Countless others have as well.

Many Americans still believe in Christian freedom, Whiggish freedom, and the freedom that they find in hope. But they are not in the mainstream and probably never were. The mainstream belongs to those who believe in do-as-you-please freedom, those who push the limits of acting without constraints. Who of these four then was the harbinger of the future?

Surely the future could not have belonged to Ryland Randolph? Sane people do not walk the streets with loaded pistols looking to settle scores. Sane people do not threaten to lynch their political opponents. Sane people do not scream for racial subordination. And yet the future *did* belong to Ryland Randolph; for it was he who embraced the people's freedom. When he stamped

"WHITE MAN—RIGHT OR WRONG—STILL THE WHITE MAN" at the top of his *Independent Monitor*, Randolph was declaring that freedom—life, liberty, and the pursuit of happiness—is an inalienable birthright. Nothing could be more American, nor more ancient, than the people's freedom.[4]

The people's freedom is appealing, no doubt, because it seems so natural and effortless—unlike the constant job of self-creation that engages the Whig. The people's freedom seems so obvious—unlike the paradoxes at the heart of Christian faith. And the people's freedom is concrete—unlike the flimsy and often unmet hopes of such men as Shandy Jones.

The people's freedom gives us self-confidence. Ryland Randolph's status as a white Southerner emboldened him to act without constraint. We too gain confidence because freedom is ours by virtue of being members of a free people. This kind of freedom asks little—only that we, in John Stuart Mill's classic formulation, avoid harming others. Because the people's freedom is so self-confirming, its lure is immediate and obvious. Our modern version of freedom may be quiet, yet in it we can still hear distant echoes of Ryland Randolph's thundering words.

But a free people will always need a contrast—an antithesis, an external evil—to blame for our frustration when our aspirations remain unrealized. Randolph found his in the gang of carpetbaggers, scalawags, and freedmen. The growth of their freedom subtracted from his. Today, this will no longer do, of course. But we do indict as enemies of the people those of privilege, or political opponents, or multinational corporations, or a distant big-spending government, or self-righteous meddlesome moralizers, or a host of others who frustrate our ambitions. The people must stay constantly vigilant else marauders, real or imagined, take away what nature has intended.

The only real question was, and is, *Who are the people?* Randolph, as his motto announced, reserved freedom for white men; indeed, the Republicans' efforts to include carpetbaggers, scalawags, and freedmen into the political process lay at the core of his rage. In that respect he was surely looking backward. During the Civil War Americans had expanded their definition of the people. We are expanding this definition still. But some will always be excluded.

Still, despite the inherent attractions of the people's freedom, not everyone will be satisfied; for in the end different people seek different paths to become who they are, or who they want to be. Goethe supposedly observed that we are happy when everything within us has its equivalent outside of us.

We feel ourselves free when our lives express our character. Freedom does that, and does more than that. Freedom gives us the opportunity to create lives well lived.

)()()(

Dust no longer rises from the Tuscaloosa streets in late August, for they are now paved with asphalt. The smells come from the rear of automobiles, not horses. The Dearing home is now the University's faculty club, and a fine Italian restaurant stands where Ryland Randolph published his newspaper. Huge oaks still shade us on sweltering summer days, except where the devastating 2011 tornado destroyed too much of the town. The political cartoons in the *Tuscaloosa News* pale by contrast to those in the Tuskaloosa *Independent Monitor*. While much has changed since 1868, much remains the same. We can still search for freedom in the City of Oaks. But we should hardly be surprised; for everyday life is saturated with ideas, values, and meaning.

Appendix A: Characters

THE PRINCIPALS

Cloud, Noah Bartlett: Scientific agriculturalist and educational reformer

Jones, Shandy Wesley: Free black barber in Tuscaloosa

Lakin, Arad S.: Methodist minister and carpetbagger

Randolph, Ryland: Klansman and editor of the Tuskaloosa *Independent Monitor*

THE OTHERS

Abbott, James: Tuscaloosa free black barber

Andrew, James O.: Southern Methodist bishop who precipitated the 1845 split over slavery

Asbury, Francis: With Thomas Coke, the first Methodist bishop in America

Barnard, Frederick Augustus Porter: Professor of the sciences at the University of Alabama, 1838–1854

Barr, John Gorman: Antebellum Tuscaloosa humorist

Bell, John: 1860 presidential candidate of the Constitutional Union Party

Benton, Sandford: Minister in the Forks of the Delaware

Berry, Ned: Tuscaloosa free black teamster

Birney, James Gillespie: Liberty Party presidential nominee, 1840 and 1844

Blackford, William T.: Scalawag Greensboro physician

Blair, Francis P.: Democratic nominee for vice president in 1868

Blair, Robert: Mayor of Tuscaloosa in the late 1850s

Boyd, Alexander: Republican solicitor of Greene County

Bradstreet, Daniel: Blacksmith in the Forks of the Delaware

Busteed, Richard: US district judge for Alabama

Byrd, William H.: Tuscaloosa's keeper of the scales

Callis, John Benton: Head of the Freedmen's Bureau in Huntsville

Chalfant, James F.: Northern Methodist minister and Lakin's immediate supervisor

Chambliss, N. R.: Interim University of Alabama president in 1869

Clanton, James Holt: Confederate brigadier general and postwar Democratic leader in Alabama

Clark, Davis Wasgatt: Northern Methodist bishop from Ohio who sent Lakin to Alabama

Clay, John Withers: Editor of the *Huntsville Democrat*

Clay, Virginia Tunstall: Wife of C. C. Clay

Cleveland, George: Eutaw hotelkeeper

Cloud, John: Father of Noah Bartlett Cloud

Cloud, Mary Barton: Wife of Noah Bartlett Cloud

Cloud, Noah B., Jr.: Son of Noah Bartlett Cloud

Cobbs, Nicholas Hamner: Alabama's first Episcopal bishop

Cocke, John Hartwell: Antebellum reformer and supporter of colonization

Colfax, Schuyler: Republican nominee for vice president in 1868

Cowin, Tood: Former Greensboro guard who shot an occupying Union soldier

Crawford, Samuel W.: Military commander of the North Alabama district

Croom, Isaac: Greene County planter and president of the Alabama Agricultural Society

Crossland, Meredith T.: Republican member of the state house from Tuscaloosa County; murdered in the Sipsey swamp

Croxton, John T.: Union brigadier general directing the invasion of west Alabama

Davis, Nicholas: Democratic lawyer from Huntsville

Deloffre, André: Librarian and professor of modern languages at the University of Alabama in 1865

Dorman, Isaac W.: MEC local preacher from Wetumpka

Douglas, Stephen A.: US senator from Illinois and 1860 national Democratic presidential candidate

Dykous, Dennis: Ryland Randolph's printer who became editor of the rival Tuscaloosa *Reconstructionist*

Eddins, Balus: Black man stabbed by Ryland Randolph

Everett, Edward: 1860 vice presidential candidate of the Constitutional Union Party

Finley, Peyton: Black member of the board of education

Forney, John H.: Former Confederate major general appointed professor of mathematics at the University of Alabama in 1869

Forrest, Nathan Bedford: Confederate lieutenant general of cavalry and an organizer of the Ku Klux Klan

Forsyth, John: Editor of the *Mobile Register*

Fowler, William Henry: Editor of several west Alabama newspapers

Garland, Landon Cabell: President of the University of Alabama, 1854–1867

Glascock, John: Owner of the store below Ryland Randolph's *Independent Monitor*

Grant, Ulysses S.: Republican nominee for president in 1868

Guild, James: Prominent Tuscaloosa physician

Harper, R. D.: Superintendent of education for the Freedmen's Bureau in Alabama and in late 1868 Arad Lakin's successor as president of the University of Alabama

Harris, John James: Tuscaloosa lawyer, merchant, politician, and editor of the *Independent Monitor*

Haven, Gilbert: Bishop of the Alabama Conference of the MEC in 1873

Hill, J. B. F.: White Northern Methodist minister and schoolteacher attacked in Greene County

Hodgson, Joseph: Colonel of the Seventh Alabama Cavalry, editor of the *Montgomery Mail*, and state superintendent of education 1870–1872

Hollingsworth, John: Tuscaloosan assailed by Balus Eddins

Hood, John Bell: Confederate commander of the Army of Tennessee

Horton, Mr. and Mrs. Benjamin: Parents of a deformed child

Houston, George S.: Democratic governor of Alabama from 1874 to 1878

Howard, O. O.: Commissioner of the Freedmen's Bureau

Jemison, Robert: Tuscaloosa businessman and Confederate senator

Johnson, Rev.: MEC local preacher in Fayetteville

Johnston, Thomas W.: Colonel whose troops burned the University of Alabama

Jones, Edward: Jackson County member of the MEC

Jones, Evalina Love: Wife of Shandy Jones

Jones, William Henry: Son of Shandy and Evalina Jones who served the Confederacy aboard ship

King, Horace: Free black bridge builder

Lakin, Achsah Labar Newton: Wife of Arad Lakin

Lakin, Jonas: Father of Arad Lakin

Lakin, Mary Martha: Daughter of Arad and Achsah Lakin, and wife of John Wigel Raines

Lakin, Prudence: Mother of Arad Lakin

Lakin, Robert: Youngest brother of Arad Lakin

Lane, A. O.: Editor of the *Birmingham Iron Age* and rival of Ryland Randolph

Langdon, Charles Carter: Whig editor of the *Mobile Daily Advertiser*

Leonard, Charles: Neighbor of the Lakin family in the Forks of the Delaware

Lewis, David Peter: Republican governor of Alabama from 1872 to 1874

Lindsay, Robert Burns: Democratic governor of Alabama, 1870–1872

Loomis, J. C.: University of Alabama professor of belle lettres

Love, Zadock: Tuscaloosa free black and father-in-law of Shandy Jones

Lupton, Nathaniel: Southern University professor asked to become president of the University of Alabama in 1869

Mallory, Stephen Russell: Confederate secretary of the navy

Manly, Basil: Second president of the University of Alabama, 1837–1855

Manly, Charles: Pastor of Tuscaloosa Baptist Church and son of Basil Manly

Mann, Horace: Creator of the Massachusetts public school system and president of Antioch College

Martin, John M.: Tuscaloosan who nearly fought a duel with Ryland Randolph

Maury, Dabney Herndon: Confederate commander of the Department of the Gulf and nephew of Matthew Fontaine Maury

Maury, Matthew Fontaine: Oceanographer and Confederate chief of Sea Coast, River and Harbor Defenses asked to be president of the University of Alabama in 1869

McConnell, W. K.: Former colonel of the Thirtieth Alabama, appointed University of Alabama commandant of cadets in 1869

McKee, Robert: Editor of the Selma *Southern Argus*

Meade, George Gordon: Hero of Gettysburg and commander of the Third Military District

Minor, Robin W.: Poor Walker County resident

Moore, Andrew Barry: Alabama's secessionist governor, 1857–1861

Morell, Prince: Tuscaloosa black Baptist minister

Morgan, John Tyler: Organizer of the Fifty-First Alabama Partisan Rangers, brigadier general, and later US senator

Nichols, William: English-born architect

Northrop, Cyrus: Yale professor of rhetoric and English literature asked to become president of the University of Alabama in 1869

Orrick, John C.: Former Greensboro guard and killer of Alex Webb

Paine, Robert: Southern Methodist bishop

Palmer, Phoebe: American Methodist leader of the holiness movement

Parsons, Lewis Eliphalet: Appointed provisional governor of Alabama from June to December 1865

Patton Robert M.: Governor of Alabama from December 1865 to March 1867

Peabody, George: Banker and philanthropist who created a fund for the intellectual, moral, and industrial education of poor Southern children

Pease, Lewis M.: First Methodist missionary to Five Points

Peck, Elisha Wolsey: Chief justice of the Alabama Supreme Court from 1868 to 1874

Perteet, Solomon: Prosperous Tuscaloosa free black plasterer and real estate investor

Pierce, George F.: Southern Methodist bishop

Pinney, John B.: Agent of the American Colonization Society

Pratt, Daniel: Autauga County manufacturer of cotton gins and developer of Alabama's mineral district

Price, William S.: Marengo County author of "Moral Benefits of Slavery"

Raines, John Wigel: Union captain and husband of Mary Martha Lakin

Randolph, Katharine Clay Withers: Adopted daughter of C. C. Clay and wife of Ryland Randolph

Randolph, Robert Beverley: Distant relative of Ryland Randolph who pulled Andrew Jackson's nose

Randolph, Robert Carter: Freethinking physician and uncle of Ryland Randolph

Randolph, Victor M.: Naval officer and father of Ryland Randolph

Rhett, Robert Barnwell, Sr.: South Carolina secessionist

Richards, J. DeForest: University of Alabama professor and president appointed in 1869

Roberts, Dossie: Black barber once owned by Shandy Jones

Ruffin Edmund: Virginia scientific agriculturalist and secessionist

Rust, Richard S.: Secretary to the Freedmen's Aid Society of the Methodist Episcopal Church

Semmes, Raphael: Captain of the CSS *Alabama*

Semple, Henry Churchill: Montgomery lawyer and Confederate officer

Seymour, Horatio: Democratic nominee for president in 1868

Shepard, William: Poor white farmer and Unionist from Blount County

Shepherd, Oliver Lathrop: Alabama's military commander and director of the Alabama Freedmen's Bureau during part of 1868

Smith, Gustavus Adolphus: Former Union brigadier general elected in 1868 to board of education and father of William Smith

Smith, William: Student at the University of Alabama, attempted assassin of Ryland Randolph, and son of Gustavus Adolphus Smith

Smith, William Hugh: Republican governor of Alabama, 1868–1870

Soulouque, Faustin-Élie: Self-proclaimed Faustin I, Emperor of Haiti

Speed, Joseph H.: Alabama superintendent of education, 1872–1874

Spencer, George E.: Republican Alabama US senator, 1868–1879

Spiller, Captain: Steamboat captain on the Tennessee River

Stanton, Edwin: Secretary of War under Abraham Lincoln

Stephens, Alexander Hamilton: Vice president of the Confederacy

Stephens, Henry: Member of the MEC in Madison County

Stone, George W.: James Holt Clanton's law partner

Sullivan, Moses B.: MEC minister in Alabama

Swayne, Wager T.: Head of the Freedmen's Bureau in Alabama beginning in 1865 and military governor from March 1867 to July 1868

Talley, J. W.: Presiding elder of Talladega and delegate to the 1868 General Conference

Tattnall, Josiah: Commander of the Pensacola Navy Yard, 1851-1854, and later a Confederate naval officer

Taylor, George: Freedman and MEC local preacher

Taylor, Joseph W.: Purchaser of the Tuskaloosa *Independent Monitor*

Thurlow, Silas: Republican Limestone County probate judge

Toombs Robert: US senator from Georgia and the Confederacy's first secretary of state

Tuomey, Michael: Professor and Alabama's first state geologist, 1846–1857

Tutwiler, Henry: Early professor at the University of Alabama and later proprietor of the Greene Springs School

Vaughan, Vernon Henry: University of Alabama professor of history, logic, and metaphysics involved in attempt to assassinate Ryland Randolph, appointed governor of Utah Territory

Webb, Alex: Black Greensboro registrar

Whitfield, Hampton S.: Lawyer, University of Alabama professor, editor of the Tusca-
   loosa *Reconstructionist*, and superintendent of education for Tuscaloosa County
Williams, L.: Missionary Baptist minister in Jasper
Wilson, James Harrison: Union cavalry commander of the 1865 raid through
   Alabama.
Wirz, Henry: Commandant of the Tuscaloosa prison camp and later of Andersonville
Woodruff, David: Bookseller and Republican mayor of Tuscaloosa
Wyman, William Stokes: University of Alabama's professor of ancient languages
Yancey, William Lowndes: Leading Alabama secessionist

Appendix B: Chronology

1809

January 26   Noah Bartlett Cloud born in Edgefield, South Carolina
February 12   Abraham Lincoln born in Kentucky

1810

May 7   Arad Lakin born in Delaware County, New York

1816

December 20   Shandy Wesley Jones born in Huntsville, Alabama

1825

December 6   Alabama General Assembly designates Tuscaloosa as
                    the seat of government

1831

April 18   University of Alabama enrolls its first students

1835   Cloud graduates from Jefferson University, marries,
                    and opens a pharmacy
October 28   Ryland Randolph born in Clinton, Alabama

1837

July 19   Lakin marries Achsah Labar Newton
December 4   Jones marries Evalina Love

1838   Cloud moves to Alabama

1847

November 1   Alabama's seat of government moves from Tuscaloosa to
                    Montgomery

1850   Ryland Randolph visits Haiti

1852

September 18   Cloud publishes first issue of *American Cotton Planter*

1854

January   Lakin appointed to the Five Points Mission
May 30   President Pierce signs the Kansas-Nebraska Bill

1855

May   Lakin gone from the Five Points Mission
October 23   First Alabama state fair opens

1858   Randolph moves to Montgomery

1861

January 11   Alabama secedes

1865

March 3   Freedmen's Bureau established by Congress in War Department
April 4   University of Alabama burned by Croxton's Raiders
May 9   Nathan Bedford Forrest surrenders his forces at Gainesville,
                     Alabama
July 26   Wager Swayne appointed Commissioner of Freedmen's Bureau
                     for Alabama
September 12   Constitutional Convention convenes
October 1   Lakin preaches in Huntsville
November 20   Alabama General Assembly convenes

1866

June 1   Swayne becomes military commander of Alabama

1867

March 2   First Reconstruction Act passes, over the president's veto,
                     dividing the South into military districts and calling for
                     state constitutional conventions
March 23   Second Reconstruction Act passes, over the president's veto
April 12   Work begins on new UA buildings

June 4	First Alabama Republican Convention convenes
July 19	Third Reconstruction Act passes, over the president's veto, giving commanding generals power to remove state offices and appoint others in their place
August 8	Democratic Conservative Party stops appealing to black voters
October 1	Randolph purchases the *Independent Monitor*
October 1–3	Alabama decides to hold a constitutional convention and selects delegates
October 17	Alabama Conference of the Methodist Episcopal Church established
November 5	Constitutional convention convenes
December 2	Cloud announces intention to run as Republican for superintendent of education
December 30	Klan's first appearance in Tuscaloosa

1868

February 4–7	Referendum to ratify constitution results in thirteen thousand votes short of required minimum
March 11	Fourth Reconstruction Act changes law to provide that majority of votes actually cast would determine ratification of the state constitution
March 28	Balus Eddins attacked by Randolph
March 30	Impeachment trial of President Johnson begins
March 31	O. L. Shepherd succeeds Swayne
May 4	Trial of Randolph begins in Selma
May 14	Randolph returns to Tuscaloosa in triumph
May 26	Senate votes not to convict President Johnson
June 23	Randolph prints an issue of the *Tuscaloosa Monitor* that results in the newspaper's suppression
June 25	Congress declares Alabama's constitution passed with Fourth Reconstruction Act
July 13	Alabama's Republican-dominated general assembly convenes
August 6	Arad Lakin elected president of the University of Alabama
August 28	Arad Lakin and Noah Cloud rebuffed in their attempts to assume leadership of the University of Alabama
September 1	*A Prospective Scene* appears in the Tuskaloosa *Independent Monitor*
September 19	*Cincinnati Commercial* reprints Randolph's woodcut
October 31	Klan attack Republicans in the Huntsville courthouse square
November 3	Presidential election results in victory for Republican U. S. Grant

1869

January 1	All functions of the Freedmen's Bureau discontinued except education
November 15	General Assembly convenes with Randolph in the House

1870

January 25	House votes to expel Randolph
February 2	Randolph marries Katharine Clay Withers
March 31	Republican solicitor Alexander Boyd killed in Eutaw
April 1	Smith-Vaughan-Randolph gunfight ends with Byrd being killed and Randolph losing a leg
April 27	Smith escapes
July 15	Freedmen's Bureau's educational work terminated
November 8	Cloud defeated for reelection as superintendent of education

1871

June 13–14	Lakin testifies before Joint Congressional Committee on Klan activities
September 26	James H. Clanton killed in Knoxville gunfight

1872

January 1	Randolph sells *Independent Monitor*

1875

October 18	Randolph publishes last issue of Tuskaloosa *Blade* and eventually moves to Birmingham
November 5	Noah Cloud dies in Montgomery

1876

October 18	Central Alabama Conference of the Methodist Episcopal Church established with Lakin as secretary

1880

August 28	Randolph shot by A. O. Lane, ending his career

1886

February 4   Shandy Jones dies in Mobile

1890

January 21   Arad Lakin dies in Rockport, Missouri

1903

May 7   Ryland Randolph dies in Birmingham

Appendix C: *A Prospective Scene in the "City of Oaks," 4th of March, 1869*

"Hang, curs, hang! * * * * * *Their* complexion is perfect gallows. Stand fast, good fate to *their* hanging! * * * * * If they be not born to be hanged, our case is miserable."

The above cut represents the fate in store for those great pests of Southern society—the carpet-bagger and the scallawag—if found in Dixie's Land after the break of day on the 4th of March next.

The genus carpet-bagger is a man with a lank head of dry hair, a lank stomach and long legs, club knees and splay feet, dried legs and lank jaws, with eyes like a fish and mouth like a shark. Add to this a habit of sneaking and dodging about in unknown places—habiting with negroes in dark dens and back streets—a look like a hound and the smell of a polecat.

Words are wanting to do full justice to the genus scallawag. He is a cur with a contracted head, downward look, slinking and uneasy gait; sleeps in the woods, like old Crossland, at the bare idea of a Ku-Klux raid.

Our scallawag is the local leper of the community. Unlike the carpet-bagger, he is native, which is so much the worse. Once he was respected in his circle; his head was level, and he would look his neighbor in the face. Now, possessed of the itch of office and the salt rheum of Radicalism, he is a mangy dog, slinking through the alleys, haunting the Governor's office, defiling with tobacco juice the steps of the Capitol, stretching his lazy carcass in the sun on the Square, or the benches of the Mayor's Court.

He waiteth for the troubling of the political waters, to the end that he may step in and be healed of the itch by the ointment of office. For office he "bums" as a toper "bums" for the satisfying dram. For office, yet in prospective, he hath bartered respectability; hath abandoned business, and ceased to labor with his hands, but employs his feet kicking out boot-heels against lamp-post and corner-curb, while discussing the question of office.

It requires no seer to foretell the inevitable events that are to result from the coming Fall election throughout the Southern States.

The unprecedented reaction is moving onward with the swiftness of a velocipede, with the violence of a tornado, and with the crash of an avalanche—sweeping negroism from the face of the earth.

Woe, woe, woe to the inhabiters of Alabama, who have recently become squatter sovereigns, carpet-bags in hand, and they filled with dirty electioneering documents!

And twenty times woe to those so-called Southrons, who have turned their narrow heads, infinitesimal hearts, and filthy hands against the land of their nativity!

Hereafter, when future generations shall contemplate the fate that these white-skinned wretches had in store for us, they will wonder at the extraordinary degree of forbearance manifested by us of the present dark day.

But the happy day of reckoning with these white-cuticle scoundrels approacheth rapidly. Each and every one who has so unblushingly essayed to lower the Caucasian to a degree even beneath the African race, will be regarded as *hostis sui generis*, and be dealt with accordingly, if found hereabout when the time is ripe for action.

The carpet-bagger already begins to sniff the coming ill-wind, and is sneaking out of the country *a la* Harrington, of Mobile. But we hope some boreal stragglers may be left far from their "hums," to swing alongside of their meridional coadjutors in infamy.

We candidly believe, that the picture, given to our readers *ut supra*, correctly represents the attitude and altitude of all foreign and domestic foes of our land, who shall have the folly to remain "down South" after the ides of March. The contract for hanging will be given to the negro; who, having mounted the carpet-bagger and scallawag on the muse that he *didn't* draw at the elections, will tie them to a limb, and, leading the said mule from under them over the *forty acres of ground* that he also didn't get, will leave the vagabonds high in mid air, a feast for anthropophagous vermin.

P.S. It will be seen, that there is room left on the limb for the suspension of any bad Grant negro who may be found at the propitious moment.

Notes

Preface

1. See for example Paul Cimbala and Randall M. Miller, eds., *The Great Task Remaining before Us: Reconstruction as America's Continuing Civil War* (New York: Fordham University Press, 2010). For a general discussion of Reconstruction violence, see George C. Rable, *But There Was No Peace: The Role of Violence in the Politics of Reconstruction* (Athens: University of Georgia Press, 1984).

2. In addition to drawing on R. G. Collingwood's idea of re-enactment (*The Idea of History*, 1946), I am struck by the microhistorians' approach. Among the many theoretical works on the subject, see Edward Muir, "Introduction: Observing Trifes," in *Microhistory and the Lost Peoples of Europe*, edited by Edward Muir and Guido Ruggiero, translated by Eren Branch (Baltimore: The Johns Hopkins University Press, 1991): vii–xxviii; Matti Peltonen, "Clues, Margins, and Monads: The Micro-Macro Link in Historical Research," *History and Theory* 40, no. 3 (2001 October): 347–359; and Richard D. Brown, "Microhistory and the Post-Modern Challenge," *Journal of the Early Republic* 23, no. 1 (2003 spring): 1–20. I dissent from the microhistorians' stress on the utter differences between the past and the present. I am instead very much struck by the relevance of these four individuals' understandings of freedom to our own day.

3. This study of Randolph, Lakin, Cloud, and Jones could have focused on other issues that engage historians today, including masculinity, remembrance, cupidity, violence, resentment, and custom to name but a few. These issues are the subject of excellent books and articles. I have chosen to confine this study to freedom, however, because it is fundamental.

4. Because Randolph, Lakin, Cloud, and Jones did not leave explicit writings on freedom, it was necessary to work backward from actions to motivations; nevertheless, I am convinced that their efforts over many decades attest to their commitment to freedom as they understood it. Revealing their ideas thus proceeds by a process most rigorously developed by the American philosopher Charles Sanders Peirce, who called it *abduction*. Other terms, such as *conjecture* and *historical imagination*, even when heavily qualified, convey an utterly unwarranted caprice and lack of rigor on the part of the historian. Abduction is not guessing, but is rather the mature effort to integrate innumerable, seemingly disjointed details into a whole.

Prologue

1. Market Street is now Greensboro Avenue; Broad Street, sometimes called Main

Street, is now University Boulevard. Let me state plainly that I do not know exactly where Cloud and Lakin met on August 28. Unless otherwise noted, the descriptions of Tuscaloosa in this chapter are taken either from the *Autobiography of James Robert Maxwell of Tuskaloosa, Alabama* (New York: Greenberg, 1926): 31–46; or from Thomas P. Clinton's series of undated newspaper articles collected in a scrapbook deposited in the W. S. Hoole Special Collections Library, University of Alabama. Both Maxwell and Clinton were living in Tuscaloosa in 1868. The general history of Tuscaloosa can be found in many sources, most easily in G. Ward Hubbs, *Tuscaloosa: Portrait of an Alabama County* (Northridge, California: Windsor, 1987).

2. Thomas Maxwell, *Tuskaloosa: The Origin of Its Name* (1876): 81.

3. Tuskaloosa *Independent Monitor* March 7, 1871. The reference to "mouldering ruins" was ironic in that it came from William Wells Brown's *Clotel, or, The President's Daughter* (1853), the first novel written by a black American. Note that instead of littering quotations with "[*sic*]," I have chosen to reproduce quotations in the text exactly as found in the original and to rely on the good sense readers to infer the modern standard equivalent.

4. One of the Leach and Avery cannons stands in front of the Perry County courthouse, Marion.

5. Some of the flavor of Washington Hall and its proprietors can be found in several pieces by southwestern humorist John Gorman Barr, collected in *Rowdy Tales from Early Alabama: The Humor of John Gorman* edited by Hubbs (Tuscaloosa: University of Alabama Press, 1981).

6. The Tuscaloosa prison was under the administration of Henry Wirz. He proved so adept at managing the Yankee prisoners in Tuscaloosa that he was given the camp at Andersonville, Georgia. The "Butcher of Andersonville" became the only Confederate hanged for war crimes after the war's end.

7. David P. Lewis to William Hugh Smith 1868 August 12, Governors' Correspondence, Alabama Department of Archives and History [herinafter ADAH].

8. *Cochran v. The State, Supreme Court of Alabama*, January term, 1857 (30 Ala. 542; 30 Ala 550).

9. *Tuscaloosa Observer* 1871 March 25. Monroe Street, the next street east of Market, toward the university, is now 23rd Avenue; and Madison Street is now 22th Avenue.

10. In 1871 the building housing Glascock's store and the offices of the *Monitor* above it was replaced by the brick First National Bank building, currently a restaurant.

11. Greensboro *Alabama Beacon* 1868 August 22.

12. *Tuscaloosa Times* 1874 September 9.

13. Tuskaloosa *Independent Monitor* 1871 April 26 and May 10.

14. The remaining account of Lakin and Cloud's day is taken from Lakin's testimony, 1871 June 13, as recorded in US Congress, *Testimony Taken by the Joint Select Committee to Inquire into the Condition of Affairs in the Late Insurrectionary States*, 42nd Congress, 2nd session, House Report 22, vol. 8, Alabama [hereinafter *KKK Tes-*

timony, Alabama] (Washington, DC: Government Printing Office, 1872), 112–114.

15. Tuskaloosa *Independent Monitor* 1869 April 13.

16. J. Lawrence Brasher, *The Sanctified South: John Lakin Brasher and the Holiness Movement* (Urbana: University of Illinois Press, 1994), 69; "No. 5—Ala. Conference Members," John Lakin Brasher Papers, Duke University Rare Book, Manuscript, and Special Collections Library.

17. East Margin Street is now Queen City Avenue.

18. If the water were high, he could have boarded either the *Jennie Rogers* or the *Reindeer*, the two steamboats that handled the Black Warrior River traffic. See Tuskaloosa *Independent Monitor* 1869 February 16.

Chapter 1

1. *Ryland Randolph's Scribbles* (c. 1894), unpublished manuscript in the Randolph Papers, Samford University Special Collections: I (p. 1). Randolph gave each essay a roman numeral and, perhaps later, assigned page numbers.

2. The nature of society in the cotton towns is covered in G. Ward Hubbs, *Guarding Greensboro: A Confederate Company in the Making of a Southern Community* (Athens: University of Georgia Press, 2003).

3. Unless otherwise noted, the descriptions and quotations from Ryland Randolph's life through the Civil War are from Randolph's letters to John W. DuBose written between May 1900 and May 1903 now in the John W. DuBose Papers at the Alabama Department of Archives and History (ADAH). These letters have been authoritatively transcribed and arranged into a convenient and scholarly narrative by Sarah Woolfolk Wiggins in "The Life of Ryland Randolph as Seen through His Letters to John W. DuBose," *Alabama Historical Quarterly* 30, nos. 3 and 4 (1968 fall and winter): 145–180.

4. Ryland Randolph seems to have had at least five siblings, three of whom did not live long. See Ellen Goode Winslow, *History of Perquimans County* (Raleigh: Edwards & Broughton, 1931), 357.

5. This incident is recounted in Kenneth S. Greenberg, *Honor & Slavery: Lies, Duels, Noses, Masks, Dressing as a Woman, Gifts, Strangers, Humanitarianism, Death, Slave Rebellions, the Proslavery Argument, Baseball, Hunting, and Gambling in the Old South* (Princeton: Princeton University Press, 1996), 20–22.

6. Randolph, *Scribbles*, III (p. 25).

7. From Victor Randolph's obituary in the *Tuskaloosa Gazette* 1876 February 10, almost certainly written by Ryland Randolph.

8. See Hubbs, *Guarding Greensboro*, 57–61.

9. What Ryland Randolph did not know was that Lemonade and Marmalade were actual places in Haiti.

10. Captain Victor M. Randolph to Richard Randolph, Forkland, Alabama, 1858 October 2, typescript in Randolph Papers, Samford University.

11. The incident is also recounted in an unidentified fragment, written in Ryland Randolph's hand, in the Randolph Papers, Samford University.

12. Where Randolph, both father and son, saw a ludicrous imposter, modern historians have seen in Soulouque a capable ruler who used the trappings of European royalty to great advantage. See John E. Baur, "Faustin Soulouque, Emperor of Haiti: His Character and His Reign," *The Americas* 6, no. 2 (1959 October): 131–166; and Murdo MacLeod, "The Soulouque Regime in Haiti, 1847–1859: A Reevaluation," *Caribbean Studies* 10, no 3 (1970 October): 35–48. MacLeod concludes that "Soulouque was a man of high intelligence, a realist, a pragmatist, and a superb, if ruthless politician and diplomat" (p. 47).

13. Randolph, *Scribbles*, IV (pp. 27–29); 1860 US Manuscript Census, Slave Schedule, First District, Montgomery County, Alabama, p. 189.

14. Randolph, *Scribbles*, IV (pp. 29–30).

15. *Montgomery Mail* 1860 November 22, 26, December 7, 14, as quoted in Nancy Anne Sindon, "The Career of Ryland Randolph: A Study in Reconstruction Journalism" (master's thesis, Florida State University, 1965), 11.

16. Randolph, *Scribbles*, III (p. 25). For more detail on a corresponding elite company, the Greensboro Guards, its relationship to slavery, and activities during the secession crisis, see Hubbs, *Guarding Greensboro*, chapter 4, "Guards and Slaves," and chapter 5, "One Voice."

17. Notes entitled "Record of the service of former Capt Victor M. Randolph, US Navy," in the Randolph Papers, Samford University; Randolph, *Scribbles*, III (p. 26); "The Mounted Rifles," reprinted in the *Birmingham Argus* from an undated *Montgomery Advertiser* article, in V. M. Randolph, Jr., Scrapbook 413, Birmingham Public Library; *Montgomery Mail* 1861 April 23, 27; *Tuskaloosa Gazette* 1876 February 10; private correspondence from Alan Pitts; *Montgomery Advertiser* 1861 May 1; US National Archives, Compiled Military Service Records, "First Alabama Cavalry" (reel #3) and "Goldwaite's Battery, Light Artillery (reel #74).

18. Gladys Ward, "Life of Ryland Randolph," (master's thesis, University of Alabama, 1932), 5.

19. *The War of the Rebellion: A Compilation of the Official Records of the Union and Confederate Armies* [hereinafter cited as *O.R.*] (Washington, DC: Government Printing Office, 1880–1901), series 1, volume 26, part 2, pp. 548–557; series 1, volume 39, part 2, pp. 588–589; *Mobile Tribune* 1864 January 10. The Peace Society and Alabama's Unionist movement in general is the chief subject of Christopher Lyle McIlwain's forthcoming work, *Civil War Alabama*.

20. *Mobile Tribune* 1864 April 10; *Mobile Register and Advertiser* 1864 April 21; William Stanley Hoole, ed., *History of the Seventh Alabama Cavalry Regiment, Including Capt. Charles P. Storrs's Troop of University of Alabama Cadet Volunteers* (University, Alabama: Confederate Publishing Company, 1984), 4; *O.R.*, series 1, volume 35, part 1, pp. 413–419; *Montgomery Advertiser* 1864 November 25.

21. *O.R.*, series 1, volume 39, part 2, p. 874.

22. Randolph's account of his "dangerous service" has all the hallmarks of self-promotion. For a more sympathetic view of soldiers writing of their experiences, see Carol Reardon, "Writing Battle History: The Challenge of Memory," *Civil War History* 53, no. 3 (2007 September): 252–263.

23. Montgomery *Alabama State Journal* 1869 September 20; Thomas P. Clinton, "Clinton Relates Yank Professors' Local Struggles," *West Alabama Breeze* 1928 March 15. See Randolph's response to Forrest in the *Mobile Register* 1869 October 16.

24. *Montgomery Advertiser* 1865 October 27, reprinted from the *New York Tribune*.

25. Greensboro *Alabama Beacon* 1865 September 15.

26. This account of Greensboro following the Civil War is taken from Hubbs, *Guarding Greensboro*, chapter 10, "The Loyal Community."

Some might question black voting in Alabama before the ratification of the Fifteenth Amendment. The Reconstruction Act of March 1867 empowered black males to vote in the election of delegates to state constitutional conventions. Alabama's Constitution of 1868 extended black suffrage to subsequent elections. The Fifteenth Amendment, ratified in 1870, preserved those rights by disallowing amendments to future state constitutions that would restrict voting on the basis of race.

27. Randolph, *Scribbles*, XIV (p. 97); *Montgomery Advertiser* 1867 April 17.

28. Unless otherwise noted, this description of Tuscaloosa is taken from G. Ward Hubbs, *Tuscaloosa: Portrait of an Alabama County* (Northridge, California: Windsor, 1987), chapter 3, "Alabama's Capital."

29. G. Ward Hubbs, "'Dissipating the Clouds of Ignorance' The First University of Alabama Library, 1831–1865," *Libraries and Culture* 27, no. 1 (1992 winter): 20–35.

30. John Witherspoon DuBose, *Alabama's Tragic Decade: Ten Years of Alabama, 1865–1874*, ed. James K. Greer (Birmingham: Webb, 1940), 232; *Report of the Ladies' Southern Relief Association of Maryland, September 1st, 1866* (Baltimore: Kelly and Piet, 1866), 12.

31. Now University Boulevard and Twenty-Third Street.

32. Probably false. Glascock and Randolph, for example, were of similar minds. As soon as the Union garrison had temporarily left in 1866, Glascock "headed a party of 'roughs,' (late Rebel Soldiers &c) some of them armed" who started trying to run politically active freedmen out of town. See Mobile *Nationalist* 1866 May 17; Wm. H. H. Peck to Col. C. Cadle, 1866 April 18, Records of the Assistant Commissioner for the State of Alabama, Bureau of Refugees, Freedmen, and Abandoned Lands, 1865–1870 (hereinafter Freedmen's Bureau Papers), reel 809, roll 18, "Reports of Operations from the Subdivisions from the Subdistricts September 1865–December 1868."

33. Randolph, *Scribbles*, XIV (p. 98).

34. *Montgomery Advertiser* 1863 December 5; Wiggins, "Life of Ryland Randolph," 157.

35. See Samuel L. Webb, "A Jacksonian Democrat in Postbellum Alabama: The Ideology and Influence of Journalist Robert McKee, 1869–1896," *Journal of Southern*

History 62, no. 2 (1996 May): 239–274; Ted Tunnell, "Creating 'the Propaganda of History': Southern Editors and the Origins of Carpetbagger and Scalawag," *Journal of Southern History* 62, no. 4 (2006 November): 789–822. Hodgson became editor of *Montgomery Mail* in fall 1865.

36. My thanks to Frances Roberts for her willingness to share her expertise in these and other matters.

37. Tuskaloosa *Independent Monitor* 1867 October 30; 1869 January 12; Randolph, *Scribbles*, XIV (pp. 101, 102).

38. My understanding of Romanticism is based on Isaiah Berlin's essay, "The Romantic Revolution: A Crisis in the History of Modern Thought," in *The Sense of Reality: Studies in Ideas and Their History* (New York: Farrar, Straus and Giroux, 1996). The Romantic Revolution began the late eighteenth century, writes Berlin, when some asserted that values were not to be discovered but to be created. Expressing one's will then moved front and center; being free thus became "the condition of being human" (p. 179).

39. Ryland Randolph, "Autobiographical Episodes," in Ryland Randolph to John W. DuBose 1900 May 21, Dubose Papers, ADAH. Only two months before Randolph took over the reins of the *Monitor*, the state Democratic Conservative Party had decided no longer to appeal to black voters and to become entirely a white man's party. See the Mobile *Nationalist* 1867 August 8.

40. Other more or less formal duels would include John Mason Martin, G. Garnett Andrews, George D. Johnston, and J. C. Loomis; see his *Scribbles*, XIV (p. 105); His many less structured personal confrontations included those with Dennis Dykous, William Smith, Joseph W. Taylor (a committed Democrat), and Balus Eddins.

41. Tuskaloosa *Independent Monitor* 1867 October 30; *Scribbles*, XIV (p. 105), XVI (p. 115); Randolph, "Autobiographical Episodes," ADAH. No copies of the Tuscaloosa *Reconstructionist* have survived.

42. Tuscaloosa *Independent Monitor* 1867 December 4; Michael W. Fitzgerald, "Radical Republicanism and the White Yeomanry during Alabama Reconstruction, 1865–1868," *Journal of Southern History* 54, no. 3 (1988 November): 586–590.

43. Tuscaloosa *Independent Monitor* 1867 December 4; 1868 February 19, March 4; Fitzgerald, "Radical Republicanism," 593.

44. Tuscaloosa *Independent Monitor* 1868 January 22, March 18, 25, April 1.

45. Randolph, *Scribbles*, XIII (pp. 84–86); Randolph to Walter L. Fleming, 1901 August 21, Walter L. Fleming Papers, New York Public Library Manuscripts and Archives Division. Randolph's memory of the Klansmen's sheets is inconsistent with contemporary images that depict Klansmen disguised in varied, vaguely Oriental robes. See the photograph in chapter 2.

46. For a general discussion of Reconstruction violence, see Rable, *But There Was No Peace*. Rable agrees but argues further that the Klan's stature exceeded its achievements (pp. 95, 110).

47. This account of the Balus Eddins attack is taken from Randolph, *Scribbles*, XIII (pp. 86–91); and Randolph, "Autobiographical Episodes," ADAH.

48. This account of Randolph's trial is taken from Mike Daniel, "The Arrest and Trial of Ryland Randolph, April–May 1868," *Alabama Historical Quarterly* 49, nos. 3–4 (1978 fall and winter): 127–143.

49. Shepherd quickly issued orders against the Klan, which drove the secret organization further underground. See Allen W. Trelease, *White Terror: The Ku Klux Klan Conspiracy and Southern Reconstruction* (New York: Harper and Row, 1971), 87.

50. Tuskaloosa *Independent Monitor* 1868 May 10.

51. *Montgomery Advertiser* 1868 May 15; Greensboro *Alabama Beacon* 1868 May 16.

52. Tuskaloosa *Independent Monitor* 1867 December 18; see also 1868 June 16. All of Randolph's woodcuts are reproduced, along with well researched commentary, in Sarah Van V. Woolfolk, "The Political Cartoons of the Tuskaloosa *Independent Monitor* and Tuskaloosa *Blade*, 1867–1873," *Alabama Historical Quarterly* 27, nos. 3 and 4 (1965 fall and winter): 140–165.

53. *Mobile Register* 1868 June 27, July 29; *Montgomery Advertiser* 1868 June 27; Randolph, "Autobiographical Episodes," ADAH; R. Blair to O. L. Shepherd, 1868 August, Freedmen's Bureau Papers, reel 809, roll 14, "Letters Received, 1865–1870."

54. *Montgomery Advertiser* 1865 October 18.

55. Alabama had created a rudimentary system of public education in the 1850s, but it was not revived after the war.

56. *Montgomery Advertiser* 1868 August 8; Tuskaloosa *Independent Monitor* 1868 August 11, 18.

57. *Cincinnati Campaign Commercial* 1868 September 21, 28; Tuskaloosa *Independent Monitor* 1871 May 10; *Cleveland Herald* 1868 September 23.

58. *Montgomery Advertiser* 1868 September 27.

59. *Mobile Register* 1868 September 14, 19, 26, 29; Montgomery *Alabama State Journal* 1868 October 1.

60. *Mobile Register* 1868 October 10; *Cincinnati Commercial* Supplement 1868 October 10. *Devil* is a colloquial term for an apprentice in a print shop; Randolph may have used the term here as a pun.

61. Randolph had even been a delegate to the state convention; see *Montgomery Advertiser* 1868 June 1.

62. Montgomery *Alabama State Journal* 1868 October 2, 1869 May 21; *San Francisco Evening Bulletin* 1868 November 2; *Bangor Whig & Courier* 1868 October 30.

63. Montgomery *Alabama State Journal* 1868 November 18; R. Blaire to Edwin Beecher, 1868 November 15, Freedmen's Bureau Papers, microfilm 809, reel 18, "Reports of Operations from the Subdivisions from the Subdistricts, September 1865–December 1868." Crossland was apparently replaced by C. C. Page. Montgomery *Alabama State Journal* 1869 May 13, 22; Mobile *Nationalist* 1869 May 17.

64. Tuskaloosa *Independent Monitor* 1869 January 5.

65. *Ibid.,* 1869 February 9, 16.

66. Randolph, "Autobiographical Episodes," ADAH; Tuskaloosa *Independent Monitor* 1869 April 6, July 5; James B. Sellers, *History of the University of Alabama,* Volume I, 1818–1902 (University: University of Alabama Press, 1953), 303–304; Tuskaloosa *Independent Monitor* 1869 July 13.

67. Randolph, "Autobiographical Episodes," ADAH; Randolph, *Scribbles,* V (pp. 31–35), IX (p. 70).

68. Randolph, *Scribbles,* XV (pp. 109–113); Randolph to Dubose, 1903 March 10, Dubose Papers, ADAH; Montgomery *Alabama State Journal* 1869 November 6.

69. Randolph to Dubose, date unknown, Dubose Papers, ADAH; Tuskaloosa *Independent Monitor* 1869 August 10; Ryland Randolph to "Miss Kate," 1869 December 4, Randolph Papers, Samford University.

70. Ward, "Life of Ryland Randolph," 44–47.

71. Tuskaloosa *Independent Monitor* 1870 February 1. My thanks to Chris McIlwain of Tuscaloosa for explaining the significance of Randolph's bill.

72. "Speech delivered by R. Randolph . . . ," DuBose Papers, ADAH, reprinted in DuBose, *Alabama's Tragic Decade,* 282–285; Tuskaloosa *Independent Monitor* 1870 February 1; *Journal of the Session of 1869–70 of the House of Representatives of the State of Alabama Held in the City of Montgomery Commencing on the Third Monday in November, 1869* (Montgomery: Stokes, 1870), 319–320.

73. "Mrs. Ryland Randolph," unidentified obituary notice in the Randolph papers, Samford University; Randolph, *Scribbles,* VII (p. 48); Virginia Clay-Clopton, *A Belle of the Fifties: Memoirs of Mrs. Clay of Alabama, Covering Social and Political Life in Washington and the South, 1853–66* (New York: Doubleday, Page, 1904), 127.

74. Montgomery *Alabama State Journal* 1869 November 6; Randolph, *Scribbles,* I (pp. 1–8).

75. Unless otherwise noted, this account of the attempted assassination of Randolph is taken from Randolph, *Scribbles,* XVII (pp. 117–126); Randolph, "Autobiographical Episodes," ADAH; Tuskaloosa *Independent Monitor* 1870 April 5, April 26; D. W. McIver, "Col. Ryland Randolph Dies in Birmingham," *Montgomery Advertiser,* undated but approximately 1903 May 10; Jerome Schweitzer, "Ryland Randolph's Life Shows Vivid Record of Many Battles," *West Alabama Breeze* 1927 July 7. It is important to remember that virtually every account of the assassination attempt is written by either Randolph or his defenders.

76. Unidentified fragment dated 1902 October 28 in the Randolph Papers, Samford University.

77. Tuskaloosa *Independent Monitor* 1869 July 20.

78. William Warren Rogers, Jr., *Black Belt Scalawag: Charles Hays and the Southern Republicans in the Era of Reconstruction* (Athens: University of Georgia Press, 1993), 63; Tuskaloosa *Independent Monitor* 1870 April 12.

79. Tuskaloosa *Independent Monitor* 1869 November 9.

80. Cornelia Bibb Vaughan to William Hugh Smith, 1870 April 20, Governors' Correspondence, ADAH.

81. Tuskaloosa *Independent Monitor* 1870 April 12, May 3, 17, July 26, November 8; Montgomery *Alabama State Journal* 1870 April 29, July 17.

82. Montgomery *Alabama State Journal* 1870 September 13; *Mobile Register* 1870 September 6.

83. Susan Lawrence Davis, *Authentic History, Ku Klux Klan, 1865–1877* (New York: published by the author, 1924), 45.

84. Randolph, *Scribbles*, XVIII (pp. 126–129); Randolph, "Autobiographical Episodes," ADAH. Before starting the *Blade*, Randolph made a trip to Waco, Texas, presumably to visit family; see [Chicago] *Pomeroy's Democrat* 1872 February 10.

85. He seems first to have moved to St. Clair Springs, Alabama, where he constructed a small hotel and seven cottages; see James Frederick Sulzby, *Historic Alabama Hotels and Resorts* (University: University of Alabama Press, 1960), 219.

86. Sindon, "Career of Ryland Randolph," 99–102.

87. Fischer, *Liberty and Freedom*, 4–13. The world *liberty*, by contrast, comes from a Latin word that means either unbounded or released from restraint. That English confounds the meaning of the two words is significant, and I have concluded to continue in that vein.

88. These new and impersonal economic forces require some explanation because they often seem to loom larger than others. Farmers and those in household economies saw a direct relationship between effort and results. But when wealth started to be based on investments, management of accounts and workers, banking, and those sorts of things, the relationship of effort to result was hard to fathom. Wealth had traditionally been thought largely incapable of being created except through labor. Those who were getting rich, those who were becoming powerful, could only be advancing at the expense of those who toiled. If this were not unnatural, nothing was. Economic inequality would remain a ready gauge for the people to use in naming their tyrants.

89. That those who were not included in the community were presumed to lack freedom was the essence of the 1857 *Dred Scott v. Sandford* decision rendered by the majority Jacksonian Supreme Court justices. The French Revolution provides a striking example of the way that the people's freedom required an opposite. Despite the Declaration of the Rights of Man and Citizen, the French quickly "required outsiders in order to define its limits and to give insiders a sense of their own bonds." Because a citizen's moral obligations became to unmask these outsiders, these conspiring enemies of the people masquerading as honest Frenchmen, the country was quickly divided into two camps: patriots and the traitors who were quickly identified with the aristocrats. The success of liberty came to depend on rooting out "Uncitizens," first through humiliation and abuse, often through the manipulation of visual images,

and then the guillotine—the ultimate machine of liberation. Here was Randolph's people's freedom with a vengeance. See Simon Schama, *Citizens: A Chronicle of the French Revolution* (New York: Knopf, 1989), 291–292, 492, 859–860.

90. Among many fine works, Edmund Sears Morgan's *American Slavery, American Freedom: The Ordeal of Colonial Virginia* (New York: Norton, 1975) stands out.

91. Wade Hampton III to President Andrew Johnson, 1866 August 25, in *Family Letters of the Three Wade Hamptons, 1782–1901*, ed. Charles Edward Cauthen (Columbia: University of South Carolina Press, 1953), 135–136.

92. Hubbs, *Guarding Greensboro*, 202.

93. Randolph, *Scribbles*, XIX (pp. 132–133).

94. Randolph's wife died 1901 April 27 according to an undated clipping in the Randolph Papers, Samford University; Randolph to Dubose, 1903 April 29, Dubose Papers, ADAH; *West Alabama Breeze* 1927 July 7.

Chapter 2

1. "Manuscript Number One Concerning Dr. Arad S. Lakin . . . ," Lakin Collection, North Alabama Conference Archive of the United Methodist Church, Birmingham-Southern College (NAC Archive); the introductory first chapter has long been missing. The story behind this typescript is long; suffice it to say that the original manuscript passed down through the family until a typescript was presented to the North Alabama Conference Archive in the 1950s. The location of the original is unknown. Because the typescript shows unmistakable errors of transcription (reversed letters and the like), I have taken the liberty of correcting what I believe are obviously introduced mistakes and of adding punctuation. Internal evidence suggests that Manuscript Number One was written in the third person by Lakin himself while he was at the Five Points mission, probably late 1854. Unless otherwise noted, this biographical account of Lakin's life until he left New York City, closely paraphrases this manuscript.

2. The standard work, upon which others have built, is Whitney R. Cross, *The Burned-Over District: The Social and Intellectual History of Enthusiastic Religion in Western New York, 1800–1850* (New York: Harper & Row, 1950).

3. Discrepancies in Lakin's New York Conference appointments abound. Relying on the New York Conference journals from 1840–1855 and on other contemporary documents, he seems to have served: the Deposit Circuit, Delaware District (first appointed 1835); Bloomville Circuit, Delaware District (1837); Jefferson Circuit, Delaware District (1838); Prattville Circuit, Delaware District (1841); Durham Circuit, Greene County (1844); Second Street Church, New York City District (1846); New Paltz and Plattekill, Newburg District (1848); Montgomery Church, Orange County (1850); Manhattanville Mission, Harlem (1852); Five Points Mission, New York City District (1854). He withdrew from the New York Conference in 1855 and in 1858 was listed as a local preacher in Peru, Indiana.

4. Lakin would be appointed to the New York Conference's "mite-money and ten cent collection committee" in 1850; see *Zion's Herald and Wesleyan Journal* 1850 May 15.

5. Jonas died about a year later, in his eighty-fourth year.

6. Ladies of the Mission, *The Old Brewery and the New Mission House at Five Points* (New York: Stringer & Townsend, 1854), 34. The Old Brewery at Five Points figures prominently in Martin Scorsese's unspeakably violent 2002 motion picture *Gangs of New York*.

7. *Ibid.*, 36–37; in addition to Lakin's account in Manuscript Number One, this description of the Five Points Mission is taken from Tyler Anbinder, *Five Points: The 19th-Century New York City Neighborhood That Invented Tap Dance, Stole Elections, and Became the World's Most Notorious Slum* (New York: Free Press, 2001), 241–268. See also Carroll Smith Rosenberg, *Religion and the Rise of the American City: The New York City Mission Movement, 1812–1870* (Ithaca: Cornell University Press, 1971), chapter 8, "The Five Points House of Industry."

8. Ladies of the Mission, *The Old Brewery*, 40–41, 300–301.

9. *Ibid.*, 49, 53.

10. There is some confusion on this point. The *New York Christian Advocate and Journal* of 1855 February 22 and others have him replacing Pease, but this is contradicted by Lakin and other sources. In 1853 the Reverend B. M. Adams was also appointed to the Five Points Mission along with Lakin.

11. *New York Christian Advocate and Journal* 1854 October 19, November 2, 9, 16, 1855 February 22; *New York Times* 1853 February 3.

12. The standard work is Timothy L. Smith, *Revivalism and Social Reform: American Protestantism on the Eve of the Civil War* (New York: Harper and Row, 1957). I have also relied on J. Lawrence Brasher, *The Sanctified South: John Lakin Brasher and the Holiness Movement* (Urbana: University of Illinois Press, 1994), especially chapter 4, "Popular Perfectionism: The Holiness Movement."

13. Five Points Mission Records, General Commission on Archives and History, Drew University; *New York Christian Advocate and Journal* 1855 May 24.

14. According to the 1850 US Manuscript Census, one A. S. Lakin, age forty, was living with his wife Mary in Rush County, Indiana; but Rush County is a hundred miles from Peru. I could find no relationship between these Lakins and Arad and Achsah Lakin. Fifteen years later Democrats charged that Lakin had been forced to leave New York after an affair with a niece or sister-in-law, but no evidence was brought forth. See US Congress, *Testimony Taken by the Joint Select Committee to Inquire into the Condition of Affairs in the Late Insurrectionary States*, 42d Congress, 2d Session, House Report 22, vol. 8, Alabama (hereinafter *KKK Testimony*), 793.

15. Giles W. Smith, *History of Methodism in Peru, Indiana* (Peru: Official Board of the M.E. Church of Peru, Indiana, 1906), 34, 35, 42. I want to thank Frances Lease, Historian of the Main Street United Methodist Church for touring me around Peru and for generously providing the background on the Peru churches.

16. Unless otherwise noted, this account of Lakin's activities during the Civil War comes from *A Biographical History of Nodaway and Atchison Counties, Missouri: Compendium of National Biography* (Chicago: Lewis, 1901), 264–265.

17. *Rochester* [Indiana] *Chronicle* 1863 February 12; *Rochester* [Indiana] *Sentinel* 1863 February 21.

18. *KKK Testimony*, 8:121.

19. As quoted in Daniel W. Stowell, *Rebuilding Zion: The Religious Reconstruction of the South, 1863–1877* (New York: Oxford University Press, 1998), 28. In characterizing the Northern Methodist understanding of the war, I have relied on Stowell's *Rebuilding Zion*, and on Ralph E. Morrow's *Northern Methodism and Reconstruction* (East Lansing: Michigan State University Press, 1956).

20. Walter Clopton Harriss to Francis Harris, Jr., 1861 May 17, quoted in Sara S. Frear, "'You My Brother Will Be Glad with Me': The Letters of Augusta Jane Evans to Walter Clopton Harriss, January 29, 1856, to October 29, 185[8?]," *Alabama Review* 60, no. 2 (2007 April): 121.

21. As quoted in Stowell, *Rebuilding Zion*, p. 54; Cincinnati *Western Christian Advocate* 1865 February 22.

22. *Mobile Register and Advertiser* 1865 August 29.

23. George C. Rable, *God's Almost Chosen Peoples: A Religious History of the American Civil War* (Chapel Hill: University of North Carolina Press, 2010), 333.

24. Cincinnati *Western Christian Advocate* 1865 February 22.

25. *Forty-Sixth Annual Report of The Missionary Society of the Methodist Episcopal Church for the Year 1864* (New York: The Society, 1865), 102; Morrow, *Northern Methodism*, p. 42.

26. *Forty-Seventh Annual Report of The Missionary Society . . . 1865*, 152. Bishop Clark reorganized the Middle Department in late 1866 or early 1867, moving Superintendent J. F. Chalfant from Huntsville to Atlanta and establishing four districts. The two Alabama districts would be Talladega, under Presiding Elder J. W. Talley, and Huntsville, under Presiding Elder Lakin. For much of the time, Lakin was the only presiding elder in Alabama.

Other ministers cropped up from time to time, for example the Reverend Howell Echells, but these people generally did not last long enough to warrant mention; see *Zion's Herald and Wesleyan Journal* 1866 March 7.

27. Cincinnati *Western Christian Advocate* 1864 June 24.

28. *Huntsville Independent* 1865 September 30, November 23; *KKK Testimony*, 8:124, 154; A. S. Lakin to J. F. Chalfant 1866 October 1, as quoted in Michael W. Fitzgerald, *The Union League Movement in the Deep South: Politics and Agricultural Change During Reconstruction* (Baton Rouge: Louisiana State University Press, 1989), 19. I have been unable to locate the original of this particular letter. The original Lakin letters to Chalfant are supposed to be in the Freedmen's Aid Society Correspondence, Gammon Theological Seminary Archives, Woodruff Center Library, Atlanta Univer-

sity. Despite repeated attempts, however, the archivists were never able to find this correspondence. Fortunately, the Amistad Research Center, Tulane University, had photocopies of most of the letters, which the archivists kindly made available to me.

29. A. S. Lakin to J. F. Chalfant 1865 December 14, Freedmen's Aid Society Correspondence, Amistad; Cincinnati *Western Christian Advocate* 1866 January 17. "Occasional" also signed the article describing the establishment of the Alabama Conference in the 1867 October 30 issue of the *Western Christian Advocate*.

30. A. S. Lakin to J. F. Chalfant, 1866 February 24, Freedmen's Aid Society Correspondence, Amistad; Cincinnati *Western Christian Advocate* 1866 July 25; *Montgomery Advertiser* 1866 July 8. The lot, purchased by the Missionary Society and recorded 1866 September 7, was on North Jefferson Street; see "Highlights of the History of Lakeside United Methodist Church," 1983 September 14, unpublished manuscript, NAC Archive.

31. Lakin to Chalfant 1866 August 27, Freedmen's Aid Society Correspondence, Amistad.

32. A. S. Lakin to J. F. Chalfant, 1866 March 13, Freedmen's Aid Society Correspondence, Amistad. An interesting series of public letters castigating James Chalfant were written to the *Huntsville Independent* following the publication of excerpts from his quarterly report from April 1866 (Chalfant was then superintendent of missions of the Methodist Episcopal Church in Western Georgia and Alabama); see *Huntsville Independent* 1866 June 3, 8, 12.

33. J. B. Callis to Wager Swayne 1866 June 7, Freedmen's Bureau Papers, reel 809, roll 18, "Reports of Operations from the Subdivisions from the Subdistricts September 1865-December 1868."

34. *KKK Testimony*, 8:746.

35. *Huntsville Independent* 1866 May 1.

36. *Huntsville Advocate* 1866 August 4, as quoted in Peter Kolchin, *First Freedom: The Responses of Alabama's Blacks to Emancipation and Reconstruction* (Westport, Connecticut: Greenwood, 1972), 153.

37. Lakin to Chalfant 1866 August 24, August 27, September 5, Freedmen's Aid Society Correspondence, Amistad.

38. Cincinnati *Western Christian Advocate* 1866 August 15, 22. Other denominations—the Congregationalists, Presbyterians, Episcopalians, and Quakers—had already established their own societies.

39. *Ibid.*, 1866 August 29, November 28, 1868 August 26; Montgomery *Alabama State Journal* 1869 August 25; *Annual Report of the Freedmen's Aid Society of the Methodist Episcopal Church* (Cincinnati: Western Methodist Book Concern), Second Report for 1867–1868, Third for 1869, Fourth for 1870, and Fifth for 1871; James P. Brawley, *Two Centuries of Methodist Concern: Bondage, Freedom and Education of Black People* (New York: Vantage, 1974), 491–492; *KKK Testimony*, 8:139. Rust Institute was the third normal school established by the Freedmen's Aid Society. The

Society established many more traditional schools, including three in Alabama: in Huntsville, Decatur, and Bluffton. Rust Institute became Rust Normal Institute, Rust Biblical and Normal Institute, Central Alabama Academy, and Central Alabama College. In 1904 it was moved to Birmingham and closed its doors in 1923.

40. *New York Christian Advocate* 1866 September 13, as quoted in William W. Sweet, "Methodist Church Influence in Southern Politics," *Mississippi Valley Historical Review* 1, no. 4 (1915 March): 553; A. S. Lakin to J. F. Chalfant 1867 March 23, Freedmen's Aid Society Correspondence, Amistad.

41. A. S. Lakin to W. Swayne 1867 March 25, in Freedmen's Bureau Papers, reel 809, roll 11, "Letters Received, 1865–1870."

42. A. S. Lakin to J. F. Chalfant 1867 March 29, Freedmen's Aid Society Correspondence, Amistad.

43. Lakin nominated the Reverend Alfred Barnett, Sr.; see Joseph C. Bradley to Major Swayne 1867 April 18, Governors' Correspondence, ADAH.

44. A. S. Lakin to Maj. Genl. J[ohn] Pope 1867 October 8, Governors' Correspondence, US District of Alabama, Wager Swayne, 1867–1868, Governors' Administrative Files SG023075, folder 16, ADAH.

45. A S Lakin to Maj Gen Swayne 1867 November 25, US District of Alabama, Wager T. Swayne, 1867–1868, Governors' Administrative Files SG023075, folder 18, ADAH.

46. A. S. Lakin to J. F. Chalfant 1867 May 28, Freedmen's Aid Society Correspondence, Amistad.

47. A. S. Lakin to J. F. Chalfant 1867 May 29, June 24, Freedmen's Aid Society Correspondence, Amistad; Cincinnati *Western Christian Advocate* 1867 July 10; *KKK Testimony*, 8:135.

48. Ralph E. Morrow, "Northern Methodism in the South during Reconstruction," *Mississippi Valley Historical Review* 41, no. 2 (1954 September): 210–211; *Harper's Weekly* 1866 October 6; A. S. Lakin to J. F. Chalfant 1867 May 28, Freedmen's Aid Society Correspondence, Amistad; Greensboro *Alabama Beacon* 1867 June 1.

49. *Zion's Herald and Wesleyan Journal* 1867 June 5; Cincinnati *Western Christian Advocate* 1867 July 10.

50. Robin W. Minor to President Andrew Johnson 1867 December 14, in *The Papers of Andrew Johnson*, ed. Paul H. Bergeron, vol. 13 (Knoxville: University of Tennessee Press, 1996), 346.

51. A. S. Lakin to J. F. Chalfant 1867 September 26, Freedmen's Aid Society Correspondence, Amistad; Cincinnati *Western Christian Advocate* 1867 July 10.

52. Cincinnati *Western Christian Advocate* 1867 August 14, October 30; Manuscript Journal of the Alabama Conference of the Methodist Episcopal Church, 1867, NAC Archive; *Minutes of the Annual Conferences of the Methodist Episcopal Church for the Year 1866* (New York: Carlton & Lanahan, 1868), 270–271; Kolchin, *First Freedom*, 115. Among the thirty-six probationary clergy was Benjamin Inge, who a

few weeks later would serve as a black delegate from Huntsville to the constitutional convention.

53. John H. Parrish to Henry Watson, Jr., 1868 April 16, Watson Papers, Rare Book, Manuscript, and Special Collections Library, Duke University.

54. *Journal of the Board of Education of the State of Alabama; together with the Laws and Proceedings of the Board of Regents of the University of Alabama* (Montgomery: Stokes, 1869), 12, 13, 17, 24, 29, 44.

55. Talladega *Alabama Reporter* 1868 August 26; David P. Lewis to William Hugh Smith 1868 August 12, Governors' Correspondence, ADAH; *Huntsville Advocate* 1868 September 29.

56. "Manuscript Number Two Concerning Dr. Arad S. Lakin," NAC Archive. In his testimony, Lakin put the date of KKK activity as commencing in March and April of 1868; see *KKK Testimony*, 8:135.

57. *Mobile Register* 1868 September 29; Cincinnati *Western Christian Advocate* 1868 October 14.

58. *KKK Testimony*, 8:114–115.

59. *Ibid.*, 8:116, 142–143; *Huntsville Democrat* 1868 November 10, as quoted in *KKK Testimony*, 8:153.

60. *New York Christian Advocate* 1871 November 23.

61. This account of the Moses Sullivan episode is taken from *New York Christian Advocate* 1869 June 10 (reprinted from the *Atlanta Advocate*); and from *KKK Testimony*, 8:123–124, 127, 146–148. Several of the dates in the testimony are wrong

62. *KKK Testimony*, 8:128, 148, 155–156, 164–165, 181, 136–137. Lakin mistakenly refers to Isaac Dorman as James Dorman.

63. *Ibid.*, 117.

64. *Ibid.*, 117–118, 730–732; US District Court Records, Northern District of Alabama, Northeastern Division, Huntsville, Criminal Case Files, 1865–1877. RG21, Box 1, Case Number 67.

65. *KKK Testimony*, 8:118–121, 732, 759.

66. *Ibid.*, 180, 208, 219.

67. *Ibid.*, 238, 253.

68. *Ibid.*, 784–785.

69. *Ibid.*, 148, 575–576.

70. *Ibid.*, 744–761.

71. *Ibid.*, 426, 430, 433–434, 440; Speed's testimony is found on pp. 417–462.

72. *Ibid.*, 1168–1169.

73. Northwest Indiana Conference, *Minutes of the Fourteenth Annual Session of the North-West Indiana Conference of the Methodist Episcopal Church, Held at Attica, Indiana, September 6–11, 1865* (Cincinnati: R. P. Thompson, 1865), 39–40; *Montgomery Advertiser* 1865 July 30; George Prentice, *The Life of Gilbert Haven: Bishop of the Methodist Episcopal Church* (New York: Philips & Hunt; Cincinnati: Walden & Stowe,

1884), 414; untitled John Lakin Brasher statement (1935), John Lakin Brasher Papers, Box 42, Church History A-G, Duke University Rare Book, Manuscript, and Special Collections Library.

74. *Mobile Register* 1874 September 16.

75. Mobile *Nationalist* 1866 July 12.

76. Methodist Episcopal Church General Conference, 1864 *Journal*, 252–253; Cincinnati *Western Christian Advocate* 1865 June 7, 1868 May 27; Methodist Episcopal Church, *Journal of the General Conference* (New York: Nelson & Phillips, 1876), 113, 329–332.

77. From at least 1879 to 1882, however, Lakin was the presiding elder in the Marion District, on the edge of the Black Belt and with the highest concentration of freed people; 1880 US Manuscript Census, Huntsville, #395/450.

78. Among the many works on this subject, Ronald G. Walters, *American Reformers, 1815–1860* (New York: Hill and Wang, 1978), remains one of the best.

79. *Tuskaloosa Gazette* 1880 June 17, July 29, 1878 May 30.

80. *New York Christian Advocate* 1883 May 17; *Huntsville Gazette* 1883 March 31; *A Biographical History of Nodaway and Atchison Counties, Missouri: Compendium of National Biography* (Chicago: Lewis, 1901), 262–265; New Orleans *Southwestern Christian Advocate* 1886 November 11, *New York Christian Advocate* 1883 May 17; *Huntsville Gazette* 1883 March 31; "A Short Family History for the Descendants of Arad and Achsah Lakin," unpublished manuscript written by Joan Raines Ritter, 1977, Lakin Collection, NAC Archive; *A Biographical History of Nodaway and Atchison Counties*, 262–265; New Orleans *Southwestern Christian Advocate* 1886 November 11, 1890 May 8. *See also* 1890 Central Alabama Conference *Journal*, 38–40, and 1890 Missouri Conference *Journal*, 66–67.

81. New Orleans *Southwestern Christian Advocate* 1886 April 22.

82. Marguerite D. Lacey, "Lakeside United Methodist Church," unpublished manuscript, NAC Archive; *Huntsville Gazette* 1890 February 1.

Chapter 3

1. *Dictionary of American Biography*, s.v. "Noah B. Cloud"; *Catalogue of Graduates of the Jefferson Medical College, from its Organization* (Philadelphia: Collins, 1879), 14; unpublished genealogical materials supplied by Joe and Wendy Slaton. Weymouth T. Jordan wrote most extensively on Cloud; see for example his "Noah B. Cloud's Activities on Behalf of Southern Agriculture," *Agricultural History* 25, no. 1 (1951 January): 53–58; "Noah B. Cloud and the *American Cotton Planter*," *Agricultural History* 31, no. 4 (October 1957): 44–49; "The Peruvian Guano Gospel in the Old South," *Agricultural History* 24, no. 4 (1950 October): 211–221; and "The Crusade for Agricultural Reform," chapter 6 in *Ante-bellum Alabama: Town and Country* (Tallahassee: Florida State University, 1957), 106–139.

2. *Southern Cultivator* (Augusta, Georgia) 6, no. 1 (1848 January): 6.

3. Henry Watson to mother, 1836 September 27, Henry Watson, Jr., Papers, Duke.

4. Henry Watson, Sr., to Henry Watson, Sr., 1836 February 6, and Henry Watson to mother, 1836 September 27, in Henry Watson, Jr., Papers, Duke; William B. Beverley to father, 1831 April 1, and William B. Beverley to father, 1831 August 1, Beverley Family Papers, Virginia Historical Society. See Hubbs, *Guarding Greensboro*, chapter 2, "A Land of Strangers"; and James David Miller, *South by Southwest: Planter Emigration and Identity in the Slave South* (Charlottesville: University of Virginia Press, 2002).

5. *American Cotton Planter and Soil of the South*, new series 1, no. 10 (1857 October): 293.

6. Cloud was hardly the only Southern scientific agriculturalist; Edmund Ruffin in Virginia was better known. Unlike Ruffin, whose energies increasingly moved toward creating a separate Southern state that would preserve slavery, Cloud voiced no interest in moving the South out of the American mainstream.

7. This account of Cloud's first experiments is taken from his "Experiments in Manuring Cotton," first published in the *American Cotton Planter* and republished in the *Alabama Planter* (Mobile) 1854 August 21.

8. This statement is subject to revision. In the 1846 December issue of the *Southern Cultivator*, Cloud listed his address as Cross Keys, which was located east of Polecat Springs and west of LaPlace; but he may have been living in LaPlace and put his mailing address as Cross Keys. Ten months later he listed his home as LaPlace in the same publication. LaPlace was restored and renamed Cloud Nine by its current owners Joe and Wendy Slaton, who generously entertained Mills Thornton and me one fall afternoon.

9. *The Cultivator* 9, no. 12 (1842 December): 191; 10, no. 2 (1843 February): 33; 11, no. 1 (1844 January): 28; William Warren Rogers, Jr., "'The Husbandman that Laboureth Must Be First Partaker of the Fruits' (2 Timothy 2:6): Agricultural Reform in Ante Bellum Alabama," *Alabama Historical Quarterly* 40, nos. 1 and 2 (1978 spring and summer): 47.

10. For example, the *American Farmer, and Spirit of the Agricultural Journal of the Day*; the *Southern Agriculturalist, Horticulturalist, and Register of Rural Affairs*; and the *Louisville Journal*.

11. See Philip Mills Herrington, "Agricultural and Architectural Reform in the Antebellum South: Fruitland at Augusta, Georgia," *Journal of Southern History* 78, no. 4 (2012 November): 858.

12. *Southern Cultivator* 1, no. 2 (1843 March 15): 12–13; *ibid.*, 1, no. 16 (1843 August 2): 121.

13. Jordan, "Noah B. Cloud's Activities," 55; Weymouth T. Jordan, "Cotton Planters' Conventions in the Old South," *Journal of Southern History* 19, no. 3 (1953): 323. The planters' convention movement, and Cloud's rise in it, is extensively covered in Weymouth T. Jordan's *Rebels in the Making: Planters' Conventions and Southern Propaganda* (Tuscaloosa, Alabama: Confederate Publishing, 1958).

14. *Southern Cultivator* 5, no. 12 (1847 December): 182.

15. Jordan, "Cotton Planters' Conventions," 323–333, 336, 339–341; Jordan, "Noah B. Cloud's Activities," 56. The agricultural reform movement is surveyed in Elizabeth McTyeire Essler, "The Agricultural Reform Movement in Alabama, 1850–1860," *Alabama Review* 1, no. 4 (1948 October): 243–260.

16. *Southern Cultivator* 12, no. 1 (1854 January): 28; *American Cotton Planter and Soil of the South*, new series 2, no. 1 (1858 January): 38.

17. *Mobile Advertiser* 1851 December 23, 1852 January 30; *Montgomery Advertiser and State Gazette* 1853 February 3, 1858 March 26; *New York Herald* 1856 December 8; Edmund Ruffin, *The Diary of Edmund Ruffin*, ed. William Kauffman Scarborough (Baton Rouge: Louisiana State University Press, 1972), volume 1, "Toward Independence," 184–187 (1858 May 8–11); Jordan, "Cotton Planters' Conventions," 341–342.

18. *Mobile Advertiser* 1852 January 15; Rogers, "'The Husbandman that Laboureth,'" 47, 48; *Montgomery Advertiser and State Gazette* 1855 May 16, 1856 November 25.

19. *Southern Cultivator* 5, no. 12 (1847 December): 182.

20. See Daniel Walker Howe, *What Hath God Wrought: The Transformation of America, 1815–1848* (New York: Oxford University Press, 2007).

21. Herrington, "Agricultural and Architectural Reform," 858.

22. Quoted in Daniel Walker Howe, *Making the American Self: Jonathan Edwards to Abraham Lincoln* (New York: Oxford University Press, 2009), 141.

23. *Tuscaloosa Independent Monitor* 1840 June 5.

24. Dr. Cloud's cooperative spirit was broad. In addition to attending agricultural reform meetings too numerous to list, he was a Freemason (like Arad Lakin), attended at least one temperance meeting and several barbecues of the Decatur and Montgomery Railroad, in which he was a stockholder. He was also a member of the Mount Vernon Association, pledged to purchase George Washington's home for the country as a whole. See Jordan, "Noah B. Cloud's Activities," 56; Thomas Hubbard Hobbs, *The Journals of Thomas Hubbard Hobbs*, ed. Faye Acton Axford (University: University of Alabama Press, 1976), 212 (1858 August 18); *Montgomery Advertiser and State Gazette* 1857 May 14.

25. *Southern Cultivator* 6, no. 1 (1848 January): 6.

26. *American Cotton Planter*, 1, no. 1 (1853 January): pp. 20–22.

27. *Mobile Advertiser* 1851 December 18.

28. Macon County Courthouse, Deed Record, Book E, 1843 March 13, p. 159; 1850 US Manuscript Census, Slave Schedule, District 21, Macon County, Alabama, p. 164. In 1850 he purchased a thirty-five-year-old male slave from John Britton, proprietor of the *Montgomery Advertiser; see* Macon County Courthouse, Deed Record, Book G, 1850 July 27, p. 502.

29. *American Cotton Planter* 1, no. 6 (1853 June): 172–174; *American Cotton Planter and Soil of the South*, new series 1, no. 10 (1857 October): 295; new series 3, no. 6 (1856 June): 171–173.

30. In December 1851 Dr. Cloud was a delegate to the state convention of the short-lived Constitutional Union Party, pledged to support the Compromise of 1850. (James H. Clanton, friend of Ryland Randolph and future head of the Democratic Party, served as secretary.) See the *Mobile Advertiser* 1851 December 18, 1852 January 25. During the next ten years Southern Whigs would join the American Party (Know-Nothings) and in 1860 a second Constitutional Union Party.

31. Jordan, "Noah B. Cloud's Activities," 58; *Huntsville Southern Advocate* 1856 October 30; *Montgomery Advertiser and State Gazette* 1856 June 7, 1857 April 7, 1856 November 26, 1859 September 21.

32. Robert Russell, *North America: Its Agriculture and Climate* (Edinburgh: Adam and Charles Black, 1857), 290, 296–300.

33. Stowell, *Rebuilding Zion*, 34.

34. *Montgomery Post* 1860 July 25; Montgomery *Alabama State Journal* 1869 July 30; *Tuscaloosa Independent Monitor* 1860 July 28. Curiously, Cloud's fellow members of the club not only included other Masons but James H. Clanton, friend of Ryland Randolph and future head of the Democratic Party.

35. *Montgomery Post* 1860 December 11.

36. At least he was serving as Senior Warden in Montgomery's Andrew Jackson Lodge No. 173; see Fletcher D. Martin and Fenton G. Fly, *History of Andrew Jackson Lodge No. 173, Montgomery, Alabama, 1852–1986* (Montgomery: Lodge, 1987), A-1.

37. US National Archives, Compiled Service Records of the Confederate General and Staff Officers and Nonregimental Enlisted Men, microfilm #331, roll 57. His obituary stated that he "entered the Confederate army at the commencement of the struggle, a statement that must be taken skeptically, and that he was "in charge of the post at Savannah, Ga. during a great portion of the war," a statement that sounds more likely; see Montgomery *Alabama State Journal* 1875 November 7. Cloud apparently also spent much time in Augusta, Georgia (across the river from his native Edgefield District, South Carolina); see for example the *Augusta Daily Constitutionalist* 1865 January 6.

38. *Mobile Register and Advertiser* 1865 August 29 December 17.

39. *Mobile Times* 1865 October 20; *Montgomery Advertiser* 1865 October 18, November 23, 24, 26, December 22. The second speaker was probably Jefferson Manly Falkner. My thanks to J. Mills Thornton, III, whose study of the Presidential Reconstruction legislature fundamentally questions its conventional assessment; see his "Alabama's Presidential Reconstruction Legislature," in *A Political Nation: New Directions in Mid-Nineteenth Century American Political History*, edited by Gary W. Gallagher and Radchel A. Shelden (Charlottesville: University of Virginia Press, 2012), 167–187.

40. *Montgomery Advertiser* 1865 November 25, 1866 February 28, 1867 March 19; *New Orleans Picayune* 1866 February 3.

41. *Southern Cultivator* 25, no. 12 (1867 December): 364.

42. *Mobile Register and Advertiser* 1867 December 5.

43. *Acts of Alabama*, no. 493, p. 426 (1854 February 18); *Tuskegee South-Western Baptist* 1855 July 26; *American Cotton Planter and Soil of the South* new series 2, nos. 5–9 (1858), 137–139, 169–171, 201–203, 233–236, 265–268; new series 2, nos. 1, 5 (1859), 9–11, 165–168.

44. Stephen Beauregard Weeks, *History of Public School Education in Alabama* (Washington, DC: Government Printing Office, 1915), 65.

45. *Minutes of the Convention, which Formed the Alabama Educational Association, in Selma, Alabama, July 24–25, 1856* (Selma: Selma Reporter, 1857), 13; *American Cotton Planter and Soil of the South*, new series 2, no. 8 (1858 August): 233. My understanding of education has been informed by Robert Eno Hunt, "Organizing a New South: Education Reformers in Antebellum Alabama" (Ph.D. dissertation, University of Missouri, 1988), and his "Home, Domesticity, and School Reform in Antebellum Alabama," *Alabama Review* 46, no. 4 (1996 October): 253–275.

46. Mobile *Nationalist* 1865 December 14. As the *Nationalist* was calling for better education, the legislature was selecting a superintendent of education. Dr. Cloud came in third in the voting. See *Mobile Register and Advertiser* 1865 December 17.

47. The strongest predictor that a white Southerner would join the Republican Party was Unionist sympathies, according to Sarah Woolfolk Wiggins, *The Scalawag in Alabama Politics, 1865–1881* (University: University of Alabama Press, 1977).

48. *Montgomery Advertiser* 1868 April 16.

49. Weeks, *History of Public School Education*, 84–85, 89; see also J. Mills Thornton, III, "Fiscal Policy and the Failure of Radical Reconstruction in the Lower South," in *Region, Race, and Reconstruction: Essays in Honor of C. Vann Woodward*, J. Morgan Kousser and James M. McPherson, eds., 349–394 (New York: Oxford University Press, 1982).

50. *Montgomery Alabama State Journal* 1868 October 29, and the *Moulton Advertiser* 1868 November 13, October 30; *Journal of the Board of Education of the State of Alabama* (1869).

51. See Hubbs, "'Dissipating the Clouds of Ignorance,'" 20–35.

52. Robert J. Norrell, *A Promising Field: Engineering at Alabama, 1837–1987* (Tuscaloosa: University of Alabama Press, 1990), 14–31.

53. William Warren Rogers, "The Founding of Alabama's Land Grant College at Auburn," *Alabama Review* 40, no. 1 (1987 January): 15.

54. *Ibid,.* 36. With the turmoil surrounding the reopening of the university, local interests began throwing out alternatives. "The State University," began an article in the *Tuskegee News* reprinted in the *Montgomery Advertiser* 1868 August 15, "has been turned over to a set of worthless, characterless carpet-baggers." The sons of Southern gentlemen were looking elsewhere for a school, and a solution could be found in purchasing the East Alabama Female College building in Tuskegee and there founding

another military institute. Those members of the university's faculty who had quite properly resigned would form the nucleus of the new school.

55. *Journal of the Board of Education of the State of Alabama* (1869), 39–44.

56. Selma *Southern Argus* 1870 June 2.

57. *Montgomery Advertiser* 1868 August 8.

58. *Mobile Register* 1868 September 21.

59. *Montgomery Alabama State Journal* 1869 August 16, 26. This idea of putting the location up for bid was typical for the time. In 1856 the Methodists had chosen Greensboro as the site of Southern University because its citizens had pledged the most money. The seat of government had been moved from Tuscaloosa to Montgomery for the same reason.

60. Tuskaloosa *Independent Monitor* 1869 September 7, 14, 21.

61. *Journal of the Board of Education* (1869), 46, 47; Tuskaloosa *Independent Monitor* 1869 January 5, April 13. Some accounts have Harper as a Presbyterian.

62. As quoted in the *Charleston* [South Carolina] *Courier* 1869 September 23.

63. *Montgomery Alabama State Journal* 1869 May 26, November 9, May 5.

64. *Ibid.*, 1869 November 27, 1869 December 1, 1870 March 23, March 10.

65. *Ibid.*, 1870 July 1, 2, 1870 September 1; Sellers, *History of the University of Alabama*, 308. It would not be until October 1871, under a new Democratic administration, that students would return in anything like sufficient numbers to judge the University of Alabama sufficiently reestablished.

66. *Montgomery Alabama State Journal* 1870 September 4.

67. Weeks, *History of Public School Education*, 85–86. See also Tuskaloosa *Independent Monitor* 1870 October 11.

68. *Mobile Register* 1870 September 27.

69. *Montgomery Alabama State Journal* 1870 September 6, 20, 25.

70. *Ibid.*, 1870 September 20.

71. *Montgomery Alabama State Journal* 1870 April 30.

72. *Ibid.*, 1870 November 22; Tuskaloosa *Independent Monitor* 1870 November 29, December 6.

73. Weeks, *History of Public School Education*, 89–100; *Montgomery Alabama State Journal* 1871 September 29; *Journal of the House of Representatives of the State of Alabama, Session 1872-'73* (Montgomery: Bingham, 1874), 77.

74. While the Whig Party last fielded a presidential candidate in 1852, the Whig impulse certainly continued and, I argue, can even be found today. See, for example, Thomas B. Alexander "Persistent Whiggery in Alabama and the Lower South, 1860–1867," *Alabama Review* 12, no. 1 (1959 January): 35–52. For a fuller understanding of the Whig and Jacksonian worldviews, see especially Lawrence Frederick Kohl, *The Politics of Individualism: Parties and the American Character in the Jacksonian Era* (New York: Oxford University Press, 1989).

75. Whiggish freedom seems to bear a close resemblance to positive liberty. The orientation, however, is quite different because positive liberty is often associated with the structures created by a large and overbearing state, whereas Whiggish freedom expresses the individualistic aspirations that are usually assigned to negative liberty. See Isaiah Berlin, "Two Concepts of Liberty," delivered as a lecture in 1958 and reprinted often, including *Four Essays on Liberty* (New York: Oxford University Press, 1970), 118–172.

The overlap of Whiggery and Methodism can be seen in the Methodist ministers selected for the presidency of the University of Alabama by the University of Alabama's board of regents.

76. *Montgomery Alabama State Journal* 1872 August 9, 12, 1873 March 1, 10, 13, April 13; *Journal of the House . . . Session 1872-'73*, 7, 590–591, 900–901.

77. *Montgomery Alabama State Journal* 1875 September 5, October 13, November 7. The newspapers have his death as November 5, but his tombstone reads November 6. According to information assembled by Joe and Wendy Slaton, as late as 1933 his estate was still being administered for the benefit of the Baptist Orphanage.

Chapter 4

1. Unless otherwise noted, this account of Shandy Jones's early life is taken from Ophelia Taylor Pinkard and Barbara Clayton Clark, *Descendants of Shandy Wesley Jones and Evalina Love Jones: The Story of An African American Family in Tuscaloosa, Alabama* (Baltimore: Gateway Press, 1993), 1–20. Mrs. Pinkard, of Silver Spring, Maryland, has generously shared her knowledge of her ancestor and has allowed me to reproduce the photograph of Shandy Jones.

2. *Acts of Alabama* 1820 December 11; the descendants identify John N. S. Jones as the probable father.

3. Marriage certificate reproduced in Pinkard and Clark, *Descendants of Shandy Wesley Jones*, 159; James B. Sellers, "Free Negroes of Tuscaloosa County Before the Thirteenth Amendment," *Alabama Review* 23, no. 2 (1970 April), 111, 119, 123.

4. *Ibid.*, 111, 115; Charles Lyell, *A Second Visit to the United States of North America* (London: John Murray, 1850), 2:71.

5. Douglas Walter Bristol, Jr., *Knights of the Razor: Black Barbers in Slavery and Freedom* (Baltimore: The Johns Hopkins University Press, 2009), 104; *Tuscaloosa Flag of the Union* 1837 June 14. See also William Johnson, *William Johnson's Natchez: The Ante-Bellum Diary of a Free Negro*, ed. William Ransom Hogan, and Edwin Adams Davis (Baton Rouge: Louisiana State University Press, 1993); Edwin Adams Davis and William Ransom Hogan, *The Barber of Natchez* (Baton Rouge: Louisiana State University Press, 1954); and Ira Berlin, *Slaves without Masters: The Free Negro in the Antebellum South* (New York: Pantheon, 1974), 235–236.

6. *African Repository and Colonial Journal* 5, no. 12 (1830 February): 379; Hubbs,

Guarding Greensboro, 64–66. On Cocke and his experiment, see Randall M. Miller, ed., *Dear Master: Letters of a Slave Family* (Ithaca: Cornell University Press, 1978). The colonization movement in Tuscaloosa is largely taken from John W. Quist's remarkable work, *Restless Visionaries: The Social Roots of Antebellum Reform in Alabama and Michigan* (Baton Rouge: Louisiana State University Press, 1998), 310–337.

7. *African Repository and Colonial Journal* 6, no. 3 (1830 May): 75; Betty Fladeland, *James Gillespie Birney: Slaveholder to Abolitionist* (Ithaca: Cornell University Press, 1955), 65–69; Robert Paul Lamb, "James G. Birney and the Road to Abolitionism," *Alabama Review* 47, no. 2 (1994 April): 122, n. 58; Quist, *Restless Visionaries*, 318.

8. Quist, *Restless Visionaries*, 329.

9. S. Wesl[e]y Jones to Rev. Wm. McLain 1848 June 12, in *African Repository and Colonial Journal* 24, no. 9 (1848 September), 268–270.

10. S. Wesley Jones to Revd. Wm. Mclain 1849 May 2, reprinted in Carter G. Woodson, ed., *The Mind Of The Negro As Reflected In Letters Written During The Crisis 1800–1860* (Washington, DC: Association for the Study of Negro Life and History, 1926), 65–67.

11. S. Wesl[e]y Jones to "Revd & dear Sir" 1849 August 4, reprinted in Woodson, ed., *Mind Of The Negro*, 67–68.

12. *African Repository and Colonial Journal* 26, no. 9 (1850 September), 276–277.

13. Quist, *Restless Visionaries*, 333–334.

14. S. W. Jones to Rev. W. McLain 1851 December 29, in *African Repository and Colonial Journal* 28, no. 5 (1852 May): 148.

15. S. Wesl[e]y Jones to Revd Wm McLain 1852 April 18, reprinted in Woodson, ed., *Mind Of The Negro*, 71–72; S. Wesley Jones to Revd Wm Mclain 1856 November 7, *ibid.*, 72–73. Jones' next letter (S Wesl[e]y Jones to Revd Wm M[c]Lain 1859 April 10, *ibid.*, 73–74) reported on a man who was ready to go to Liberia but his wife would have none of it, fearing starvation or cannibalism, and would rather remain a slave in Alabama.

16. A few were reading Baynard Rush Hall's *Frank Freeman's Barber Shop* (1852), a novel written in response to *Uncle Tom's Cabin*, in which a disillusioned escaped slave and barber eventually makes his way to Liberia.

17. *Mobile Herald and Tribune* 1853 March 22, April 1, 27, June 18, 19. An Old Methodist specified the Denmark Vesey and Nat Turner rebellions alongside the legendary John A. Murrell who, along and his band, would kidnap slaves and use them for criminal purposes.

18. James Robert Maxwell, *Autobiography of James Robert Maxwell* (New York: Greenberg, 1926), 12–13.

19. *Tuscaloosa Gazette* 1844 May 8; 1850 US Manuscript Census, Tuscaloosa County, District 1, #319, 320, and 321. Jones lived on the southwest corner of Sixth Street and Twenty-Ninth Avenue. See also Pinkard and Clark, *Descendants of Shandy Wesley Jones*, 181–186. Sellers, "Free Negroes," 112–113.

20. John Gorman Barr, "Relief for Ireland! or, John Brown's Bad Luck With His Pickled Beef," *Porter's Spirit of the Times* 1 (1857 February 21), 393–395; reprinted in *Rowdy Tales from Early Alabama: The Humor of John Gorman Barr*, ed. G. Ward Hubbs (University: University of Alabama Press, 1981), 143–161.

21. Tuscaloosa *Independent Monitor* 1857 August 6.

22. *Ibid.*, 1859 August 13. The following year they would place a poll tax on slaves and free blacks; see Tuscaloosa *Independent Monitor* 1860 April 7.

23. *West Alabama Breeze* 1920 January 1. My personal thanks to Jim Ezell for finding this gem.

24. *Mobile Register* 1860 February 4; *Montgomery Mail* 1860 February 21.

25. The editor of the Tuscaloosa *Independent Monitor* pressed for passage, declaring on 1861 February 1 that "the sooner our slaves are freed from their influence, the better." The Alabama Senate did adopt the bill, but it was then apparently amended in the House. When the amended bill returned to the Senate, Tuscaloosa's Robert Jemison and several other senators attempted to kill it by offering more amendments. Jemison's amendment would have exempted three black men and their families from its provisions: Shandy Jones, Horace Ware, and Solomon Perteet. In the end, no bill was passed. Jemison's efforts on behalf of Jones and the others may not have been motivated by more than altruism, for he was heavily in debt and close to bankruptcy; these wealthy free black men were among the many who may have loaned him money. If they had been forced leave to Alabama, then they would have collected all monies owed to them before doing so, bringing Jemison's financial house of cards tumbling down. Alabama Senate *Journal* (1862 February 1): 71–72. My thanks to Chris McIlwain for this discovery and insight.

26. Loren Schweninger, *Black Property Owners in the South, 1790–1915* (Urbana: University of Illinois Press, 1990), 243–244. Schweninger based his assessment of Jones on an analysis of the manuscript census. At least seven lots were put up for sale in Tuscaloosa in order to settle his estate; see *Tuscaloosa Times* 1887 April 6, June 8, December 7; 1888 January 9, November 9.

27. Pinkard and Clark, *Descendants of Shandy Wesley Jones*, 13; Barr, *Rowdy Tales*, 146. The location of the Jones home is now the southwest corner of Sixth Street and Twenty-Ninth Avenue.

28. That was the charge in 1846, according to the Basil Manly diary, W. S. Hoole Special Collections Library, University of Alabama, 1844 February 28. About 135 years later I had a haircut in Jones's barbershop, still going but relocated to the 2300 block of Sixth Street; it cost me more than twenty-five cents.

29. Tuscaloosa *Independent Monitor* 1858 February 18; *Cochran v. The State*, Supreme Court of Alabama, January term, 1857 (30 Ala. 542; 30 Ala 550). The court cases mentions that Shandy Jones had used the rooms for experimenting in taking daguerreotypes and thus could have taken his own portrait.

30. Pinkard and Clark, *Descendants of Shandy Wesley Jones*, 25.

31. As quoted in Kolchin, *First Freedom*, 7; and John B. Myers, "Black Human Capital: The Freedmen and the Reconstruction of Labor in Alabama, 1860–1880" (Ph.D. dissertation, Florida State University, 1974), 24.

32. Mobile *Nationalist* 1865 December 14.

33. *Ibid.*, 1866 April 5, 1867 December 19, 1866 May 3; as quoted in Kolchin, *First Freedom*, 84–85.

34. Unidentified newspaper clipping in William Hugh Smith, Governors' Administrative Files SG023109, folder 7, ADAH.

35. My understanding of the black interpretation of the Civil War is taken from Stowell, *Rebuilding Zion*, and from Morrow, *Northern Methodism and Reconstruction*.

36. Mobile *Nationalist* 1866 May 10, 17. The three churches were Sandy Springs, Union Chapel, and Bone Camp.

37. *Ibid.*, 1866 April 5; James B. Sellers, *The First Methodist Church of Tuscaloosa, Alabama, 1818–1968* (Tuscaloosa: Weatherford, 1968): 24; Pinkard and Clark, *Descendants of Shandy Wesley Jones*, 15; Robert L. Glynn, *"How Firm a Foundation": A History of the First Black Church in Tuscaloosa, County, Alabama* (Tuscaloosa: Friends of the Hunter's Chapel African Methodist Church, and the City of Tuscaloosa, Alabama Bicentennial Committee, 1976). The following year, the seventy-one ministers who met as the Alabama Conference would represent some 6,700 members. See Mobile *Nationalist* 1867 May 2; Kolchin, *First Freedom*, 111.

38. Basil Manly diary, 1866 June 24, Hoole; testimony of Prince Morrell and Jim Caldwell, 1867 April 24, Freedmen's Bureau Papers, reel 809, roll 18, "Reports of Operations from the Subdivisions from the Subdistricts September 1865–December 1868."

39. Mobile *Nationalist* 1867 May 9.

40. Mobile *Nationalist* 1867 May 16; Greensboro *Alabama Beacon* 1867 June 1. The Tuscaloosa delegation, which surely would have included Jones, was not present for the opening session. These conventions are extensively covered in Judy Bussell LeForge's "Alabama's Colored Conventions and the Exodus Movement, 1861–1879," *Alabama Review* 63, no. 1 (2010 January): 3–29.

41. Kolchin, *First Freedom*, 162, 93–95, 170. For an analysis of the delegates, see James D. Thomas, Jr., "The Alabama Constitutional Convention," (master's thesis, Alabama Polytechnic Institute [Auburn University]), 1947.

42. Fitzgerald, *The Union League Movement*, 83, 172; Kolchin, *First Freedom*, 170; Hubbs, *Guarding Greensboro*, 211, 212, 218; Mobile *Nationalist* 1868 February 27.

43. Mobile *Nationalist* 1868 March 26.

44. Randolph, *Scribbles*, XIV (pp. 107–108); *Tuscaloosa News* 1953 March 1; Tuscaloosa *Independent Monitor* 1868 April 1, May 5, June 16, July 28; 1870 US Manuscript Census, p. 15/409, 14/408. Randolph's prediction for Roberts's success came in the same issue of the *Monitor*, April 1, that devoted many column inches to explaining for the first time the origins, oaths, and ceremonies of the Ku Klux Klan to the Tuscaloosa readers.

45. Tuskaloosa *Independent Monitor* 1868 July 28, May 5; Randolph, *Scribbles*, XIV (p. 107).

46. Randolph, *Scribbles*, XIV (pp. 107–108).

47. My thanks to Margaret Storey for this observation.

48. *Montgomery Advertiser* 1866 April 15; *African Repository* 46, no. 7 (1868 July): 220. Black Americans' interest in emigration to Liberia continued well into the 1890s only to be revived by Marcus Garvey; see Steven Hahn, *A Nation under Our Feet: Black Political Struggles in the Rural South from Slavery to the Great Migration* (Cambridge: Harvard University Press, 2003).

49. *Journal of the Session of 1869–70, of the House of Representatives*, 456–457. Many in the legislature used this particular bill for personal gain.

50. Tuskaloosa *Independent Monitor* 1868 July 28, August 11, 1869 March 2; Pinkard and Clark, *Descendants of Shandy Wesley Jones*, 25; *Tuscaloosa News* 1953 March 1.

51. Tuskaloosa *Independent Monitor* 1868 July 28, June 2.

52. *Ibid.*, 1869 March 2, 23.

53. *Ibid.*, 1869 April 6; Sellers, *History of the University of Alabama*, 310–311. Some opposed the idea of separate black and white agricultural colleges; see Montgomery *Alabama State Journal* 1872 January 23.

54. Tuskaloosa *Independent Monitor* 1870 February 1, November 15; Montgomery *Alabama State Journal* 1870 November 20.

55. Tuskaloosa *Independent Monitor* 1871 March 28; Pinkard and Clark, *Descendants of Shandy Wesley Jones*, pp. 16–17, 23. According to Pinkard and Clark, Jones lived in various residences in Mobile: on Bay Shell Road in 1871, on the south side of St. Michael between Joachim and Jackson streets in 1872, and on Spring Hill Road in 1873. His whereabouts between 1875 and 1882 are unclear, for he does not show up in the census or the Mobile city directories, and in 1874 he was listed as a delegate from Tuscaloosa to the state Republican convention in Montgomery (Montgomery *Alabama State Journal* 1874 August 22). From 1883 to 1884, he lived in the parsonage of the Little Zion AME Zion Church on the northwest corner of Church and Bayou streets.

56. Examination certificate reproduced in Pinkard and Clark, *Descendants of Shandy Wesley Jones*, 157. The source of Jones's appointment is not altogether clear. It is thought that he received an appointment as inspector of customs in September 1871 as part of a plan by former senator Willard Warner to gain political advantage over his rival Republican, senator George E. Spencer; however, the *Tuscaloosa Times* reported 1872 July 31 that Jones was appointed by Spencer. The role of patronage is covered in Michael W. Fitzgerald, *Urban Emancipation: Popular Politics in Reconstruction Mobile, 1860–1890* (Baton Rouge: Louisiana State University Press, 2002), chapter five, "The Mainspring of It All: The Racial Politics of Federal Employment."

57. See for example *Tuscaloosa Times* 1872 September 18, October 9.

58. The church, still at the same address, is now Big Zion AME Zion Church.

59. Mobile *Nationalist* 1865 December 14. Tuscaloosa was represented at the meeting, almost certainly by Jones, although I cannot verify it. The resolutions prompted the editor of the *Nationalist* to write an essay on social and governmental relations two issues later, on 1865 December 28. Society, he began, "is not a mere accidental collection of independent human beings, but a divinely constituted corporation, possessing organic relations—having a common social life and moral attributes and responsibilities." Because government is "the divinely appointed complement of this social identity," John Locke was simply wrong. Government was not an aggregate of individual rights surrendered for the common good, "any more than are the duties and prerogatives of the parent the result of a compact among the children by which each child surrenders up for the common family weal certain individual rights and privileges."

60. Alexis de Tocqueville, *Democracy in America* II (1840), second book, chapter 13, "Causes for the Restless Spirit of the Americans in the Midst of Their Prosperity."

61. Hope may not have been freedom itself, but it was a necessary condition for freedom. "Abandon hope all ye who enter here," were the words above the entrance to Dante's Hell, from which there was certainly no freedom.

62. J. C. Saunders's account of Jones's last days and funeral is found in the *Star of Zion* 10, no. 8 (1886 February 19), 1, as transcribed in Pinkard and Clark, *Descendants of Shandy Wesley Jones*, 165–166.

63. Perhaps originally a hymn, the poem was published in the *Guardian* 30, no. 12 (1879 December): 363.

Epilogue

1. David Hackett Fischer, *Albion's Seed: Four British Folkways in America* (New York: Oxford University Press, 1989), 199–205, 410–418, 595–603, 777–782. Fischer expands on some of these ideas in *Liberty and Freedom: A Visual History of America's Founding Ideas* (New York: Oxford University Press, 2005). See also Eric Foner's *The Story of American Freedom* (New York: Norton, 1998).

2. Abraham Lincoln, "Address at Sanitary Fair, Baltimore," 1864 April 18. This passage is the subject of James M. McPherson's article, "Lincoln and Liberty," in *Abraham Lincoln and the Second American* (New York: Oxford University Press, 1990), 43–64. See also his related "Liberty and Power in the Second American Revolution," in the same volume, 131–152.

3. Lawrence Frederick Kohl's insights were especially helpful here.

4. Michael J. Sandel arrives at the same conclusion by a different route. See "The Public Philosophy of Contemporary Liberalism," in *Democracy's Discontent: America in Search of a Public Policy* (Cambridge: Harvard University Press, 1996), pp. 3–24, and esp. 21–24.

Bibliography

MANUSCRIPTS

Alabama Department of Archives and History (ADAH)
Governors' Administrative Files
Governors' Correspondence
John W. DuBose Papers

Amistad Research Center, Tulane University
Freedmen's Aid Society Correspondence

Birmingham Public Library
V. M. Randolph, Jr., Scrapbook 413

Duke University Rare Book, Manuscript, and Special Collections Library
John Lakin Brasher Papers
Henry Watson, Jr., Papers

New York Public Library Manuscripts and Archives Division
Walter L. Fleming Papers

North Alabama Conference Archive of the United Methodist Church, Birmingham-Southern College (NAC)
Lakin Collection
Manuscript Journal of the Alabama Conference of the Methodist Episcopal Church

Samford University Special Collections
Randolph Papers

United Methodist Church General Commission on Archives and History, Drew University
Five Points Mission Records

University of Alabama Hoole Special Collections Library
Basil Manly Diary

Virginia Historical Society
Beverley Family Papers

PUBLIC DOCUMENTS

Acts of Alabama

Alabama Senate *Journal*

Journal of the Board of Education of the State of Alabama; together with the Laws and Proceedings of the Board of Regents of the University of Alabama. Montgomery: Stokes, 1869.

Journal of the House of Representatives of the State of Alabama, Session 1872-'73. Montgomery: Bingham, 1874.

Journal of the Session of 1869–70 of the House of Representatives of the State of Alabama Held in the City of Montgomery Commencing on the Third Monday in November, 1869. Montgomery: Stokes, 1870.

Macon County Courthouse, Deed Record, Books E and G.

US Bureau of Refugees, Freedmen and Abandoned Lands [Freedmen's Bureau Papers], Records of the Assistant Commissioner for the State of Alabama.

US Congress. *Testimony Taken by the Joint Select Committee to Inquire into the Condition of Affairs in the Late Insurrectionary States.* 42nd Congress, 2nd session, House Report 22. Volume 8, Alabama [*KKK Testimony*]. Washington, DC: Government Printing Office, 1872.

US District Court Records, Northern District of Alabama, Northeastern Division

US Government, Manuscript Census

US National Archives. *Compiled Military Service Records*

The War of the Rebellion: A Compilation of the Official Records of the Union and Confederate Armies [*OR*]. Washington: Government Printing Office, 1880–1901.

PERIODICALS

Alabama Newspapers

Birmingham Argus

Greensboro *Alabama Beacon*

Huntsville Advocate

Huntsville Democrat

Huntsville Gazette

Huntsville Independent

Huntsville Southern Advocate

Mobile Advertiser

Mobile Herald and Tribune

Mobile *Nationalist*

Mobile Register

Mobile Register and Advertiser

Mobile Times

Mobile Tribune
Montgomery Advertiser
Montgomery Advertiser and State Gazette
Montgomery *Alabama State Journal*
Montgomery Mail
Montgomery Post
Moulton Advertiser
Talladega Alabama Reporter
Tuscaloosa Flag of the Union
Tuscaloosa Gazette
Tuscaloosa Times
Tuskaloosa *Blade*
Tuskaloosa Gazette
Tuskaloosa *Independent Monitor* (the Tuscaloosa *Independent Monitor* before 1867
    October)
West Alabama Breeze

Out-of-State Newspapers
Augusta [Georgia] *Daily Constitutionalist*
Bangor [Maine] *Whig & Courier*
Charleston [South Carolina] *Courier*
Cincinnati Campaign Commercial
Cincinnati Commercial
Cleveland Herald
New York Herald
New York Times
Rochester [Indiana] *Chronicle*
Rochester [Indiana] *Sentinel*
San Francisco Evening Bulletin

Agricultural Journals
Alabama Planter
American Cotton Planter
American Cotton Planter and Soil of the South
Cultivator
Southern Cultivator

Other
African Repository and Colonial Journal
Guardian
Harper's Weekly
Porter's Spirit of the Times

Star of Zion
Tuskegee South-Western Baptist

Methodist Episcopal Church Publications

Alabama Conference. *Journal.* In *Minutes of the Annual Conferences.* New York: Carlton & Lanahan, 1868. (Manuscript version housed in the North Alabama Conference Archive, Birmingham-Southern College.)
Central Alabama Conference. *Journal.*
Cincinnati *Western Christian Advocate*
Freedmen's Aid Society of the Methodist Episcopal Church. *Annual Reports.* Cincinnati: Western Methodist Book Concern.
Methodist Episcopal Church. *Journals of the General Conference.* New York: Nelson & Phillips.
Minutes of the Annual Conferences of the Methodist Episcopal Church for the Year 1866. New York: Carlton & Lanahan, 1868.
Missionary Society of the Methodist Episcopal Church. *Annual Reports.* New York: The Society.
Missouri Conference. *Journal.*
New Orleans *Southwestern Christian Advocate*
New York Christian Advocate
New York Conference. *Journals.*
Northwest Indiana Conference. *Minutes of the Fourteenth Annual Session of the North-West Indiana Conference of the Methodist Episcopal Church, Held at Attica, Indiana, September 6–11, 1865.* Cincinnati: R. P. Thompson, 1865.
Zion's Herald and Wesleyan Journal

Books, Articles, Dissertations, and Theses

Alabama Educational Association. *Minutes of the Convention, which Formed the Alabama Educational Association, in Selma, Alabama, July 24–25, 1856.* Selma: Selma Reporter, 1857.
Alexander, Thomas B. "Persistent Whiggery in Alabama and the Lower South, 1860–1867." *Alabama Review* 12, no. 1 (1959 January): 35–52.
Anbinder, Tyler. *Five Points: The 19th-Century New York City Neighborhood That Invented Tap Dance, Stole Elections, and Became the World's Most Notorious Slum.* New York: Free Press, 2001.
Barr, John Gorman. *Rowdy Tales from Early Alabama: The Humor of John Gorman Barr.* Edited by G. Ward Hubbs. University: University of Alabama Press, 1981.
Baur, John E. "Faustin Soulouque, Emperor of Haiti: His Character and His Reign." *The Americas* 6, no. 2 (1959 October): 131–166.

Berlin, Ira. *Slaves without Masters: The Free Negro in the Antebellum South.* New York: Pantheon, 1974.

Berlin, Isaiah. "The Romantic Revolution: A Crisis in the History of Modern Thought." In *The Sense of Reality: Studies in Ideas and Their History*, pp. 168–193. New York: Farrar, Straus and Giroux, 1996.

———. "Two Concepts of Liberty." In *Four Essays on Liberty.* New York, 118–172: Oxford University Press, 1970.

A Biographical History of Nodaway and Atchison Counties, Missouri: Compendium of National Biography. Chicago: Lewis, 1901.

Brasher, John Lawrence. *The Sanctified South: John Lakin Brasher and the Holiness Movement.* Urbana: University of Illinois Press, 1994.

Brawley, James P. *Two Centuries of Methodist Concern: Bondage, Freedom and Education of Black People.* New York: Vantage, 1974.

Bristol, Douglas Walter, Jr., *Knights of the Razor: Black Barbers in Slavery and Freedom.* Baltimore: The Johns Hopkins University Press, 2009.

Brown, Richard D. "Microhistory and the Post-Modern Challenge." *Journal of the Early Republic* 23, no. 1 (2003 spring): 1–20.

Catalogue of Graduates of the Jefferson Medical College, from Its Organization. Philadelphia: Collins, 1879.

Cauthen, Charles Edward, ed. *Family Letters of the Three Wade Hamptons, 1782–1901.* Columbia: University of South Carolina Press, 1953.

Cimbala, Paul A. and Randall M. Miller, eds. *The Great Task Remaining before Us: Reconstruction as America's Continuing Civil War.* New York: Fordham University Press, 2010.

Clay-Clopton, Virginia. *A Belle of the Fifties: Memoirs of Mrs. Clay of Alabama, Covering Social and Political Life in Washington and the South, 1853–66.* New York: Doubleday, Page, 1904.

Cross, Whitney R. *The Burned-Over District: The Social and Intellectual History of Enthusiastic Religion in Western New York, 1800–1850.* New York: Harper & Row, 1950.

Daniel, Mike. "The Arrest and Trial of Ryland Randolph: April-May, 1868." *Alabama Historical Quarterly* 40, nos. 3–4 (1978 fall and winter): 127–143.

Davis, Edwin Adams, and William Ransom Hogan. *The Barber of Natchez.* Baton Rouge: Louisiana State University Press, 1954.

Davis, Susan Lawrence. *Authentic History, Ku Klux Klan, 1865–1877.* New York: author, 1924.

DuBose, John Witherspoon. *Alabama's Tragic Decade: Ten Years of Alabama, 1865–1874.* Edited by James K. Greer. Birmingham: Webb, 1940.

Essler, Elizabeth McTyeire. "The Agricultural Reform Movement in Alabama, 1850–1860." *Alabama Review* 1, no. 4 (1948 October): 243–260.

Fischer, David Hackett. *Albion's Seed: Four British Folkways in America.* New York: Oxford University Press, 1989.

———. *Liberty and Freedom: A Visual History of America's Founding Ideas.* New York: Oxford University Press, 2005.

Fitzgerald, Michael W. "Radical Republicanism and the White Yeomanry during Alabama Reconstruction, 1865–1868." *Journal of Southern History* 54, no. 3 (1988 November): 586–590.

———. *The Union League Movement in the Deep South: Politics and Agricultural Change During Reconstruction.* Baton Rouge: Louisiana State University Press, 1989.

———. *Urban Emancipation: Popular Politics in Reconstruction Mobile, 1860–1890.* Baton Rouge: Louisiana State University Press, 2002.

Fladeland, Betty. *James Gillespie Birney: Slaveholder to Abolitionist.* Ithaca: Cornell University Press, 1955.

Foner, Eric. *Free Soil, Free Labor, Free Men: The Ideology of the Republican Party before the Civil War.* New York: Oxford University Press, 1970.

———. *Reconstruction: America's Unfinished Revolution, 1863–1877.* New York: Harper & Row, 1988.

———. *The Story of American Freedom.* New York: Norton, 1998.

Frear, Sara S. "'You My Brother Will Be Glad with Me': The Letters of Augusta Jane Evans to Walter Clopton Harriss, January 29, 1856, to October 29, 185[8?]." *Alabama Review* 60, no. 2 (2007 April): 111–141.

Glynn, Robert L. *"How Firm a Foundation": A History of the First Black Church in Tuscaloosa, County, Alabama.* Tuscaloosa: Friends of the Hunter's Chapel African Methodist Church, and the City of Tuscaloosa, Alabama Bicentennial Committee, 1976.

Greenberg, Kenneth S. *Honor & Slavery: Lies, Duels, Noses, Masks, Dressing as a Woman, Gifts, Strangers, Humanitarianism, Death, Slave Rebellions, the Proslavery Argument, Baseball, Hunting, and Gambling in the Old South.* Princeton: Princeton University Press, 1996.

Hahn, Steven *A Nation under Our Feet: Black Political Struggles in the Rural South from Slavery to the Great Migration.* Cambridge: Harvard University Press, 2003.

Hall, Baynard Rush. *Frank Freeman's Barber Shop: A Tale.* New York: Scribner, 1852.

Herrington, Philip Mills. "Agricultural and Architectural Reform in the Antebellum South: Fruitland at Augusta, Georgia." *Journal of Southern History* 78, no. 4 (2012 November): 855–886.

Hobbs, Thomas Hubbard. *The Journals of Thomas Hubbard Hobbs.* Edited by Faye Acton Axford. University: University of Alabama Press, 1976.

Hoole, William Stanley, ed. *History of the Seventh Alabama Cavalry Regiment, Including Capt. Charles P. Storrs's Troop of University of Alabama Cadet Volunteers.* University, Alabama: Confederate Publishing Company, 1984.

Howe, Daniel Walker. *What Hath God Wrought: The Transformation of America, 1815–1848.* New York: Oxford University Press, 2007.

———. *Making the American Self: Jonathan Edwards to Abraham Lincoln.* New York: Oxford University Press, 2009.

Hubbs, G. Ward. "'Dissipating the Clouds of Ignorance': The First University of Alabama Library, 1831–1865." *Libraries & Culture* 27, no. 1 (1992 winter): 20–35.

———. *Guarding Greensboro: A Confederate Company in the Making of a Southern Community.* Athens: University of Georgia Press, 2003.

———. *Tuscaloosa: Portrait of an Alabama County.* Northridge, California: Windsor, 1987.

Hunt, Robert Eno. "Home, Domesticity, and School Reform in Antebellum Alabama." *Alabama Review* 46, no. 4 (1996 October): 253–275

———. "Organizing a New South: Education Reformers in Antebellum Alabama, 1840–1860." Ph.D. dissertation, University of Missouri at Columbia, 1988.

Johnson, Andrew. *The Papers of Andrew Johnson.* Edited by Paul H. Bergeron. Knoxville: University of Tennessee Press, 1996.

Johnson, William, *William Johnson's Natchez: The Ante-Bellum Diary of a Free Negro.* Edited by William Ransom Hogan and Edwin Adams Davis. Baton Rouge: Louisiana State University Press, 1993.

Jordan, Weymouth T. *Ante-bellum Alabama: Town and Country.* Tallahassee: Florida State University, 1957.

———. "Cotton Planters' Conventions in the Old South." *Agricultural History* 19, no. 3 (1953 August): 321–345.

———. "Noah B. Cloud and the *American Cotton Planter*." *Agricultural History* 31, no. 4 (1957 October): 44–49.

———. "Noah B. Cloud's Activities on Behalf of Southern Agriculture." *Agricultural History* 25, no. 1 (1951 January): 53–58.

———. "The Peruvian Guano Gospel in the Old South." *Agricultural History* 24, no. 4 (1950 October): 211–221.

———. *Rebels in the Making: Planters' Conventions and Southern Propaganda.* Tuscaloosa, Alabama: Confederate Publishing, 1958.

Kohl, Lawrence Frederick. *The Politics of Individualism: Parties and the American Character in the Jacksonian Era.* New York: Oxford University Press, 1991.

Kolchin, Peter. *First Freedom: The Responses of Alabama's Blacks to Emancipation and Reconstruction.* Westport, Connecticut: Greenwood, 1972.

Ladies of the Mission. *The Old Brewery, and the New Mission House at the Five Points.* New York: Stringer & Townsend, 1854.

Ladies' Southern Relief Association of Maryland. *Report . . . September 1st, 1866.* Baltimore: Kelly and Piet, 1866.

Lamb, Robert Paul. "James G. Birney and the Road to Abolitionism." *Alabama Review* 47, no. 2 (1994 April): 83–134.

LeForge, Judy Bussell. "Alabama's Colored Conventions and the Exodus Movement, 1861–1879." *Alabama Review* 63, no. 1 (2010 January): 3–29.

Lester, John C., and D. L. Wilson. *Ku Klux Klan: Its Origin, Growth and Disbandment*. New York: Neale, 1905.

Lyell, Charles. *A Second Visit to the United States of North America*. 2 vols. London: John Murray, 1850.

MacLeod, Murdo. "The Soulouque Regime in Haiti, 1847–1859: A Reevaluation." *Caribbean Studies* 10, no 3 (1970 October): 35–48.

Martin, Fletcher D., and Fenton G. Fly. *History of Andrew Jackson Lodge No. 173, Montgomery, Alabama, 1852–1986*. Montgomery: Lodge, 1987.

Maxwell, James Robert. *Autobiography of James Robert Maxwell*. New York: Greenberg, 1926.

McIlwain, Christopher Lyle, Sr. *Civil War Alabama*. Forthcoming.

McPherson, James M. *Abraham Lincoln and the Second American* Revolution. New York: Oxford University Press, 1990.

Miller, James David. *South by Southwest: Planter Emigration and Identity in the Slave South*. Charlottesville: University of Virginia Press, 2002.

Miller, Randall M., ed. *Dear Master: Letters of a Slave Family*. Ithaca: Cornell University Press, 1978.

Morgan, Edmund Sears. *American Slavery, American Freedom: The Ordeal of Colonial Virginia*. New York: Norton, 1975.

Morrow, Ralph E. "Northern Methodism in the South during Reconstruction." *Mississippi Valley Historical Review* 41, no. 2 (1954 September): 197–218.

———. *Northern Methodism and Reconstruction*. East Lansing: Michigan State University Press, 1956.

Muir, Edward and Guido Ruggiero, eds. *Microhistory and the Lost Peoples of Europe*. Translated by Eren Branch. Baltimore: The Johns Hopkins University Press, 1991.

Myers, John B. "Black Human Capital: The Freedmen and the Reconstruction of Labor in Alabama, 1860–1880." Ph.D. dissertation, Florida State University, 1974.

Norrell, Robert J. *A Promising Field: Engineering at Alabama, 1837–1987*. Tuscaloosa: University of Alabama Press, 1990.

Peltonen, Matti. "Clues, Margins, and Monads: The Micro-Macro Link in Historical Research." *History and Theory* 40, no. 3 (2001 October): 347–359.

Pinkard, Ophelia Taylor, and Barbara Clayton Clark. *Descendants of Shandy Wesley Jones and Evalina Love Jones: The Story of an African American Family of Tuscaloosa, Alabama*. Baltimore: Gateway, 1993.

Prentice, George. *The Life of Gilbert Haven: Bishop of the Methodist Episcopal Church*. New York: Phillips & Hunt; Cincinnati: Walden & Stowe, 1884.

Quist, John W. *Restless Visionaries: The Social Roots of Antebellum Reform in Alabama and Michigan*. Baton Rouge: Louisiana State University Press, 1998.

Rable, George C. *But There Was No Peace: The Role of Violence in the Politics of Recon-struction.* Athens: University of Georgia Press, 1984.

———. *God's Almost Chosen Peoples: A Religious History of the American Civil War.* Chapel Hill: University of North Carolina Press, 2010.

Reardon, Carol. "Writing Battle History: The Challenge of Memory." *Civil War History* 53, no. 3 (2007 September), 252–263.

Rogers, William Warren. "The Founding of Alabama's Land Grant College at Auburn." *Alabama Review* 40, no. 1 (1987 January): 15–37.

Rogers, William Warren, Jr. *Black Belt Scalawag: Charles Hays and the Southern Republicans in the Era of Reconstruction.* Athens: University of Georgia Press, 1993.

———. "'The Husbandman that Laboureth Must be First Partaker of the Fruits' (2 Timothy 2:6): Agricultural Reform in Ante Bellum Alabama." *Alabama Historical Quarterly* 40, nos. 1 and 2 (1979 spring and summer): 37–50.

Rosenberg, Carroll Smith. *Religion and the Rise of the American City: The New York City Mission Movement, 1812–1870.* Ithaca: Cornell University Press, 1971.

Ruffin, Edmund. *The Diary of Edmund Ruffin.* Edited by William Kauffman Scarborough. Baton Rouge: Louisiana State University Press, 1972.

Russell, Robert. *North America: Its Agriculture and Climate.* Edinburgh: A. and C. Black, 1857.

Sandel, Michael J. *Democracy's Discontent: America in Search of a Public Policy.* Cambridge: Harvard University Press, 1996.

Schama, Simon. *Citizens: A Chronicle of the French Revolution.* New York: Knopf, 1989.

Schweninger, Loren. *Black Property Owners in the South, 1790–1915.* Urbana: University of Illinois Press, 1990.

Sellers, James B. *The First Methodist Church of Tuscaloosa, Alabama, 1818–1968.* Tuscaloosa: Weatherford, 1968.

———. "Free Negroes of Tuscaloosa County Before the Thirteenth Amendment." *Alabama Review* 23, no. 2 (1970 April): 110–127.

———. *History of the University of Alabama,* Volume I, 1818–1902. University: University of Alabama Press, 1953.

Shain, Barry Alan, ed. *The Nature of Rights at the American Founding and Beyond.* Charlottesville: University of Virginia Press, 2007.

Sindon, Nancy Anne. "The Career of Ryland Randolph: A Study in Reconstruction Journalism." Master's thesis, Florida State University, 1965.

Smith, Giles W. *History of Methodism in Peru, Indiana.* Peru: Official Board of the M.E. Church of Peru, Indiana, 1906.

Smith, Timothy L. *Revivalism and Social Reform: American Protestantism on the Eve of the Civil War.* New York: Harper and Row, 1957.

Stowell, Daniel W. *Rebuilding Zion: The Religious Reconstruction of the South, 1863–1877.* New York: Oxford University Press, 1998.

Sulzby, James Frederick. *Historic Alabama Hotels and Resorts*. University: University of Alabama Press, 1960.

Sweet, William W. "Methodist Church Influence in Southern Politics." *Mississippi Valley Historical Review* 1, no. 4 (1915 March): 546–560.

Thomas, James D., Jr. "The Alabama Constitutional Convention." Master's thesis, Alabama Polytechnic Institute [Auburn University], 1947.

Thornton, J. Mills, III. "Alabama's Presidential Reconstruction Legislature." In *A Political Nation: New Directions in Mid-Nineteenth Century American Political History*. Edited by Gary W. Gallagher and Radchel A. Shelden, 167–187. Charlottesville: University of Virginia Press, 2012.

———. "Fiscal Policy and the Failure of Radical Reconstruction in the Lower South." In *Region, Race, and Reconstruction: Essays in Honor of C. Vann Woodward*. Edited by J. Morgan Kousser and James M. McPherson, 349–394. New York: Oxford University Press, 1982.

Trelease, Allen W. *White Terror: The Ku Klux Klan Conspiracy and Southern Reconstruction*. New York: Harper and Row, 1971.

Tunnell, Ted. "Creating 'the Propaganda of History': Southern Editors and the Origins of *Carpetbagger* and *Scalawag*. *Journal of Southern History* 62, no. 4 (2006 November): 789–822.

Walters, Ronald G. *American Reformers, 1815–1860*. New York: Hill and Wang, 1978.

Ward, Gladys. "Life of Ryland Randolph." Master's thesis, University of Alabama, 1932.

Webb, Samuel L. "A Jacksonian Democrat in Postbellum Alabama: The Ideology and Influence of Journalist Robert McKee, 1869–1896." *Journal of Southern History* 62, no. 2 (1996 May): 239–274.

Weeks, Stephen Beauregard. *History of Public School Education in Alabama*. Washington, DC: Government Printing Office, 1915.

Wiggins, Sarah Woolfolk. "The Life of Ryland Randolph as Seen through His Letters to John W. DuBose." *Alabama Historical Quarterly* 30, nos. 3 and 4 (1968 fall and winter): 145–180.

———. *The Scalawag in Alabama Politics, 1865–1881*. University: University of Alabama Press, 1977.

Winslow, Ellen Goode. *History of Perquimans County*. Raleigh: Edwards & Broughton, 1931.

Woodson, Carter G. ed. *The Mind Of The Negro As Reflected In Letters Written During The Crisis 1800–1860*. Washington, DC: Association for the Study of Negro Life and History, 1926.

Woolfolk, Sarah Van V. "The Political Cartoons of the Tuskaloosa *Independent Monitor* and Tuskaloosa *Blade*, 1867–1873." *Alabama Historical Quarterly* 27, nos. 3 and 4 (1965 fall and winter): 140–165.

Index